The Alderman

Photograph showing members of Sinn Féin with
Back row (from left): Dan McCarthy, Darrell Figgis, Fr. Browne, Alderman Tom Kelly, Austin Stack, Éamon de Valera, Seán Milroy
Front row (from left): Laurence Ginnell, Countess Markiewicz, W.T. Cosgrave, Mrs. Ginnell
Private Collection

The Alderman

Alderman Tom Kelly (1868-1942)
and Dublin Corporation

Sheila Carden

First published 2007 by
Dublin City Council
Dublin City Library & Archive
138-144 Pearse Street
Dublin 2

Text © Sheila Carden, 2007

A catalogue record is available for this book
from the British Library.

ISBN
Casebound   10-Digit 0 946841 88 8
            13-Digit 978 0 946841 88 2

Paperback   10-Digit 0 946841 89 6
            13-Digit 978 0 946841 89 9

Design and origination: Environmental Publications
Cover design: Katrina Bouchier

Printed in Ireland

'The Alderman – there was only one to Dublin's poor… many illiterates voted simply for the Alderman, that was the best they could do'

Hanna Sheehy-Skeffington, *Irish Press*, 22 April 1942

Table of Contents

List of Illustrations

Acknowledgements

I should like to acknowledge the help and co-operation I received from many people in the nine years it has taken me to research and write Tom Kelly's story. The Housing Department of Dublin City Council has been most generous in sponsoring this book, and I am indebted to Deirdre Ellis-King, the Dublin City Librarian and Mary Clark, City Archivist, for their interest and support, and the assistance I received from Mary in the matter of preparing my material for publication. I am also grateful to Divisional Librarian Alastair Smeaton for his technical advice in the preparation of illustrations for the book.

I thank most sincerely Kevin B. Nowlan, who has always encouraged me and who gave me a belief in my own capacity to deal with the subject. He made many wise and important suggestions, and, apart from his eminence as a historian, he occupies a unique position as one of few people alive to have known my grandfather in the early days of the Old Dublin Society. I also owe a great debt of gratitude to my former RTÉ colleague Louis McRedmond, who in the last two years has given of his time and knowledge unstintingly and supplied me with valuable advice, not least in the matter of achieving historical balance, which I hope I did.

Members of my own family have been always supportive. I thank my cousins the Cullen family, also grandchildren of Tom Kelly, for their encouragement, and in partic-ular Harriett Cullen Fay, who passed on much family knowledge and many documents. She also researched the material from the Convent of the Sisters of St. Joseph of Peace in Grimsby. I could never have finished the text without the editorial and technical skills of my sister, Mary Canning, who was most generous with her time and expertise in the last crucial months. I thank Timothy King for the financial conversions.

Over the years I have benefited greatly from those with whom I came in contact in the libraries and archives of Dublin. I wish to record the assistance I received from the fol-lowing institutions and individuals:

The Dublin City Library and Archive, in particular Andrew O'Brien; staff of The National Library of Ireland; The National Archives of Ireland; Trinity College Dublin, Manuscripts Room; University College Dublin Archives; The National Archives, Kew London; Allen Library, CBS North King Street; Patrick Melvin, Librarian Oireachtas Library; Philip Hannon, Fianna Fáil Party Archive; Niall Mooney and Committee Dublin Workmen's Club; Niamh O'Sullivan, Kilmainham Jail; David Sheehy, Dublin Diocesan Archives; Teresa Whitington, Central Catholic Library; Mary Kelleher, RDS

Library; the Registry of Friendly Societies; Edward McParland, Brian Farrell, W.E. Vaughan, Liam Cosgrave, R.K. Gahan. Helen Carden, Max Keane, Ann Martha Rowan, Robert Monks, Marie O'Neill, Patrick O'Byrne; the late Seán Ó Lúing, the late Brother Malachy Thomas of CBS Westland Row; the late James Plunkett Kelly. I am also indebted to the following for permission to reproduce illustrations in the book: Dublin City Gallery; the Hugh Lane Gallery; David Keating and the Keating family for permission to reproduce Seán Keating's painting 'Homage to Hugh Lane'; the Royal Society of Antiquaries of Ireland for permission to reproduce images from the Darkest Dublin Collection; the *Irish Independent*; and *The Irish Times*.

Tá focal buíochais speisialta ag dul do Mháire Ní Mhurchú agus do Dhiarmuid Breathnach, beirt a sprioc i gcónaí mé.

I dedicate the book to the memory of my grandfather.

Sheila Carden

Foreword

Alderman Tom Kelly was one the significant figures in the shaping of the capital of the modern Irish state. He was a man of the people, coming from a very modest background, and for a lifetime he retained a deep love of the city and its history.

The reform of local government, at the end of the nineteenth century, made it possible for men like Kelly to enter public life and in his case to bring to it high principles and a deep sense of the social realities. He was a nationalist, but one who saw in the improvement of the living and working conditions of the people issues of central importance. Better housing at a reasonable rent were objectives he felt that local authorities should pursue without concern about vested interests.

Kelly associated with men such as Arthur Griffith, Willie Rooney and other members of the early Sinn Féin movement, and with some of the most significant figures in the making of modern Ireland. His interests had a largely educational aspect to them. His deep commitment to a public art gallery for Dublin brought him into close association with Hugh Lane and Sarah Cecelia Harrison and others. The results of their efforts was a Gallery which has enriched the cultural life of the city of Dublin. Again, his deep interest in the history of Dublin was to be seen in the Old Dublin Society, of which he was the first President when it was founded in the 1930s.

Tom Kelly was in many ways the all-round citizen concerned with social, political and cultural matters. It is not surprising that he was elected as Lord Mayor of Dublin but, as the narrative will reveal, he was never able to assume office. He remains one of the most interesting persons elected to the highest office in the city.

Kelly's memory and his contribution to Irish public life deserve to be remembered and I believe that this book will help to establish his place in the history of a critical phase in the shaping of Dublin and of Ireland.

Kevin B. Nowlan, MRIA,
Professor Emeritus of Modern History
National University of Ireland, Dublin (UCD)

Introduction

Thomas Kelly was born in Dublin in 1868 and died in 1942 after a long and eventful life. Over the course of forty years, his work in Dublin Corporation contributed to the alleviation of poverty and social exclusion in the city and left it a better place at his death. His contributions to the intellectual and cultural life of the city, which began in the early days of the twentieth century, continue to enrich Dublin to the present day.

The passage of the Local Government Act of 1898, which reformed the structure of local government in Ireland, made it possible for Thomas Kelly to become a city councillor and then an alderman. Dublin Corporation became a training ground in practical political activities for men such as Kelly, W.T. Cosgrave and Seán T. O'Kelly, all of whom became significant figures in the shaping of modern Irish political life. New skills had to be learned in the servicing of the city's needs, ranging from housing and water services to the provision of libraries and art galleries. Kelly, as a newly-elected councillor, immersed himself in the work of the Corporation, and, from the beginning, displayed a strong concern for the needs of his fellow citizens. As the father of a large family living near the centre of his work, he understood the importance of access to education in the lives of Dublin's poor and worked exhaustively to ensure that such facilities would be provided. As Chairman of the Public Library Committee, his relationship with Hugh Lane led him to play a pivotal role in establishing the Municipal Gallery. Kelly's career in municipal development enabled him to contribute seriously to the wider political questions of the day as the new state evolved and led him to play a significant role in national politics. The creation of the institutions and the beginnings of the modern political party system, together with the wide range of local and national issues in which he was involved, makes it desirable for this book to examine his place in the history of the early twentieth century in Ireland.

Kelly's friends were some of the finest of the thinkers and social reformers of his generation. But the Rising of 1916 and subsequent developments leading to the Anglo-Irish conflict, together with the Civil War, took a huge toll on him and the other survivors of his generation. His health was seriously undermined as a result of being imprisoned twice, initially in Kilmainham Gaol and then in Richmond Barracks after the Rising, and subsequently in Wormwood Scrubs in 1919. His imprisonment in Wormwood Scrubs caused a severe nervous breakdown, and that incarceration, coupled with a terrible sense of sorrow because of the loss of so many close personal friends and companions, adversely affected his health and his career. He also experienced more than his fair share of family grief. His brother was shot dead by the Auxiliaries (the British Emergency Police) in Dublin in March 1921, near the steps of the family home in what was then Great Brunswick Street. Both his eldest son and his eldest daughter died at relatively young ages of diseases which now would be eminently treatable.

Kelly held the position of Chairman of the Housing Committee from 1914 until December 1919. On his return to Dublin Corporation in 1931, he was re-elected to the same office which he continued to hold until 1940 when the administrative structures were changed. He actively pursued his work for the Corporation until his death.

In addition to his political career, Kelly was acknowledged during his lifetime to be an expert on the history of Dublin and, from the early days of the twentieth century, he contributed many articles to various journals and periodicals. In 1934 he became a founding member and first president of the Old Dublin Society. He had his own antiquarian bookshop at No. 8 Trinity Street, which he ran during the latter years of his life, and where he entertained many of the city's more colourful personalities, knowing well that few could afford to purchase his books. A perceptive visitor to Dublin today can still discern Kelly's influence not just in the Hugh Lane Gallery and the magnificent library in Pearse Street, but also in the many public housing schemes throughout the city which he would have considered his greatest legacy.

Kelly died almost penniless and the contents of his shop were sold to defray the costs of his funeral. Subsequently, Dublin Corporation Libraries fittingly purchased some of his books, a fact which would have given him great pleasure.

Chapter One: Early Years

Thomas Kelly was born on 13 September 1868 into a Catholic working-class family. His parents, Isaac Kelly and Sarah (née Pitts), lived at the time at 51 Townsend Street. Five days after his birth, Kelly was baptised in St. Andrew's Church, Westland Row. He went to school at the Christian Brothers, next door to that church, where the records show that he first attended on 12 January 1874. The available records are somewhat erratic. They list him as attending the school up to 13 August 1875 and not again until February 1884 when he seems to have left. He himself mentions that he was a pupil-teacher, or monitor, at the school, a fact confirmed in the school records made available to the author in 1998 by Brother Malachy Thomas. These list Kelly in the Sixth School (or class), on 28 March 1886 when he would have been eighteen. For information on this early period of his life, the only other existing account appears to be the memoir he himself dictated to Fr. Senan, Editor of the *Capuchin Annual,* shortly before he died, and published in the *Annual* of 1942. From this personal account, it appears that in 1882 the Kelly family inhabited the drawing room of 13 Cumberland Street, for which they were paying three shillings a week. Clearly, therefore, he was no stranger to the hardships being suffered by the tenement dwellers of the city.

Kelly's family had strong nationalistic tendencies and he describes vividly various events in which he had participated as a youth. The house in which the Kellys lived in Cumberland Street belonged to James Carey, known afterwards as the 'Informer', who was the owner of several other tenement properties in the area. The 'Invincibles', of whom Carey was a member, drew their inspiration from the Fenian movement, and were arrested as the perpetrators of the Phoenix Park murders in 1882. The victims were Sir Frederick Cavendish and Thomas Burke (the Chief Secretary and Under-Secretary for Ireland), who were stabbed to death while walking in the Phoenix Park near the Vice-Regal Lodge. Carey betrayed four of his fellow members to the authorities and they were subsequently charged, convicted and executed. Kelly recalls the election of Carey as a Corporation councillor for the Trinity Ward in 1882, and describes the local rejoicing around a bonfire to celebrate the event. He remembers Carey inviting the neighbours to his house to celebrate the release from prison of Michael Davitt that same week. When it became known nearly a year later that Carey had been the informer, he had to flee Ireland and went with his wife and family to South Africa. Patrick O'Donnell, a member of the Invincibles, followed him there and shot him dead en route to Natal. O'Donnell was subsequently tried and hanged.

Kelly vividly recalled these turbulent times. He lived through the Land Wars, the Land League, the Parnell Movement and, in his own words, 'through the period which saw Britain's policy change from one of coercion to one of concession'. He walked in the

Annie Glynn and her brother James, photographed in New York. Private Collection

great procession to commemorate the centenary of Daniel O'Connell's birth in 1875, wearing a green sash. He remembered the election of 1885 when the Home Rule policy once again appeared to be in the ascendant and all Dublin rejoiced in the election of Edward Dwyer Gray, a Home Ruler and the editor of the *Freeman's Journal*, who defeated the future Lord Iveagh for the St. Stephen's Green seat. He heard Parnell's last public speech from the window of Conarchy's Hotel and took part in Parnell's funeral where he was one of the guards at the graveside to prevent the taking of mementoes from the grave.[1] It is easy to understand how his interest in nationalism and his subsequent concern for the welfare of Dublin's poor took shape.

Kelly married Anne Glynn in St. Kevin's Church, Harrington Street on 2 September 1894. On his marriage certificate Kelly is described as a bookkeeper, while Annie, as she was known, is described as a dressmaker. They started their married life at 1a Bloomfield Cottages, whence they moved to 23 Longwood Avenue and finally to 37 St. Teresa's Terrace, all on the South Circular Road. By 1911, Kelly was describing himself as an alderman and company manager. The description 'Company Manager' derives from his work for the co-operative clothing company which he helped to found in 1901, the Dublin Workmen's Industrial Association. He was known to have had an aptitude for figures, and his bookkeeping skills no doubt stood him in good stead in this work and subsequently for his committee work in the Corporation. As mentioned, he had attended the Christian Brothers school at Westland Row. The *Westland Row CBS Centenary Record,* published in 1964, carries an account of the death in 1899 of Brother Francis Clifford, who for thirty years had made a most significant contribution to the community in the area as well as to the school. Immediately after his interment in Glasnevin Cemetery, a group of past pupils gathered to suggest that Brother Clifford deserved a memorial to his life's work. Kelly presided over this group. A committee was set up to organise concerts and lectures in Brother Clifford's honour, and to distribute prizes to the boys 'who had shown the greatest proficiency in the ancient language of Ireland'. The list of subscribers included many prominent citizens, one of whom was Patrick Pearse, who together with his brother Willie, attended the school. This committee actively helped the school for many years.[2]

---

[1] Kelly, Tom, Alderman. 'I Remember', in *The Capuchin Annual,* Dublin, 1942, pp. 589-593
[2] *Westland Row CBS Centenary Record,* 1964, p. 63

Apart from what Kelly dictated himself for the *Capuchin Annual,* the only existing records to be found of this early period appear to be those of the Workmen's Club at 41 York Street, of which he had been a member since the early 1890s. In 1897, he was elected secretary of the Amnesty Association, where he worked with Maud Gonne and others for the release of political prisoners held in British prisons, of whom there were approximately twenty at the time, all charged with treason-felony, and nearly all undergoing penal servitude for life. The Association, set up in 1891, had the objective not only of securing their release, but also of providing for their families who were badly in need of financial support. Progress at first was very slow, but by degrees the prisoners were released, some in impaired health, and it became possible to help them and their families with Amnesty Association funds. Large amounts were collected by the Irish abroad in America and South Africa.[3]

Tom Kelly's beautiful and elegant wife Annie was a dressmaker at the time of their marriage in 1894. Private Collection

The total amount raised was about £2,300 (approximately €286,000 at 2005 prices).[4]

Kelly recalled a request for a member of the Association to visit Thomas Clarke who had been imprisoned in Portland prison since 1883. Clarke specifically asked for someone who could write in shorthand so that he could dictate some information that he wished to be made public. Kelly knew shorthand, and he and a companion went to England to visit Clarke. Kelly described graphically their visit to the prison. He called it a terrifying big prison on the top of a hill.

> The heat reflected from the white stone quarries was very trying. An immense horse lay on the road, dead. In the vast quarry there were hundreds and hundreds of convicts at work. Warders stood on raised platforms in their midst, fully armed. It was a most depressing sight.

Only Clarke's head and chest could be seen through a wire frame; the shorthand, however, proved unnecessary as the warders were listening to every word that was spoken

---

3 *United Irishman,* 16 December 1899, Irish National Amnesty Association Final Report, dated 30 November 1899

4 This calculation and others throughout this book were made by by applying the UK price index in Dominic Webb, *Inflation: the value of the pound 1750-2005* (London, House of Commons Library Research Paper, 06/09, February 2006) to estimate a 2005 sterling equivalent and converting this to euros using the average 2005 sterling-euro exchange rates reported on the Bank of England website. These figures are approximate and are based on the latest available data at time of writing.

and Clarke therefore could not speak freely. This visit occurred in 1897, and Clarke was released the following year.[5]

Maud Gonne has also left an account of her visit to Portland in connection with her work for the Amnesty Association. She had obtained a permit to visit eight of the seventeen Irish treason-felony prisoners, three of whom had never received a visit from a friend during the ten years of their captivity. She wrote that she would never forget that visit, as on the way she saw gangs of convicts chained like beasts of burden pulling great carts of stones from the quarries.

> Among the treason-felony prisoners, some like John Daly, James Egan and Tom Clarke, who were often in the punishment cells came out of that hell of Portland with minds keen and ready for the joys and sorrows and battles of Irish life. But others, who were never on the punishment list, came out broken men, unfit for life; in Portland five out of seventeen lost their reason.

Maud Gonne approached T.P. O'Connor, a member of the Irish Parliamentary Party, and asked for his help in obtaining their release. To her astonishment, he refused, saying that it would embarrass the Liberal Home Rule Government. She threatened him that she would appeal to the English and French press, which she did, and within a year over a thousand articles appeared in the newspapers to the embarrassment of the Prime Minister, Lord Salisbury, who appealed to John Redmond to stop her. Redmond replied that nothing but the release of the prisoners would stop Maud Gonne.[6]

The work of the Amnesty Association ended in November 1899, and the final report and accounts were issued on 30 November, and were signed by Michael Lambert, Chairman, and Thomas Kelly, Hon. Secretary. Tribute was paid to all those individuals and groups who had supported the Association's work, including the Irish National Members of Parliament, and the publicity given to the Amnesty Association by the *Irish Daily Independent, Freeman's Journal,* and *Daily Nation* was also acknowledged.

In 1897, planning began for the commemoration of the Rising of 1798, on its centenary. This stirring of nationalist feeling had developed from the language and literary movements, such as the Celtic Literary Society and the Young Ireland Society, whose president was the old Fenian, John O'Leary. It is reasonable to assume that Kelly would have been actively supporting the nationalist movement because of his Amnesty Association work. 1798 Clubs, or '98 Clubs as they were called, were formed all over the country, and as far afield as America and Australia. These clubs were responsible for identifying potential candidates for the elections, anticipating the passing of the Local Government Act in 1898, and for ensuring nationalists had a voice in the new county councils. In England, W.B. Yeats and Dr. Marcus Ryan worked for the 1798 commemoration and Maud Gonne continued to work actively in both America and France.

---

[5] Kelly, Tom, Alderman. 'I Remember', in *The Capuchin Annual*, Dublin, 1942, pp. 595-596
[6] *The Voice of Ireland,* ed. William G. Fitzgerald, Dublin & London, Virtue & Co. Ltd., pps. 112-113

While visiting America as part of her Amnesty Association work, she was collecting also for a monument to Wolfe Tone to be erected in Dublin during 1898, and, in all, put together a sum of over \$4,000 (about €105,000 at 2005 prices). The 1798 commemoration, which took place in Dublin on 15 August 1898, was a great success and attracted huge crowds to the laying of the foundation stone for the monument to Wolfe Tone. At this time, Kelly had come in contact with Arthur Griffith, recently returned from South Africa, and also with Willie Rooney, a young man who was making a name for himself because of his nationalist writings and his commitment to the Irish language.

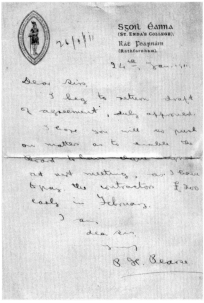

Letter from Patrick Pearse, dated 26 January 1911, with reference to completion of loan in relation to St. Enda's 'as I have to pay the contractors £200 early in February.' Pearse and Tom Kelly were both past-pupils of Westland Row CBS. Private Collection

From 1892 onwards, Kelly was joint treasurer of the Dublin Total Abstinence League and Workmen's Club of 41 York Street, which had been established in 1872, a position for which his numerical skills fully equipped him. As one of the aims of this club was the promotion of temperance, all its members were required to take 'the pledge', a solemn promise to abstain from alcohol. Apart from dealing with temperance issues, the club also provided a range of social services to the many needy families which patronised it, such as grants of small loans, family outings in the summertime and goose clubs at Christmas. The experience of working there would have certainly heightened Kelly's awareness of the havoc wreaked by alcohol in the homes of Dublin working-class families. The first mention of Kelly's name in the minutes of the club occurs in March 1892, and he is subsequently referred to as one of the two certifying signatories of the club accounts in the same year. For the greater part of his life he contributed to its activities in many capacities, acting as treasurer, secretary, and also as the club librarian, over the years. It was the Workmen's Club that nominated him to contest a seat in the Mansion House Ward in the first municipal election following the establishment of the Local Government Act in 1898. This election was to launch his career in politics.

Before describing the events leading to the passing of the Local Government Act of 1898, which extended the franchise to a large number of men and women and proved to be an important stage in the evolution of Irish independence, it is necessary to give some account of its background. To do so we must return to the Act of Union in 1800. This had resulted in the extinction of the Irish parliament and the creation of the new parliament of the United Kingdom of Great Britain and Ireland with a single Parliament at Westminster. The results of this amalgamation had been disastrous for the

Irish economy. The Union had helped to open up the Irish market to the full impact of the British industrial revolution. The economic consequences of this factor, and the serious defects in the Irish land system, gave strength to the forces of nationalism. Famine and emigration further increased the distress of the people. There were demands for the repeal of the Union and the restoration of the Irish parliament, and some went further in demanding complete separation from Great Britain. Looking back to the United Irishmen of the late eighteenth century, the demand for political and social change came to dominate the Irish political scene in the nineteenth century.

In England in the 1870s, Gladstone was doing his best to modify the effects of the Union and to deal with the increasing violence caused by agrarian agitation in both Ireland and England. It is important to remember that conditions in Great Britain were similar to those existing in Ireland at the time. There was a depression in prices obtained for grain, and a combination of bad weather together with cheap imports, caused many to leave the land, unable to pay their rents. It is fair to say that the Westminster Parliament was concerned about the effects that the ensuing unrest was having in both countries. Gladstone's best efforts to achieve Home Rule were to be further undermined tragically by the events which led to the death of Parnell in 1891. First there came the disclosure of Parnell's relationship with Mrs. O'Shea, which destroyed his credibility with many in England and Ireland, including most significantly with the Irish Catholic bishops. This, in turn, led to attempts to remove him from the leadership of the Irish Parliamentary Party. The Party split into two groups – a small number who were loyal to Parnell, led by John Redmond, and the remainder and much larger group, led by John Dillon. Ten years of bitter and divisive wrangling ensued before the Irish Party was reunited under the leadership of John Redmond in February 1900.

The Local Government Act of 1898 was introduced in order to do two things: to bring the corporations and district councils under a democratic franchise by allowing the vote to all male citizens regardless of status and also to women over thirty; and secondly, to deal with the demand for Home Rule. A similar act had been passed ten years earlier creating elected county councils in England, Scotland and Wales, and only the land agitation had prevented it from being implemented in Ireland at the same time. There were mixed feelings about it in Ireland, as it was feared that its implementation might distract attention from the priority of achieving Home Rule. While the Act had obvious limitations, its practical effect was, for the first time since the Act of Union, to provide a platform for dealing with certain functions of a national nature, apart from the provision of a whole range of municipal services which were previously administered by the Grand Juries. The latter, which had come into existence in the reign of James the First, comprised of local landowners appointed by the High Sheriffs in each county and had responsibility for the erection and maintenance of buildings such as courthouses and dispensaries, roadways and other local administrative services.

The plight of nationalists at the end of the century was bleak. After the debacle of Parnell, there was very little hope left in the downtrodden elements of the population except for the existence of the small nationalist societies such as the Young Ireland

League and the Leinster Debating Club, later the Celtic Literary Society. The resurgence of interest in the Irish language had resulted in the founding of Connradh na Gaedhilge, the Gaelic League, in 1894. However, some saw the potential of the pending local government legislation. A letter dated 10 September 1898 from George Noble Count Plunkett to Archbishop William Walsh expresses his fears that the Catholic population might not take full advantage of the Act's possibilities.

> It is our duty to call the attention of our flock to the Revision of the Voters' Lists which commences tomorrow. To secure Catholic interests and to safeguard our poor we have asked you, year after year, to vote for Catholic Poor Law Guardians. The Franchise being much extended under the Local Government Act, a large number of Catholics, men and women are on the new lists, and for the first time. Objections have been freely served all over the City to deprive the Catholics of this increase of power to which they are entitled by law, but which they will lose if they do not appear in Court when summoned to prove their claims. For Catholics to neglect this duty is to leave many Catholic interests at the mercy of those who may be opposed to them. It is also important for you to remember that under the new Act, Guardians elected next March will hold office for three years.

Count Plunkett wished to have the above read at all Masses on 11 September 1898.[7]

Thus, with the pending local government legislation, together with the growing interest in the linguistic and cultural heritage of Ireland, a major and most significant change was to come about which greatly enhanced the position of nationalists as the twentieth century dawned. Thomas Kelly was to play a significant role in these historic events.

---

[7] *Archbishop William Walsh papers*, 1898, 364/2, DDA

Chapter Two: The Councillor

Under the new Local Government Act, the Total Abstinence and Workmen's Club, 41 York Street, proposed Tom Kelly as a candidate in the Mansion House Ward. In his own account of how he came to be elected, he says that he was proposed against his will at the very last minute as a substitute candidate. The candidate originally chosen by the Workmen's Club had turned out to be ineligible for the technical reason that his name was not on the voting register. This does not tally with the account in the minutes of the club for that time, which seem to suggest that Kelly was the candidate originally selected. It may be that his memory was faulty at the end of his life when he dictated his memories. However, in the election held in January 1899 he topped the poll by one vote in the Mansion House Ward, much to the chagrin of his nearest rival, a Labour candidate, who demanded a recount as he wished to be declared the alderman. When the recount produced the same result the latter demanded another recount and Kelly said he had not got the time to be waiting all day recounting votes, and ceded the aldermanship to his rival. This meant Kelly had to go forward for re-election after three years, while the alderman, his rival, could remain in office for five.

The newly elected councillors went about their business immediately. A proposal by Sir Thomas Grattan Esmonde, a newly elected councillor for Wexford County Council, resulted in the formation of the National Council of County Councils, a body which was to consolidate the position of all the councils for the benefit of the country, and which still exists. Esmonde envisaged sending two representatives from each county to regular meetings in Dublin, thus creating a form of parliament in the capital city which was his clearly stated objective. He felt that if this suggestion were to be generally adopted, the result would be a People's Parliament.

In January 1899, a Dublin Corporation motion, proposed by Councillor P. White, and seconded by Capt. William Redmond, MP (John Redmond's brother) was tabled and carried unanimously. It stated that the Lord Mayor, aldermen and councillors, constituting the first Corporation of the City of Dublin elected by popular franchise, declared their unalterable devotion to the cause of National Self-Government for Ireland and their firm determination to use every legitimate means to secure its triumph.[1] Dublin Corporation then proceeded to name three representatives to the National Council, namely Messrs. Meade, Sexton and Pile. The motion proposing them was voted on by the Corporation, and resulted in 33 votes for, and 6 against. Kelly voted against these

---

[1] *Minutes of Dublin City Council,* 23 January 1899, p. 50, DCA
[2] Ibid. p. 364

Daniel Tallon, Lord Mayor of Dublin, 1898-1900, photographed in the Mansion House garden with members of Dublin City Council and civic officials. The Lord Mayor is seated centre front, wearing the Great Chain and holding the wand of office, with his chaplain on his right and the High Sheriff on his left; the Mace Bearer and Sword Bearer are standing behind, the latter wearing the ceremonial Cap of Maintenance. Tom Kelly is in back row, extreme right. Private Collection

particular candidates.[2] Four months after the inaugural meetings of the councils, on 22 August 1899, members from 24 of the 39 authorities came together in the Antient Concert Rooms, in Brunswick Street (now Pearse Street) in Dublin, to form the general council which Esmonde had envisaged. This building still exists.

The gathering proceeded with its deliberations in a most businesslike fashion. Esmonde said he wished that politics could be excluded from the Council's business, but nationalists gave a resounding response in the negative to this suggestion and political resolutions regarding Home Rule, the Catholic University issue and other matters were voted on and carried, despite protests from the unionist councillors. The nationalists were not so foolish as to forget the anti-Home Rule resolutions of the Grand Juries.

An editorial in the *Freeman's Journal* was very strong on the aspirations of nationalists, pointing out, *inter alia*, that it was due to nationalist politics that the Local Government Act, extracted from a unionist government, had brought about the county councils and it would be from nationalist politics alone that a final settlement could be expected for the Land question, the Catholic university and most of all, an Irish parliament to deal with Irish affairs. 'A General Council of County Councils, speaking with the full authority of its representative character, can render invaluable service in the furtherance of nationalist questions. Its members have a direct mandate from the electorate which they are not at liberty to ignore.' [3]

---

[3] *Freeman's Journal,* 23 August 1899

In the Local Government elections, the nationalists fought a brave battle on political issues, and won a splendid and overwhelming victory. The next meeting was set for December, and within two years, all county and city councils were sending representatives to the General Council.

Kelly brought with him into the newly formed Corporation his experience in the Workmen's Club, a keen awareness of the lack of proper housing and the problems brought about by the heavy consumption of alcohol amongst Dublin working-class families, and a lively interest in the general welfare of the citizens. In 1890 the Archbishop of Dublin, Dr. William Walsh, who was similarly concerned about the effects of drink on the everyday lives of the deprived people of the city, had inaugurated a national temperance movement to mark the centenary of Fr. Mathew's birth. Kelly must have been dismayed to find in the new Corporation that several of his fellow councillors were publicans and tenement landlords, wielding enough power to form cliques to protect one another's interests. Not all of these were unionists, as nationalists owned public houses and tenements also, and they supported each other in many cases where their business interests coincided. This issue was rather complex because the publicans were frequently shop owners and were an important source of credit to poor families. They often provided vital support to good causes, and would have contributed to the Irish Parliamentary Party.

On his entrance to the Corporation, Kelly was elected to the Finance and Leases Committee, to the Public Libraries and School Attendance Committees, and to the Boards of the Royal Irish Academy of Music and the Royal Hospital for Incurables at Donnybrook. He was concerned from the beginning about the fact that local authority positions were not being filled by proper competition. He proposed a motion that all future appointments and offices in the gift and patronage of the Council of the City of Dublin should only be filled by burgesses[4] and sons of burgesses of the city, and that appointments be filled by open competition. This motion was defeated but nonetheless a marker had been put down, and Kelly was to return to the issue at a later date.

As a councillor, Kelly became increasingly aware of the appalling housing conditions of Dublin's poor. Housing conditions at this time in Dublin were amongst the worst in Europe, and were created by the gradual deterioration of the city after the Act of Union, which brought with it many social changes and a decline in demand for goods with a consequent loss of traditional skills. The writer of an article published in the *United Irishman*,[5] signed with the *nom de plume*, Fogey, describing himself as a 'garrulous old man with a jaundiced eye', laments the loss of the following crafts: lacemaking, rope-making, glass and glove making, hat-making, ribbon, leather and cap-making, mathematical and musical instrument making, pump-making, organ-building, boatbuilding, carpet-, comb-, button-, and whip-making. Fogey goes on to write that when he knew Dublin first it was a great and wealthy city – one of the greatest cities in the world, and

---

[4] The term 'burgesses' indicates prominent citizens, such as masters of trade, freemen etc.
[5] *United Irishman,* 9 March 1901

Gordon's Place, Dublin, c. 1890, from the Darkest Dublin Collection *at the Royal Society of Antiquaries of Ireland.*

he now sees it as a shell, a thirty-fifth rate town. The causes he attributes to foreign government and to Irish supineness. He refers to 'fishmonger baronets and illiterate knights who have bought honours by betraying the city, thanked by their fellow-corporators for the wonderful things they have done for Dublin'.

Perhaps in some ways this is an overstatement, but there is no doubt that the destruction of all these industries created huge unemployment problems which in turn led to the deterioration of the housing stock. Many of the beautiful houses erected in the latter part of the eighteenth century were situated north of the Liffey, where some of the most affluent classes had resided in Mountjoy Square, North Great George's Street and Henrietta Street, and these were the areas which first fell into decline. Some of these buildings were taken over by religious orders, but a large number became tenements, which often meant that up to fifteen people were living in one room. The larger houses frequently contained up to one hundred occupants within one dwelling. There was typically only one privy in the back yard. The level of sickness and disease was very high. Report after report listed the terrible hazards to which the residents of the tenements were exposed, sometimes arising from the deterioration of the buildings themselves which frequently collapsed, causing death and injury. As early as 1880, the Royal Sanitary Commission had documented the severe overcrowding, lack of sanitation, poor diet, damp and cold conditions and foul air. At the end of the nineteenth century, Dublin recorded the highest infant mortality rates in the British Isles. Twice as many people died of tuberculosis in Dublin as in London. About twenty per cent of all deaths in the city occurred among those less than a year old, nearly all from the poorer classes.[6]

These, then, were the circumstances in which the working people of the once-proud city of Dublin lived, and the conditions which led to the establishment of loan clubs such as the Workmen's Club in York Street, where, as we have seen, Kelly was to play a key role. There were at least four other such clubs in the city at the turn of the century, such as the Dublin Workingmen's Co-operative Loan Fund Society, established in

---

[6] *United Irishman,* 9 March 1901

1896. Interestingly 1906 saw the establishment of the Sinn Féin Loan Fund Society with an address at 27 Wellington Quay, which had nothing to do with the Sinn Féin organisation.[7]

Allied to the misery of bad housing, and helping to perpetuate it, was the existence of so many public houses, where it was all too easy for the labourers to squander their meagre earnings on their way home from work. The housing conditions were attracting severe criticism in the columns of some of the newspapers, in particular by two recently established periodicals. The slum landlords and publicans began to be attacked on a weekly basis by Arthur Griffith in the *United Irishman*, which first appeared on 4 March 1899, and secondly, in the *Leader*, owned and edited by D.P. Moran, which was first published in September 1900. Neither let an opportunity go by without criticising the many Corporation councillors who were involved in the liquor trade, using a variety of sarcastic names such as the 'Whiskey Ring', 'Boodlers', the 'Bung Corporation' and more in the same vein. In an article in the *Leader* dated 28 September 1901 Moran claimed that there were twenty-five licensed and off-licence vintner members of Dublin Corporation, and asked whether it was any wonder that the question of the housing of the working classes was not being tackled vigorously when so many members of the Corporation were interested in the drinking of the working classes. Both papers thundered each week against these and other contentious issues such as the overtaxation of the country by the British Parliament, the perfidiousness of the Irish Parliamentary Party as they saw it, the housing conditions and then, in April 1900, the imminent arrival of Queen Victoria on a State visit, her first since 1861.[8]

At a Council meeting on 21 August 1899, a motion proposed by Alderman Farrell and seconded by Kelly stated that, in view of the unsanitary conditions of the tenements which in some instances were totally unfit for human habitation, the Public Health Committee be requested to prepare a scheme to ensure that the poor be better housed, the slums cleansed and put in order, and the health and well-being of the citizens safeguarded. This motion was tabled and carried.[9] Kelly also suggested that it should be obligatory for councillors to visit and inspect the tenements in their wards once or twice a year. Councillor Pile said the real problem was the cost of sites for housing, and that the problem would not be solved until the boundaries were extended, to which there was great resistance from many sources.

It was unfortunate for Kelly that early on in his councillorship the matter of the Boer War and a proposal to grant the freedom of the city to President Kruger came up in the Corporation, a subject of great interest to Arthur Griffith who had recently returned from South Africa and who, through the *United Irishman*, campaigned for the Boer cause. The motion proposed that the freedom of the Ancient City of Dublin be conferred on His Excellency President Kruger of the Transvaal Republic, in consideration

---

[7] *Registry of Friendly Societies*, No. 125 SAL, Parnell Square, D.1
[8] *The Leader*, 28 September 1901
[9] *Minutes of Dublin City Council*, 1899 p. 243, DCA

of his patriotic and gallant efforts to maintain his country's freedom and as a protest against the characteristic action of the English Government and their sordid and brutal endeavours to enslave the brave and unconquerable Boers. Kelly had his own reasons for not wishing to support this motion, due to a lack of sympathy which he had perceived on the part of Kruger towards Amnesty Association issues. He thus drew down the wrath of Griffith who denounced in the columns of his paper the names of those 'so-called nationalist councillors in the Corporation' who refused to support the Boers. There are several caustic references to Kelly in the *United Irishman* in the issues of November 1900, but the bad feeling between himself and Griffith did not endure, and from not long afterwards an intimate friendship developed between them which was to last until Griffith's death. The Corporation passed the motion regarding President Kruger, 16 votes for, and 15 against. Kelly did not vote at all.[10] However, subsequently, at a Council meeting held on 5 November 1900, the Lord Mayor (Pile) stated that having taken eminent advice on the motion as it appeared on the Notice Paper he was obliged to rule it out of order.[11]

It was through Griffith that Kelly came into contact with Willie Rooney, a young man who devoted all his spare time to writing for the *United Irishman* and working for the restoration of the Irish language. He was employed in a menial job as a railway clerk at the North Wall, and Kelly in his reminiscences relates the efforts which had been made to get him a position more suited to his qualifications and interests. Kelly was Chairman of the School Attendance Committee within the Corporation, which had need of a secretary, and it was suggested to him that it would be an excellent post for Rooney. The post was highly sought after, and Kelly, Griffith and others did their best to canvass on Rooney's behalf, but he was beaten for the position by one vote, and he died soon after, worn out by his hard work, and his labours in furthering the national cause.[12] Rooney was greatly mourned by Dubliners, and particularly by Griffith to whom he was very close. At the time of his death Griffith published an obituary of his friend in the *United Irishmen,* and described him as a Gaeilgeoir, a fine singer, poet, archaeologist and linguist. He had worked ten hours a day as a railway clerk, teaching Irish classes to men, women and children and produced literature of a lasting kind while refusing to take a single penny in recompense. Griffith considered that in his death another Davis had been lost to Ireland.[13]

Queen Victoria, referred to contemptuously as the Famine Queen, came to Ireland in April 1900. Her visit was marked by an official welcome from the Corporation, much to the annoyance of nationalists. John Redmond, recently elected as leader of the re-united Irish Parliamentary Party, did himself no good in the eyes of the country by standing up in Westminster and assuring Her Majesty's Government that the Queen would receive a royal welcome from her subjects when she visited Ireland. Many

[10] *Minutes of Dublin City Council,* 1900, p. 111, DCA
[11] Ibid. p. 473
[12] Kelly, Tom, Alderman. 'I Remember', in *The Capuchin Annual,* Dublin, 1942, pp. 597-598
[13] *United Irishman,* 11 May 1901

thought otherwise and the nationalist newspapers indulged in much sarcastic comment while, equally predictably, papers such as the *Irish Times, Freeman's Journal, Evening Mail* and the *Express* exhorted their readers to rejoice at the Queen's coming and to turn out to welcome her on the streets. The Lord Mayor, Thomas Pile, proposed a motion that the Aldermen and Councillors of the city of Dublin begged to offer to Her Majesty, on their own behalf and on behalf of the citizens, a hearty welcome on her arrival in the Capital City of her Kingdom of Ireland. 'Your Majesty comes amongst the Irish people above and apart from all political questions, and the citizens of Dublin unite in welcoming you with that deep respect which all entertain for the person of your Majesty.' He asserted that her stay in Ireland would prove a pleasant one and of lasting benefit to her health, and that she would always receive a Céad Míle Fáilte whenever it might please her to visit this portion of her dominions. A document to this effect was to be presented to the Queen at Leeson Street Bridge, on which had been erected a wood and canvas structure decorated to represent one of the old city gates.[14]

Thirty councillors voted for this motion, and twenty-two, including Kelly, voted against. Lord Mayor Pile and the unionist councillors had their way, and the Queen was welcomed officially to Dublin. Tempers flared and arguments raged, while preparations were put in place to line the streets with policemen, and large reinforcements of military were drafted up from the Curragh in order to quell any potential disturbances. It was alleged that the Queen's secret service fund paid the fares of Orangemen to travel from Belfast and that the little children of pauper institutions were marched out to cheer her as she passed through the city.[15]

Nationalists mounted a counter-demonstration. A procession of some 15,000 men, headed by the flag of the Transvaal Republic, marched past the Mansion House on their way to Beresford Place where a rally was held. The *Marsaillaise* and *A Nation Once Again* were sung. The people were attacked by mounted police and baton-charged, in spite of the fact that notice had been given in advance to the authorities that a peaceful demonstration was going to take place. Maud Gonne organised what was called the 'Patriotic Children's treat' for 20,000 children of nationalist families in Croydon Park, Fairview, to rival the free treat given to 5,000 loyal children in the Phoenix Park. Out of this initiative of Maud Gonne's came the formation of Inghinidhe na hÉireann (The Daughters of Ireland). There was great jockeying for invitations to the social functions at Dublin Castle and the Vice-Regal Lodge. Griffith, in the columns of the *United Irishman*, enumerated Victoria's alleged crimes against Ireland: five million people banished – 43,000 in the previous year alone; three million driven into famine graves; many industries destroyed; the men who died for Ireland in prison, in exile and on the scaffold; and the £800,000 (€96.3 million at 2005 prices)[16] taken every year from Ireland in taxes.[17]

---

[14] *Minutes of Dublin City Council*, p. 134, DCA
[15] *United Irishman*, 7 April 1900
[16] See footnote 4, Chapter 1, for calculation methodology
[17] *United Irishman*, 24 March 1900

Queen Victoria's visit provoked such violent opposition and inflamed public opinion amongst the nationalist community to such a degree, that when King Edward VII and Queen Alexandra came to Dublin three years later, it was practically a foregone conclusion that there would be no official civic welcome for them.

In an attempt to retrieve the situation, on 2 April 1900, the centenary of the Passing of the Act of Union, the Council approved a motion rejecting vehemently the suggestion in 'a section of the unionist press' that an address of welcome to Queen Victoria meant abandonment of the claim for 'National Self-Government'. The motion declared that that Act of Union was passed by fraud and shameful corruption and claimed that there would be neither contentment nor loyalty in the country until the National Parliament was restored. This motion was passed by 49 votes to 9.[18]

From 1899 onwards, therefore, a tiny group of nationalist councillors constantly tried to promote reform in key issues such as housing, and fought each election courageously in the hope of increasing their numbers. They battled against corruption in the licensed trade and struggled to force the implementation of whatever small amount of protection existed under the law to compel landlords to repair their tenements. In several cases where such landlords were reported to the Corporation and the Corporation housing inspectors tried to insist on enforcing the law, the reports were suppressed, thus ensuring no further action would be taken. A case in point was a tenement house in Townsend Street, owned by Alderman Gerald O'Reilly, which had collapsed and killed or maimed eight persons. Dr. Louis Byrne, City Coroner, said no blame was attached to anyone. The previous July, this particular house had been reported to the Corporation as being in a perilous condition by one of the Corporation's own Sanitary Inspectors. The Inspector of Dangerous Buildings had subsequently surveyed it and had reported back that the house was not dangerous. Griffith was scathing in his condemnation of the Corporation's retention of the Inspector of Dangerous Buildings 'who after the sanitary officer reported that this house was falling down, certified that it was not'.[19]

By 1901, the Kelly family had moved to 23 Longwood Avenue, thus remaining in the South Circular Road area. Obviously the new house was larger than their previous one in Grantham Place, indicating that the man who had described himself as a bookkeeper in 1894 (the date of his marriage), was climbing up in the world. The family consisted at that point of two sons and a daughter, Isaac, John and Sallie, and they went on to have six more children.

Coming up to the municipal elections of January 1902, in an analysis of the candidates, Griffith was urging the electors of the Mansion House Ward to vote for Kelly, and despite their difference of opinion at the time of the Kruger resolution, he stated that

[18] *Minutes of Dublin City Council,* 1900, p. 149
[19] *United Irishman,* 15 November 1902

Tom Kelly's wife Annie with five of their nine children (left to right): Mary, Sheila, Sallie, Eileen and baby Tom.
Private Collection

Kelly had stuck to his guns as a nationalist in the Council Chamber and that his unselfish work as Secretary of the Amnesty Association should not be forgotten. However, the results of the 1902 elections were disappointing for nationalists. Three workingmen candidates for the North City and Wood Quay Wards, and the nationalist candidate for the North Dock ward, were defeated. The net result was the gain of one seat for nationalists. Kelly was re-elected to the Mansion House Ward, and his win was described by Griffith as a smashing victory.[20] This election clearly demonstrated that his reputation as a councillor was being consolidated. Obviously his experience in the Workmen's Club, together with his keen interest in the major problems of housing and his nationalist leanings, all contributed to his advancement within the Council, and he was clearly perceived by the electorate to be an effective and articulate politician. Griffith gloried in the defeat of Alderman Dowd (Kelly's opponent) who, he claimed, was working hand in glove with the whiskey ring to oust from the representation of the Mansion House Ward his colleague, a *bona fide* labour representative, Thomas Kelly. Kelly beat Dowd and the publicans by a majority of over four to one and the people of the ward then called on Dowd to resign which he refused to do.[21] Griffith claimed that half-a-dozen fearless men in the Council Chamber, acting together, would in a little time clear out the humbugs from the positions they were using to befool, boodle and betray the workingmen of Dublin.[22] He advocated a temperance movement led by the

---

[20] *United Irishman,* 25 January 1902
[21] Ibid. 6 September 1902
[22] Ibid. 25 January 1902

priests against the root of the drinking evil in Ireland, and claimed that such a move-ment, organised with the language and industrial development movements, would be hailed with joy by every man who had a heart to feel or a head to think.[23]

Meanwhile, in *The Leader,* D.P. Moran beat many of the same drums and consistently advocated that the Irish should stand on their own feet and set up their own industries. Week after week he published lists of shops which did not stock Irish goods and urged consumers to boycott them. His paper regularly contained advertisements for Irish firms that manufactured their own goods, and Moran pointed out that giving support to Irish industries would help stem the flow of emigration. He did not hesitate to raise many contentious issues with his readers whom he berated whenever he saw fit. Moran took grave exception to what he called 'Coonery', which was the name he gave to the dixie-minstrel types of stage shows featuring singers with blackened faces which were very popular with the public at the time. He heaped praise on the various brass bands from institutions such as the Workmen's Club, which played traditional music and fre-quently supplied the music at aeraíochtaí (fetes held out of doors during the summer) organised by the Gaelic League. However, he deplored the fact that they did not wear uniforms, such as the smart ones worn by the 'Tommy Atkins' (i.e., the English) bands.[24]

In July 1901, a co-operative association called the *Dublin Workmen's Industrial Association* had been formed, whose objective was to promote Irish industries and to make Irish goods available at moderate prices for the working men, as well as helping them to buy goods on convenient terms. Kelly, representing the Workmen's Club, acted as Secretary, and a capital of £1,000 was subscribed. Members were invited to apply for shares. Two-thirds of the profits were to be divided amongst the shareholders, and the remaining one-third would be allocated for the benefit or encouragement of objects of Irish industry or art, as the Committee saw fit. The Chairman was Alderman William Russell, together with a committee of twelve, many of them associated with the Dublin Workmen's Club, or representing temperance clubs from various parts of the city. The association offered clothing, boots, furniture, hats, caps, bicycles, etc., all guaranteed of Irish workmanship, and made of Irish materials, on a weekly payment system. No secu-rity was needed, but good references were required. The offices were open each day and on Saturday evenings, at hours convenient for the working men. This was a practical answer to what Kelly perceived to be a problem for workers: the ability to purchase goods on a credit basis. Up to this point, it is not known where Kelly was employed, but from 1903 onwards, he is listed in Thom's Directory as Secretary and Manager of the *Dublin Workmen's Industrial Association* with an address at 10 South William Street. The fact that this club is listed in Thom's Directory from 1903 until 1927, indicates how successful it was in dealing with the difficulties poor people often had in obtain-ing credit. A typical advertisement for the Association can be quoted:

---

[23] *United Irishman,* 1 February 1902
[24] *The Leader,* 5 July 1902

Dublin Workingmen's Industrial Association Ltd., 10 South William Street.

Sell Irish-made Clothes, Boots, Hats, Ladies' Wearing Apparel and Furniture. Hearns, Cahills Governeys and Williamson's Boots can always be had; also Dennehy's Hats. Accounts opened on Satisfactory References Manager Alderman Thomas Kelly. No connection with any other firm.

Chapter Three: The National Council

The municipal elections of January 1903 were disappointing for nationalists. Griffith thought that 25% of the voters abstained through sheer disgust at the quality of the candidates.[1] He wrote that out of eighty members, twenty-nine were publicans, ex-publicans or persons otherwise directly connected with the liquor trade, that at least twenty others were indirectly connected with it, and that Dublin was being ruled and ruined in the interests of the whiskey-sellers. He claimed that what the electorate wanted was a clean, healthy and progressive Dublin, its great streets beautified and its mean streets freed from their meanness, its slums swept away and its people taught the rights and duties of the citizen.

Another royal visit was being planned for 1903: King Edward VII and Queen Alexandra intended to visit Ireland in May. Griffith announced the formation of a National Council, the object of which was to gather representative men from all parts of the country into one loosely knit organisation, whether they were Home Rulers only or nationalists who believed in absolute independence for the country. He outlined the policies of the National Council which could be described as national self-development through the recognition of the duties and rights of citizenship consistent with the national tradition; the non-recognition of foreign authority in Irish affairs; the development of Irish firms, using Irish labour and supporting only native industries; and finally, in furtherance of these aims, using to the utmost the powers of the local representative bodies.[2]

In the pages of *United Irishman*, Griffith further elaborated on why nationalists could not participate in any welcome to the King and Queen.

> It is clear to every Nationalist that no Irishwoman, or Irishman who values National dignity or honour, who realises the condition to which our country has been reduced – a shrunken and still shrinking population – a plundered and still overtaxed people – an impoverished country – a Nation with rights stolen and still unrestored – can participate in any address of welcome to the King of England, who can come only as the existing representative of the power responsible for all our evils. We write from a National point of view, regardless of the different religious opinions of Nationalists.. Can any Catholic welcome the King who, scarce two years ago, took an oath grossly insulting to their religion? It must not be forgotten that upon the occasion of the visit of the late Queen of

---

[1] *United Irishman*, 24 January 1903
[2] Lyons, George. *Some Recollections of Griffith and his Times*, Talbot Press, 1923, pp. 64,65

England workers were, against their wills, locked out from their work, in order that the country should be misrepresented as participating in a National Holiday. Not only were the Schools under the control of the Government closed, but attempts were made to coerce children to participate in loyal displays.

The article concluded that in order that national self-respect would be upheld, and that false representations of Irish opinion would not be made, it was essential that a council, composed of representative Irishwomen and Irishmen, should be established.[3]

In the same issue of the *United Irishman,* there were some 40 signatures appended to a statement pertaining to the forthcoming royal visit of the King. These included Edward Martyn, W.B. Yeats, Henry Dixon, Walter Cole, Arthur Griffith, and Thomas Kelly. It stated that in view of the gravity of the situation caused by the reports of the visit of the King of England to Ireland, it was imperative that nationalists should ensure that the national opinion of the country should not be misrepresented, that the people should be protected from being coerced into a make-believe acquiescence in reception displays and that the children should not be used for a similar purpose.[4]

Major MacBride, in a letter quoted in the *United Irishman,* also on 30 May, wrote:

A friendly welcome to him (the King) would be a crime to Ireland. You are told Home Rule is to follow the stranger King's visit. Keep your gratitude for the gift until you receive it. Put not your trust in Saxon faith. If they meant to give you Home Rule it should have preceded the stranger's coming.

Meanwhile, the Lord Mayor, Timothy Harrington, worked covertly to organise a civic address for the King and Queen. At a public meeting on 18 May in the Rotunda, which had been arranged to appeal for funds for the Irish Parliamentary Party, a group of five, chosen from the newly established National Council, walked on to the stage where John Redmond was addressing the meeting and confronted Harrington regarding his plans for an official address to the King. This group consisted of Edward Martyn, Maud Gonne, Seamus MacManus, Henry Dixon and Thomas Kelly. Harrington did his best to evade the question, and the meeting ended with a fracas involving chair-throwing. The *United Irishman* reported graphically on what happened then. Its one-sided version of events, while undoubtedly partisan, well reflected the bitter animosities of the period between different elements within Irish nationalism. There was so much publicity about this meeting that a lot of people who beforehand had little interest in whether the King would receive an official address of welcome or not, became determined that there would be no such thing.[5]

---

[3] *United Irishman,* 30 May 1903
[4] Ibid. 30 May 1903
[5] Ibid. 23 May 1903

At a meeting of the Council on 3 June within the Corporation, it was recorded that Alderman Cotton J.P. proposed a motion that the Council would present an address of welcome and good wishes on behalf of the citizens to their Majesties, the King and Queen, on the occasion of their coming visit.[6] Subsequently, a meeting of ward representatives was convened to oppose the re-election of members of the Corporation who voted in favour of an address of welcome to the King. Kelly was a member of this group, representing the Mansion House Ward. On Thursday, 4 July, a public meeting to protest against the visit was called by the National Council. It was held in Beresford Place and was attended by a huge crowd, with Edward Martyn presiding. Only one resolution was proposed:

> That this meeting of the citizens of Dublin protest against our Municipal representatives degrading the National cause by passing any resolution to present an address of any kind to the King of England, and directs that steps be taken to look after the register of voters with the object of securing proper National representation in the Dublin Corporation.

Kelly addressed the meeting, asking that the professing nationalists who supported such an address be cleared out of the Corporation. He instanced what he had witnessed that day in Mercer Street, where he claimed to have seen supporters of the royal visit, whom he called 'the political and religious soupers[7] at work, endeavouring to persuade by promises of toys and outings to get the little children to wear British flags.'[8]

Henry Dixon ridiculed the base and baseless argument that the Irish people should receive the English monarch with cheers, because his coming meant employment for Dublin workmen. 'No one better than the intelligent Dublin workingman knew how utterly false that claim is… When a royal visitor comes to this country it costs the average Dublin workingman his day's wages. His employer, generally a loyal man, locks him out to exhibit his loyalty and in 75% of cases does not pay him for the day.'

Maud Gonne MacBride also spoke and was received with prolonged cheering. She pointed out that if the Irish people were to grovel before the King of England, they were promised that great good would come of it. They were told the same at the time of Victoria's visit. She said that the real reason for the visit was to help in the attainment of an alliance between England and the United States because the King believed that an alliance with America would save the Empire from falling apart.

'Between the English and the coveted alliance', she said, 'stand the Irish in America, and the Irish in America are hostile, because the Irish at home are hostile ... In pursuance of the plan to diminish Irish-American hostility to the alliance, the King of England comes to Ireland hoping that by the reception of addresses from such bodies as the

6 *Minutes of Dublin City Council*, 1903, p. 202, DCA
7 Pejorative – Refers to the giving of soup by Protestants to impoverished Catholics
8 *United Irishman*, 11 July 1903

Dublin Corporation – bodies supposed to represent popular feeling – the American Irish may be deceived into weakening their opposition to the alliance'.[9]

At a meeting of Dublin Corporation in July, Kelly objected to extending any official welcome to the royal couple, and referred to the Coronation Oath as 'the infamous oath of an infamous king', and despite an outcry from the unionist members, refused to withdraw as much as one syllable of what he had said.[10] An account of this meeting was published in the *Leader*. The Lord Mayor was partially praised, and the rest dismissed as rubbish with the exception of 'Mr. T. Kelly's humour (which) came as a relief to this prevailing dullness, (as) there were some telling touches in it which immensely amused the Chamber and the Gallery'. The paper of 'a hundred earls' or 'Mr. Buff' (both names frequently used by Moran when referring to *The Irish Times*) called Councillor Kelly 'the licensed clown of the City Hall', and Mr. Harrington 'the Emperor of the Municipal Gutter'.[11]

The King and Queen arrived in Dublin on 21 July, and it was reported that they were received very coolly and there were no enthusiastic crowds to cheer them through the streets. The *United Irishman* gave an account of the progress of the royal visitors, stating that on the day they had arrived there was an eight-mile stretch from Kingstown into the city where hardly a supporter was to be seen, in contrast to the visit of Queen Victoria only three years earlier, and it was only when the procession reached College Green that anything like a crowd was there to welcome them.

The English *Daily Mail*[12] commented that the truth was that the King and Queen were quietly received, that Dublin's greeting was in no sense loud and that the King afterwards expressed his disappointment at the reception he had received, saying that it had lacked warmth.[13]

The royal visit coincided with the death of the Pope, Leo XIII, and, while various nationalist celebrations were cancelled, there was criticism of the fact that the Archbishop of Dublin, William Walsh, did not order a mourning bell to toll for the Pope as would have normally happened. Maud Gonne flew a black flag from her house in Coulson Avenue, Rathgar, which was torn down by police. She hoisted another and the same thing happened. She hoisted a third, and this time there gathered such a crowd of nationalists at the house that the police had no option but to back away.[14] The only streets on which flags were displayed for the royal visit were Grafton Street, Westmoreland Street and O'Connell Street. His advisors thought it would be a good thing to bring the King down to where the poor lived and get him to profess an inter-

---

9   *United Irishman*, 11 July 1903
10 Ó Luing, *Art Ó Gríofa*, p. 114
11 *The Leader*, 18 July 1903
12 Quoted in the *United Irishman*, 1 August 1903
13 Ó Luing, *Art Ó Gríofa*, p. 116
14 Ibid.

est in the quality of their housing. So accordingly, they applied to the Corporation and the Chairman of the Estates and Finance Committee was requested to be good enough to conduct His Majesty around. The Chairman of the Estates and Finance Committee happened to be Thomas Kelly T.C. of the National Council and he declined to act. As a last resort, Sir Charles Cameron, Chief Medical Officer of the City, was accepted as cicerone. His Majesty's visit to the poor failed to arouse the enthusiasm anticipated.[15]

The royal couple visited Galway where they were presented with an address. They also went to Maynooth where they were received by the Archbishop of Dublin and a dozen other bishops, and were welcomed by a performance of *God Save the King* on the college organ. The room in which they were received was decorated with pictures of horse-racing and of the King's Derby-winner.[16] In a letter issued by Inghinidhe na hÉireann (Daughters of Ireland), Maud Gonne MacBride referred to a treat for patriotic schoolchildren which had been announced, similar to the children's treat which had been organised when Queen Victoria had visited Dublin in 1900. She claimed that the unionists were offering children a bribe of 6d. per head to cheer the King in the Phoenix Park. The effect of the royal visit was to incite further growth in the budding nationalist movement.

Meanwhile, the nationalist group within the Corporation was not idle and on 29 August, 1903, the *Leader* gave prominence to a report from James W. Drury, a Local Government Board auditor, to which grave exception was taken. The Local Government Board was originally the old Poor Law Commissioners. The name was changed and their role expanded in 1872. They authorised loans and rates and framed the rules for electoral divisions, and provided a financial basis from which local bodies were to operate. This report dealt with the accounts of the Corporation and the City of Dublin for the years ending 31 March 1901 and 1902. The Corporation had been accused of over spending and of having confused the capital and revenue accounts; in sum that it had plunged the city into debt for current expenditure to the extent of over £50,000 (€6 million at 2005 prices).[17] The *Leader* stated that were this picture proved to be correct, no censure would be too severe for such madness.

But Thomas Kelly, the Chairman of the Finance Committee, issued a report in answer to that of Mr. Drury, and it is a complete refutation of the charges brought against the Corporation. Kelly's report stated that all expenditure was provided for, but the auditor had not ascertained that it was available. The fact is that whilst Mr. Drury had audited the Corporation accounts only up to March 1902, he had taken it upon himself not only to criticise but to make the most positive and damaging assertions regarding the state of the accounts for the year ending 31 March 1903, which he had not audited at all. No wonder Mr. Kelly in his reply tears Mr. Drury's figures to pieces. The utter want of public morality displayed by the press of Dublin (excepting *The Freeman* and *Telegraph*) is appalling. *The*

---

15 *United Irishman*, 1 August 1903
16 Ibid. 8 August 1903
17 See footnote 4, Chapter 1, for calculation methodology

Irish Times, Express, Independent, Herald and Mail used it as a splendid weapon to discredit the Corporation. All ignored the facts of Kelly's reply. They want no answer to Drury's charges and would listen to none. The Tory game was to heap odium on the Nationalist Council and cry out for reform. Mr. Thomas Kelly has also earned the enmity of the Tory press and of the *Independent*. He must be put down at all costs. Even the sedate *Irish Times* forgets itself and gives way to language unbecoming a fishwife in attacking him.[18]

The dissension between the Council and the Local Government Board could have been anticipated. As early as 1901, there was a report in *The Irish Times* dated 27 March of that year to the effect that during House of Commons proceedings on a motion regarding the Consolidated Final Appropriation Bill, Sir Thomas Esmonde complained that the work of the new local authorities in Ireland was being impeded in every possible way by the unconstitutional methods and in some cases, the illegal proceedings, of the Irish Local Government Board. Very great dissatisfaction existed amongst the local bodies he went on, and said it was suggested that the Board was not competent to discharge the duties entrusted to it by the Local Government Act. Esmonde especially condemned the action of the Board in illegally raising the salaries of officials who were now the servants of the local authorities, and demanding these bodies to pay the increased salaries. Esmonde was supported by Messrs. Cullinan and Clancy. Wyndham maintained that the Local Government Act had been inspired solely by the desire to fulfil the statutory obligations laid upon it by the Act passed in 1898. It had transferred from the Grand Juries very much greater powers than had even been held by Grand Juries in England, and it had granted these powers to the elected bodies. John Dillon complained that the Board carried a spirit of partisanship into its work, ignored the county councils and stirred up local surveyors to a spirit of rebellion against their employers. John Redmond announced that to mark their disapproval of the action of the Local Government Board in Ireland, the nationalists would divide the House. The House accordingly divided, the Government winning by a majority of 92.

Drury had issued his report on 31 July 1903, dealing with the period 31 March, 1901 and 1902, setting out what he perceived as shortcomings with regard to the accounts of the Corporation. He claimed that its methods of keeping accounts were seriously flawed, and had resulted in large sums being borrowed considerably in excess of actual requirements. He urged that there should be a substantial increase in the rates so as to discharge previous liabilities and to provide for past indebtedness.[19] Kelly, as Chairman of the Estates and Finance Committee, issued his reply rebutting Drury's claims. He mentioned the two serious charges, namely the alleged neglect of the Council to make proper estimates and, secondly, that in order to provide contingent security for this overdraft 'sums considerably in excess of actual requirements were from time to time borrowed'. He provided detailed figures to demonstrate that Drury had arrived at erroneous conclusions and set out various assets made up of such items as rates, rents and

18 *The Leader*, 29 August 1903
19 *Dublin Corporation Reports*, Vol. 2, 1903, pp. 469-476

way-leaves, to the value of £66,252 14s.6d (€7.8 million at 2005 values), all of which had become due before the previous 31 March, and the greater part of which had since been realised. He also pointed out that under orders made by the Local Government Board, the commencement of the financial year for local authorities was altered from 1 January to 1 April, thus causing disruption to the system.[20]

This serious clash with Drury could have been a potential disaster for Kelly's career. Drury, after all, represented the Local Government Board to the Corporation, and his Board, in turn, had to deal with the Treasury in London. It is a measure of Kelly that by the age of thirty-five he was proving himself to be a good accountant, a seasoned politician well able to fight his corner, and both amusing and effective in public debate.

---

[20] *Dublin Corporation Reports,* Vol. 2, 1903, pp. 479-489

Chapter Four: The Evolution of Sinn Féin

The Dublin municipal elections were scheduled to take place on 17 January 1904. In preparation for these elections, the *United Irishman* was busy advising its readers to vote for as many nationalist candidates as possible to build on their existing position within the Corporation. Its leading article on 16 January stressed the importance of the Corporation's standing in the country, 'shorn as it was of a native senate and a native government'. Without doubt, the duty of a Corporation was to provide effectual local government, but in the case of the Corporation of the capital of Ireland, its duty was to guard the dignity and the honour of the Irish nation. An analysis was then given of the men going forward as councillors in each ward. Many of them were branded by Griffith as place seekers and publicans, but encouragement was given to a favoured few who were found to be of the required calibre in terms of honesty and ability.[1]

An extract from the election address of Walter Cole for the municipal elections of 1904, sums up very well how the nationalist councillors saw their function within the Council at this period. 'It is well, I think, to bear in mind that the Corporation of Dublin is the first representative body in Ireland, and speaks and acts not for this city alone, but as the capital of a nation, and until our national rights are restored, must largely take the place which a National Congress would then occupy in giving voice to the National will.'[2] Cole at this time was the leader of the nationalist councillors within the Corporation and was highly regarded by Griffith as an Irishman of brains, ability, honesty, education and patriotism.

Following the results of the election of 6 February 1904, a new National Party was formed within the Corporation. Councillor Michael Lord was elected Chairman and Thomas Kelly became Secretary. The other members of this group were Alderman Cole, Councillors Madden and P.T. Daly. Their first battle was to get Councillor Hutchinson elected as Lord Mayor. Hutchinson was a candidate favouring nationalist aspirations even though he was not a member of their group. He was pitted against Alderman Cotton, a unionist candidate who had championed the presentation of an address on the occasion of the royal visit and who was favoured by many prominent councillors. The *United Irishman* said that the nationalist councillors had lifted the debate to a new level, namely that it was now an issue between Ireland and England. Alderman Cole addressed the Council in Irish to the astonishment of the majority of

---

[1] *United Irishman*, 16 January 1904
[2] Ibid. 9 January 1904

the members. It was claimed that it was the first time in its six hundred years' history that the Corporation of Dublin had listened to a speech in the Irish language from one of its own members. When the vote was taken, Councillor Hutchinson was elected by 41 votes to 37. The result was received with prolonged cheers inside and outside the City Hall.[3] The aim of this new group, as it saw it itself, was to strengthen and consolidate the nationalists on a more formal basis. Griffith admitted that the numbers were small, but its members had pledged themselves to sustain the national cause in the Council Chamber and to oppose every attempt to misrepresent the attitude of the Irish nation towards the British Government and the British Crown. They also undertook neither to seek nor to accept for either themselves or their relatives any position or emolument under the Council and to expose jobbery and corruption in all its aspects.[4]

Kelly was listed as Chairman of the Estates and Finance Committee in the new Corporation. He was also Chairman of the Libraries' Committee, where his non-councillor colleagues included T.W. Lyster, Dr. George Sigerson, T.W. Rolleston, Henry Dixon, and the Rev. Gilbert Mahaffy. He represented the Corporation on the Committee of the Royal Irish Academy of Music, and also served on the Committee of Mercer's Hospital. On 25 April 1904, in his capacity as Chairman of the Estates and Finance Committee, Kelly proposed an amendment requesting that the Report of the Estates and Finance Committee be adopted. The amendment also proposed that, in view of the constant disagreement between Mr. Drury, the Local Government Board auditor, and the Corporation over its financial position, it would be expedient that Drury be withdrawn and another auditor be appointed in his place to audit the accounts of the Council. The amendment was tabled, and a division taken, resulting in twenty-nine votes for and thirteen votes against.[5]

The Local Government Board acknowledged receipt of the Estates and Finance Committee resolution, but found themselves unable to comply with the request to remove Drury.[6] Thereupon it was Councillor Kelly who proposed, seconded by Councillor Lord, that the accounting officers of the Council be instructed to refuse to submit their books to Mr. Drury for audit, until compelled to do so. This motion was defeated by 39 votes to 17. As we shall see, this would not be the last to be heard from Mr. Drury.

Meanwhile Kelly, as Chairman of the Public Libraries, was very involved in the search for suitable sites in order to expand the number of the existing city libraries, of which at the time there were only two – Capel Street and Thomas Street. He had already been instrumental in acquiring the site for the new library being built in Great Brunswick (now Pearse) Street, which was purchased in 1904 and opened on 1 December 1911. His remit also extended to the development of musical instruction for the city's chil-

---

3 *United Irishman*, 30 January 1904
4 Ibid. 6 February 1904
5 *Minutes Dublin City Council*, 1904, pp. 180-181
6 Ibid 1904, p. 186, DCA

dren. To that end, he had sponsored a motion to establish and maintain a school of instrumental and vocal music with a scale of fees which would make music education accessible to all. The objective also was to assist the Feis committees and the Orchestral Society in their work of developing musical talent and establishing a local orchestra on a permanent basis in which the pupils of the school might find employment. Concurrently, he was supporting very actively the proposal from Hugh Lane to provide a Municipal Art Gallery for Dublin. This was a project of major significance and will be discussed separately in Chapter Six.

January 1905 brought further municipal elections, and resulted in a gain of two more seats for the nationalist party in the Corporation. Eight candidates were put forward on the nationalist platform, of whom four were elected. There might have been more had the poll not been carried out in the worst weather experienced in Dublin for years: a gale, accompanied by an incessant downpour of rain, and freezing temperatures. The *United Irishman* claimed that the conditions adversely affected the candidates in wards such as Inns' Quay and the North Dock, which were heavily populated areas. In New Kilmainham, it reported that William Partridge and Patrick O'Carroll had simply annihilated their opponents, with a vote that was six to one in favour of the National Council candidates. But the victory in the Mansion House Ward was one to savour.

> All the forces of corruption – all the strength of the liquor ring – all the powers of Seoinínia [Shoneen was the name given to anyone who aped the manners and speech of the British] were set at work to drive Councillor Kelly out of the Corporation. Councillor Philip Little, the pious publican, carried the banner of Bung [the publicans] and the King in the Ward, and he and it are buried under the weight of 700 unbribable Nationalists as we write. Councillor Kelly is now Alderman of the Mansion House Ward, and his fellow Nationalist candidate, Mr. Clear is Councillor.[7]

The *Leader* had also carried endorsements for temperance candidates. In the issue of 14 January 1905, the battle for the seat in the Mansion House Ward is thus described:

> We hear that Mr. T. Kelly, T.C. who is a candidate for Aldermanship is being opposed by a Bung by the name of Little, who runs a 'bungery' [public house] styled the Winter Palace Gardens in Stephen's Green. Mr. Kelly is a strong temperance advocate… and we trust that after the election… Mr. Kelly, the temperance advocate, will be at the top of the poll.

Moran, in that same issue of the *Leader,* also strongly endorsed the candidature of Dr. J.C. McWalter, who was going forward in the North City Ward. He described him as a temperance advocate, a Gaelic Leaguer and a champion of tolerance, justice and fair play for Catholics. He was also a successful doctor, earning every day the love and gratitude of the poor.

---

[7] *United Irishman*, 21 January 1905

Both Moran and Griffith were delighted with the results of these elections. In a subsequent issue of the *United Irishman,* 28 January 1905, Griffith allowed himself to further enjoy the triumph:

> The West British party in the Dublin Corporation which we found five years ago
> dominating the civic life and spreading contagion around, is hopelessly shattered today.
> The introduction of a really Nationalist party into the Corporation for the first time – a
> party determined to uphold before all things the National honour and to oppose in all
> matters jobbery and corruption, has forced the weak-kneed ones to vote straight on
> National issues. To that party we look now for those reforms the capital has so long waited
> for. It has sought for night sittings of the Corporation committees, and it has been defeated
> – defeated by the votes of men whose written pledges given at election time to support that
> measure we hold in our possession. Night-sittings of the Corporation committees mean the
> extinction of the domination of the liquor trade in municipal politics. It means that
> businessmen and workingmen who are now debarred from entering the Council Chamber
> shall be enabled to do so. The business men and working men are occupied by day and free
> by night – the publican is free by day and occupied by night – hence his objection to
> night-sittings… And again`, comes up the question of the housing of the working classes.
> Now at last we have a party in the Corporation who are in earnest in this matter. In the
> city of Dublin there are 22,000 tenements of one room, some of them containing as many
> as twelve persons, and in nine-tenths of the cases the unfortunate tenement-dwellers of
> Dublin are rack-rented as harshly as the Irish tenant-farmers in the worst days of
> landlordism… We commend to the Nationalist Party the securing of the registration and
> efficient inspection of tenement houses, and the rigorous prosecution of every slumowner –
> be he who he may – who does not keep his premises in good and wholesome order.[8]

On St. Patrick's Day, 1905, the National Council issued its manifesto, headed An Chomhairle Náisiúnta, Ár dTír agus Ár Muintir (The National Council, Our Country and Our People). It outlined its principal aims which were based on the Hungarian model, i.e., national self-determination within the Austrian Empire, a policy of passive resistance and reliance on *Sinn Féin,* 'ourselves alone'. The Council pledged to support the Gaelic and industrial movements, to secure that all Irish bodies employ only Irish officials and use only Irish-manufactured goods, to develop the resources and industries of each to the utmost by using the full powers of the County and District Councils. With an eye to furthering the movement outside Dublin, attention was drawn to the forthcoming triennial local elections, where potential National Council candidates would be committed to supporting and carrying out these objectives. Candidates were invited to contact the two secretaries, Alderman T. Kelly and Joseph F. Hallinan, who had signed the manifesto, issued from an address at 22 North Gt. George's Street.[9]

The first annual Convention of the National Council was held in the Rotunda, in Dublin, on Tuesday, 28 November 1905, with Edward Martyn taking the Chair. Over a hundred delegates were present who came from all over Ireland, as well as from

---

[8] *United Irishman,* 28 January 1905
[9] Ibid. 8 March 1905

London and Liverpool. Before the meeting, entertainment was provided by the St. James's Brass Band, and the York Street (presumably the Workmen's Club) Brass Band who performed a selection of national airs. Máire de Buitléar, a friend of Arthur Griffith's has left us this account, published in *The Voice of Ireland:* [10]

> A shabby room in the old Rotunda of Dublin, with less than a hundred men and a handful of women and girls seated in rapt attention. They are listening to an earnest young man who faces them with a sheaf of papers in his hand. He is very tranquil, very modest, quite unaggressive – yet also full of suppressed flame and ardour... It began at eleven in the morning with Edward Martyn in the Chair; and near me sat Mrs. J. Wyse Power, Thomas S. Cuffe, Oliver St. John Gogarty and many more...

Griffith afterwards credited Máire de Buitléar with naming the movement *Sinn Féin.* She did not go on to have a political career, but became a nun.

Edward Martyn addressed the meeting, and reminded delegates of the progress which had been made since the foundation of the Council, arising from the King's visit in 1903 and the fight which had been put up to defeat the proposal to accord the royal visitors a civic welcome. He said that since then much had been achieved, particularly the success of the National Council within the Corporation. Thomas Martin, a London delegate, referred to the series of articles on the 'Resurrection of Hungary' advocating a dual monarchy system, which had been written and published by Griffith in the *United Irishman* and had pinpointed the need to get out of the quagmire of the business of Ireland being transacted in Westminster. Griffith now stated to the meeting that it was clear that the Union had not benefited Ireland in any way and that preparations should be made to withdraw Irish representatives from the British Parliament forthwith. He proposed a policy of national self-development through the recognition of the duties and rights of citizenship on the part of the individual. The control of Irish educational policy by the British Government was a key issue, because the language of Ireland, its history, culture and economics had no place in the school curriculum.

> Out of the primary schools come the recruits for the British armed forces... The Government Board which controls our primary schools brazenly offers bribes to the boys in our primary schools to join the British navy. [11]

Griffith also emphasised the importance of the General Council of County Councils, comprising as it did representatives of the Urban Councils, Rural Councils and Poor Law Boards and Harbour Boards, a *de facto* Irish parliament. Millions were going out of Ireland in taxation. He spoke scornfully of the Irish Parliamentary Party, and how they were being duped by the Liberals in the House of Commons.

---

[10] *The Voice of Ireland,* p.106
[11] *United Irishman,* 9 December 1905

Kelly followed with a robust speech outlining the development of the Sinn Féin movement, and laced it with a good deal of the kind of knockabout humour for which he was becoming famous, which evoked cheers and laughter. He was followed by Oliver St. John Gogarty, who delivered a thoughtful analysis of the Irish character, which blamed England for everything – poverty, laziness, dirt, want of employment, drunkenness. He said that the man who blames England for everything is never at fault because he is too stupid to see that denationalisation means demoralisation.

Alderman Cole proposed that national self-development through recognition of the duties and rights of citizenship on the part of the individual, with the aid and support of all movements originating within Ireland, was vital to the country. This attitude, he claimed, embodied the fundamental principles of the Sinn Féin policy. The motion was seconded and proposed to the meeting, and it was carried unanimously amidst vociferous cheering.

It was agreed to sanction the establishment of country branches of Sinn Féin consisting of at least ten members in every electoral district, thus ensuring that the new movement would spread its wings throughout the country and beyond. Candidates for representative positions were to be pledged to the principle of national self-development by the aid and support of all movements originating from within Ireland and not looking outside Ireland to accomplish their aims. The proceedings then concluded with three cheers for the Sinn Féin policy and the singing of *A Nation Once Again.*[12]

D.P. Moran in *The Leader* offered the following analysis which seemed to share to some extent Griffith's reservations regarding the Irish Parliamentary Party and its ability to deliver.

> The *Leader* policy, or as it is sometimes called, the Irish Ireland or Sinn Féin policy, is in its essence an attempt to turn men's minds to what can be done in the living present under existing conditions and existing national disabilities. We seldom or ever trouble our readers with what could be done if we had Home Rule. There are a good many people – be they more or less – who believe that Ireland should withdraw her representatives from the floor of the House of Commons. We who would work our policy of Sinn Féin for all it is worth, would also work the floor of the House of Commons so long as anything could be got out of it. At the present juncture when a General Election and a rearrangement of parties in England are at hand, it is highly probably that a fairly efficient Parliamentary Party may be able to do a considerable amount of efficient work... The Liberal Party will be returned to power. For some reason we associate the Liberals with hope for Ireland and the Tories with the other thing..... In the end it comes to this – that the Liberals have sympathy and the Tories power... The moral of all this is clear: give nothing for nothing. Do not keep a Government in power without a clear definite bargain as to what you are to get from it. I say bargain – no mere understanding will do...Votes are definite things, and 80 of them should not be given in return for nothing.[13]

---

12 *United Irishman*, 9 December 1905
13 *The Leader*, 2 December 1905

In January 1906, the Liberals were returned to Government and hopes were high that they would deliver. Moran offered some further advice:

> The Parliamentary Party must be left to do what they can on the floor of the British House of Commons, but while they are making such bargains as they may in that place, the work of making Ireland must go on with renewed vigour at home. It is seldom that a new year synchronises with circumstances that are full of new hopes. The year of 1906 is such a year. So much spade work has been done in recent times that we may reasonably look forward to a little reaping during the present year.[14]

In the same issue of the *Leader* Moran gave an analysis of the stock objections to Irish self-government which were: fear of rebellion, disturbance of the imperial parliament, and the government of the non-Irish half of Ulster against its will.

> The control of Irish affairs is mainly vested in the Chief Secretary, but he is subjected at every turn to that of the Treasury… the Treasury says how much they will pay and consequently can block any proposal. Under a scheme of Home Rule the power of Chief Secretary would be transferred to an Irish Prime Minister and that of the Treasury in effect to the Irish Chancellor of the Exchequer… Suppose you extend the independent control of the elected Under Secretary of the functions of the Chief Secretary, and also gave him the support of an Irish Treasury, you would have a very large measure of administrative Home Rule. There would be a possible amelioration of taxation if this were to happen… of course this is but one of the advantages of responsible Irish administration. The abolition of the Dublin Castle gang and the effecting of a real Catholic emancipation is another. But it is because I feel that it is by her fiscal administration that Ireland is being pressed to death, that I attach so much importance to that question.[15]

The results of the municipal elections in 1906 saw a further increase in Sinn Féin candidates within the Corporation. Every supporter of the Sinn Féin policy who had retired from the Corporation by rotation had been re-elected and three new seats had been won. More could have been achieved if all nationalist voters had checked that their names were on the register.[16] The *Irish Independent* of 16 January described it as 'dull voting'.

On 10 January, the first meeting of the Executive of the National Council took place in Dublin. John Sweetman from Co. Meath, an ex-MP of the Irish Parliamentary Party, presided in the absence of Edward Martyn. It was decided to choose two vice presidents for the National Council: Arthur Griffith and John Sweetman were unanimously elected to these posts. A plan was devised for the membership, which was by now very extensive and growing throughout the country. An executive committee would meet in Dublin on a monthly basis, with various other committees established to meet at regular intervals. Kelly was elected to the Organising and Press Committee. The executive

---

[14] *The Leader*, 6 January 1906
[15] Ibid. 6 January 1906
[16] *United Irishman*, 20 January 1906

unanimously decided, after the views of all the members had been considered, that no opposition should be offered at the time to the re-election of members of the Irish Parliamentary Party to Westminster, in order that no excuse might be afforded that party if it failed to redeem its promise to procure a Bill establishing an independent parliament in Ireland on the accession of the Liberal Party to power. A public meeting was held in the Council Chamber of the Cork Municipal Buildings on the following Sunday to lay the Sinn Féin principles before the citizens of Cork. The attendance was so large that scores of people failed to gain admission.[17] Nationalist hopes were high that at last something worthwhile was about to be achieved at Westminster.

Griffith surmised in the *United Irishman* on 27 January 1906 that in a fortnight's time the Bill for the establishment of an independent Irish legislature, which had passed through the House of Commons just twelve years previously, would be reintroduced. He inquired rhetorically whether the Irish Parliamentary Party had not got its price – Home Rule – in return for giving the Liberal Party political supremacy. He foresaw that the legislation could be passed for the second time in the House of Commons and for the first in the House of Lords and through all its stages by early summer of 1906, thus allowing for the preliminaries to be carried out in time for a meeting of the Irish Parliament in College Green in January 1907. Alas, the reality was to be quite different.

Moran, too, was getting impatient with the Irish Parliamentary Party. He wrote in the *Leader* on 10 February 1906:

> The present Irish Party, if it does not learn common patriotism and common sense, may wake up some day to the discovery that it does not possess the fee-simple of Irish public opinion; that it is only a tenant-at-will, and can be evicted without use of crowbar or battering-ram at the next General Election.

On 20 February, after listening to the Speech from the Throne which promised Home Rule for the Transvaal but no Home Rule for Ireland, John Redmond stood up in the Commons and announced his Party's continuing support for the Liberal Government. Griffith's reaction was scathing; he claimed that the party of Parnell was dead. He excoriated Redmond, reminding him of pledges given to the Home Rule cause over a period of twelve years and demanding an explanation, while at the same time voicing his suspicion that what the Government intended to do was to devolve certain administrative functions only.[18]

John Sweetman wrote supporting Griffith's view that Redmond had abandoned the cause of Home Rule. In a powerful letter, Sweetman recounted his own disappointments in the House of Commons stating that the reason he had resigned his seat twelve

---

[17] *United Irishman*, 27 January 1906
[18] Ibid. 24 February 1906

Alderman Tom Kelly refused to allow Local Government Auditor Drury (the figure on the right climbing onto the desk) to examine the Corporation's accounts. 'Poor Henry' is Town Clerk Campbell, behind the blackboard. Cartoon by Fitzpatrick from The Lepracaun Annual *[1906]. Courtesy National Library of Ireland.*

years previously was that he had become convinced that nobody could do anything for Ireland in the British House of Commons. Sweetman now offered himself to the National Party as a candidate, independent of all English parties, stating that he would no longer be bound to act with those whom he thought were sacrificing the cause of Home Rule to the demands of any English government.[19]

The *Leader*, on 14 April 1906, carried an analysis of the political situation since the Liberals took over, summing up the position as follows:

> Unless the Liberals are prepared to give us Home Rule or a large fraction of it, they are in effect neither more nor less than enemies. It is not worth the Irish Party's while to accept any lesser concession.

On 8 May, 1906, the *Irish Independent* carried an interesting account of a debate concerning the use of Irish within the Corporation. Councillor J.T. Kelly (Seán T. O'Kelly) proposed that Irish be used in addressing envelopes emanating from the Corporation. This suggestion caused heated exchanges between Councillors Vance and Brady, the latter stating that the principal members of the Gaelic League were civil servants in the pay of the British Government. Kelly invited them to name these people and Brady told him not to be always making a fool of himself. More heated exchanges followed, but the motion was carried by 39 votes to four. The *Irish Independent* sent a reporter around to the City Hall the following day to inquire what effect the motion regarding the use of Irish was having on the officials. He found that almost every department was equipped with one or more persons who were capable of doing the work. Some of the officials, however, were not too sympathetic and one was heard positively declaring that he would never learn Irish. Another said that he had purchased an O'Growney[20] that morning. The officials in the Town Clerk's office were not too worried. Three of the clerks there claimed to have a good working knowledge of Irish and did not anticipate any difficulties.[21]

Meanwhile, within the Corporation, the battle of the annual audit was looming again. By May, the Council was reiterating its determination not to allow the books to be submitted to Mr. Drury. Alderman Irwin said that what the Council objected to was the wholesale criticism calculated to make the general public believe that the Council was not managing its business properly, whereas the reality was that the Council had striven to have the administration of the city's affairs carried out on 'proper and square' lines. Councillor P.T. Daly said that Drury seemed to be motivated, for unknown reasons, to discredit the City Council. Kelly proposed that the books should not be made available to the auditor, and this motion was carried and by 34 votes to five.[22] The Lord Mayor, in supporting the motion, said that no one disagreed with a Local

---

[19] *United Irishman*, 3 March 1906
[20] An Irish language grammar, written by an tAthair Eoghan Ó Gramhnaigh (O'Growney)
[21] *Irish Independent*, 9 May 1906
[22] *Minutes of Dublin City Council*, 1906 pp. 299/300, DCA

A BOMB AMONGST THE PIRATES.

PIRATE CAPTAIN, from Poop;—"Stick to yer guns, men, and the day is ours!"
THE CREW; "Aye! Aye, Captain! we're d——d well stuck!"

The Court of King's Bench has granted a mandamus for the surrender of the books
by the Corporation to the L.G.B. auditor.

Alderman Tom Kelly (the Pirate Captain) had encouraged the Corporation to refuse to surrender its books to the
Local Government Auditor, until a mandamus was issued by the Court of King's Bench.
Cartoon by Fitzpatrick from The Lepracaun Annual *[1906]. Courtesy National Library of Ireland*

Government Board audit, but that Drury had gone out of his way to hamper the work of the Corporation and belittle the members of the Council.[23]

A letter from the Local Government Board, dated 29 May 1906 and recorded in the Minutes of the Municipal Council,[24] rejected the request of the Corporation to appoint another auditor in place of Drury, and urged the Corporation not to obstruct Drury in the fulfilment of his statutory obligations to audit their accounts. The Lord Mayor proposed a motion, seconded by Alderman Kelly, that the letter be inserted in the minutes, and the Local Government Board be informed that the Council would adhere to its former resolutions regarding Mr. Drury. The Local Government Board refused to change its position and lodged an application with the Lord Chief Baron, Mr. Justice Johnson, for an order of mandamus to force the Corporation to comply.

In the *Irish Independent*, 13 June 1906, the editorial dealt with the impasse regarding Drury who had gone too far in the tone of his comments which were not very judicial. The *Independent* noted that the Lord Mayor was prepared to go to jail and that Alderman Kelly was also prepared for the 'martyr's crown.' Overall, however, the editorial considered that while the Corporation might have some right on its side, its attitude could not be justified. A report carried in that paper on the same day recounted that Drury had gone to the Treasurer's Office at the City Hall on 12 June, and no books or documents had been forthcoming. The Town Clerk, Henry Campbell, said he was unable to give him the books. Drury adjourned the matter for 48 hours and departed. A special meeting of the Corporation was convened at noon. The Lord Mayor said that the Local Government Board could have shown a more conciliatory spirit. The citizens were entitled to know how their money was spent and the Corporation was fully prepared to submit their accounts to any investigation that was full and fair, but they objected to the Board sending as auditor a gentleman who by his past conduct had proved himself, in the opinion of the Council, a man of partial mind who came not merely to scrutinize the books but with the intention of belittling the Corporation of Dublin in the eyes of the citizens. He added that the Council intended to adhere to their former resolution as the members would be unworthy of their positions if they 'sat down' under Mr. Drury's imputations. Kelly said they had borne too long with the 'campaign of blackguardism', and were determined that it should end. A long discussion followed and the Lord Mayor proposed a further motion, supporting the action of the Town Clerk, Henry Campbell, as he was the instrument of the Council and therefore bound to effect their instructions. The judges knew that he was not the protagonist and that the real conflict lay between the Corporation and the Local Government Board.[25]

The case again came before the King's Bench with an application by Drury to make absolute a conditional order of mandamus to compel the Corporation, through the

[23] *Irish Independent*, 22 May 1906, p. 6
[24] *Minutes of Dublin City Council*, 12 June 1906, p. 299, DCA
[25] *Irish Independent*, 25 June 1906

Town Clerk, to deliver up the account books to him for audit. An affidavit was filed by the Lord Mayor, and the courtroom was filled with a large public audience including members of the Corporation. The affidavit stated that Drury did not confine himself to matters with which the law entitled him to deal, but had assumed an authority paramount to that of the Corporation in matters of policy and administration. Assertions by Drury about Corporation members had resulted in injuries to their reputation, financial standing and property, and had hampered the Corporation in the exercise of its borrowing powers. The affidavit also claimed that the reputation of the Corporation had been damaged with investors. It alleged that Drury had issued his report for the year ending 31 March 1903 to the press before the Council had had an opportunity to review it. The Corporation had concluded, therefore, that Mr. Drury had all along shown an unmistakable animus against it as a body and an absolute incapacity to confine himself to his own business. It considered that only the appointment of another auditor in Drury's place would ease the difficult relations that prevailed in the matter of the annual audit of Corporation accounts. The Town Clerk had no discretion but to obey the orders of the Corporation.

Mr. Ronan, Counsel for the Corporation, said that the Lord Mayor's affidavit addressed the key issues and stated that the Board had expressly sanctioned the illegal conduct of their auditor. Mr. Drury, he averred, was acting as the 'boss' of the Corporation. He had put them to enormous expense in having to repudiate his statements. Drury, in his answering affidavit, said he intended to continue to behave in the same fashion.[26]

The *Irish Independent* on 27 June, recorded how another day had been spent in court debating the role of the auditor but that no conclusion had been reached. On 2 July, the King's Bench found in favour of Drury, and an order of mandamus was issued to compel the Corporation to deliver the books. The Court found that Drury was justified in everything that he had done, and the costs were awarded against the Corporation. The past conduct of the auditor was judged irrelevant: the books were required for audit and the Corporation was obliged to produce them.

A Special Meeting of the Corporation was called on 6 July to consider the decision of the Lord Chief Baron. After a long and heated discussion, the Corporation decided to abide by its original decision. This amounted to contempt of court, and the councillors were leaving themselves open to arrest and imprisonment. The Lord Mayor complimented their Counsel, Mr. Ronan, and stated that the Lord Chief Baron's decision was very disappointing. The Corporation's affidavits were unanswerable, he said. The decision, if allowed to stand, would place the Corporation and every other body in Ireland under the heel of the Local Government Board and its auditors. If they proceeded to an appeal to the House of Lords, he was satisfied that the Lord Chief Baron's decision could not stand. He stressed he was concerned for the citizens' rights in the matter of costs but he felt that they would not be well served if this decision were not appealed.

---

[26] *Irish Independent*, 25 June 1906

He proposed a motion to appeal, which was seconded by Alderman Corrigan. Alderman Kelly agreed with the Lord Mayor's conclusions. He felt that the Local Government Board was determined to ruin the Corporation as a democratic body and it was for the Corporation to say whether they were going to allow that to be done. The unacceptable behaviour of Mr. Drury had commenced seven or eight years before, and he hoped that there was going to be no 'wobbling' on the matter. They were going to be 'spat upon' by the Chief Baron and Tim Healy who had said, he alleged, that their officials (the Corporation's) were able and clever but that they were 'a gang of parasites'. Healy had been a democrat once, but now had an enormous income and had built himself a palace on the Liffey. 'Why not stand to our guns and say: These books you won't get unless you bring in the police, artillery and militia. Bring on the Lion and the Unicorn.' All of this speech was interspersed with cheers and laughter. Kelly then claimed that the judgment of the Chief Baron was not the judgment of a calm, judicious mind but the outpouring of Dublin Castle. He proposed an amendment reiterating the Corporation's determination not to allow Drury access to the books, notwithstanding the judgment of the King's Bench, and again instructing the Town Clerk not to release them. This proposal was carried, amid heated debate, by 35 votes to 12.[27]

As things stood, however, members who had voted for continuing to refuse access to the books were liable to attachment for contempt followed by impeachment. On Monday, 9 July,[28] Drury turned up to commence the audit, and was resisted by the Town Clerk, Campbell, the Law Agent, Rice and Lord Mayor, Nannetti. Drury had to withdraw, and the affair was put on hold for a fortnight. At a meeting of the Corporation which followed, the Lord Mayor stated that the books would be produced for any impartial auditor.

The same issue of the *Irish Independent* reported that a legal difficulty had now arisen about Drury's status. Drury had been appointed to audit the accounts of the Poor Law Unions in Ireland generally, and the ambiguity was that no particular Union was specified. Under the Acts of 1871 and 1872, the greater part of the area controlled by the Corporation lay within the boundaries of the North Dublin Union, and the gentleman who was in charge of the audit in that area was a Mr. King. On 12 July, it was reported that Westminster would not interfere in the row between the Corporation of Dublin and the Local Government Board. On 17 July, the Corporation met to consider an appeal on the basis that Drury's appointment had left it open to argument that his actions for many years past were without authority. Kelly, however, felt that an appeal would be useless. The motion to appeal was lost, by fifteen votes to thirty-four. An editorial in the *Irish Independent* on 27 July, recommended that the Local Government Board take heed of what Chief Secretary Bryce had put to its officials regarding to their duties. He had advised them to study the wishes of the people. The Board should treat them like friends, he said, and take them into their confidence. There should be no spirit of bureaucratic superiority.

---

[27] *Irish Independent*, 7 July 1906
[28] Ibid. 10 July 1906

The final curtain fell on the drama and was reported in the *Irish Independent* on 5 December under the headline: 'Exit Drury, Enter King'. To a query raised by the Lord Mayor, and asked on his behalf by John Redmond in the House of Commons, whether the former audits conducted by Drury and surcharges made by him were legal, Chief Secretary Bryce answered that a decision had been taken two days previously, and that Mr. King, the auditor of the North Dublin Union, had been asked to audit the accounts. This announcement was greeted with loud cheers from the nationalist benches.

Regarding the interesting question as to whether the former audits of Drury and surcharges made by him were legal, Edward Carson asked if the auditor had been selected by the Local Government Board or by the Corporation. By neither, said Bryce, adding that he believed that Mr. King was the appropriate person under the statute. The Corporation, he stated, had had nothing to do with the matter, which he said was now closed. A prominent member of the Irish Bar consulted by the *Irish Independent* gave it as his opinion that all Corporation audits which had been conducted by Drury were now illegal, as it had emerged that he was not a legally appointed auditor, and that some action would now have to be taken to place the past Corporation audits performed by Drury on a satisfactory legal basis. As to the possibility of members of the Council being able to recover surcharges ordered by Drury, the informant felt it would be complicated, but that the Statute of Limitations would remove a number of claims and prevent their being put forward. So far, there was no indication that the Corporation as a whole or individual members of it, proposed to take any action. Ignatius J. Rice, Law Agent for the Corporation, was also interviewed, and said that undoubtedly the previous audits carried out by Drury were illegal. He added that he did not think there would be any developments in consequence, but that it was open to those surcharged in the last six years to have such surcharges remitted, and that those who had been subjected to severe strictures by Mr. Drury in his reports, could, if the circumstances so warranted, take proceedings for libel.

At this remove, it is difficult to understand why Drury had not seen fit to withdraw at a much earlier date. His character seems to have been such that once he had adopted an attitude, he became entrenched. It is to be deplored that so much valuable Council time and money had to be wasted in trying to resolve the situation. There is no description of his character to be found, other than those rather colourful accounts published in the newspapers of the proceedings within the Council, which were, of course, the perceptions of the councillors and which could not be held to be impartial. There is nothing in the Corporation minutes to give us any insight into his personality. It was a pity Drury did not see fit to take the advice offered by Chief Secretary Bryce when he urged the officials of the Local Government Board to study the wishes of the people and treat them like friends. The final verdict must surely have been very sweet to those in the Corporation who had persisted to the end in the battle to remove him.

Chapter Five: Home Rule or Devolution? And the North Leitrim Election

Whilst all these arguments were being rehearsed within the Council, the burning issue of Home Rule, or some variation of it, was being pursued on the wider stage. With the General Election of 1906, the Irish Parliamentary Party did not hold the balance of power in the House of Commons. It had won 83 seats, but because of the huge majority of 377 seats achieved by the Liberals, the Party could only rely on their goodwill, as the Liberals did not need their votes. The Party's expectations were over optimistic. In August of 1906, Sir Antony MacDonnell, Under-Secretary at Dublin Castle, who incidentally was an Irish Catholic, expressed his firm belief that the next session of Parliament would see the fruition of many of those hopes, which the best Irishmen for years had entertained. The British Government had plans under consideration for an Irish Government Bill, a measure which would be brought before Parliament in the 1907 session. This Bill was designed to give Ireland a large measure of management in local affairs. The *Irish Independent* of 1 August 1906 quoted an article by the Dublin correspondent of the English *Tribune,* who had it on reliable authority that what Sir Antony was hinting at was a development of a Central Council of County Councils to be formed of nominees from various county bodies. This proposal seemed similar to that initiated by Sir Thomas Esmonde, whose General Council of County Councils had already introduced a resolution in 1906 in favour of Home Rule, thus losing many of its Ulster members.[1]

John Dillon MP, speaking at a meeting in Co. Leitrim, expressed concern about the level of criticism being directed against the Irish Parliamentary Party, which implied that the party had done nothing for Ireland. He claimed that by persistent work in Parliament, the party had succeeded in destroying the whole system of coercion in Ireland, never in their lifetime to be revived, he believed, and had almost succeeded in emancipating the farmers from the tyranny of landlordism. Dillon declared, amid cheers, that until an Irish Government was obtained, he would never consent to the abrogation of the party pledge or the disbanding of the Irish Party. He thought that the measure of self-government promised by Sir Antony MacDonnell would be at least as good as that given to the Boers.[2]

---

[1] *Irish Independent*, 1 August 1906
[2] Ibid. 16 August 1906

On 29 August, the *Irish Independent* carried another report on the projected Irish Bill of 1907. It was understood that the legislative Union would remain unimpaired; the Irish representation at Westminster would not be interfered with, and the powers of the imperial Parliament would remain exactly as they were. The outstanding feature of the scheme would be the establishment in Dublin of an Irish Council, and the responsibilities to be devolved to the council were understood to include those generally grouped under the heading of local government, for instance, education and the police authority. On 23 September 1906, John Redmond addressed a large nationalist meeting held in Grange, Co. Limerick. He stated:

> We declare that nothing short of a complete measure of Home Rule – and by that I mean a freely-elected Parliament with an executive responsible to it – can ever be accepted as a settlement of the Irish Question, and that only a scheme of Home Rule can ever bring peace, prosperity and contentment to Ireland.

He said that he had noted that because he had remained silent in the five or six weeks since Parliament had risen, it was thought that he had been prepared to accept a scheme of administrative reform of some sort or kind as a substitute for Home Rule. He said that this assumption was without foundation. The editorial in the *Irish Independent* on the following day warned the Prime Minister that he might expect to find the members of the Irish Party in the same lobby as the opposition.[3]

An interesting diversion involving local politics occurred in Dublin on 24 September. Alderman Cotton, in his capacity as Chairman of the Improvements Committee in the Corporation, gave a lunch to celebrate the opening of a new main drainage scheme for the city, thus enabling the Liffey to be relieved of its function as an open sewer. The polluted state of the river had long been a civic nuisance, as the entire volume of the city's sewage had been pouring straight through the city sewers and into the Liffey. On the day of the inauguration of the new system, Alderman Cotton's invited guests were ferried to the pumping station by the SS. *Shamrock*, owned by the Corporation. Alderman Kelly was among those invited, and the sight of the Union Jack flying from the stern of the ship annoyed him so much that he cut down the flag with his penknife. Subsequently, a group of nationalist guests, including Kelly, refused to drink a toast to 'The King' at the luncheon that followed. This action gave rise to much unfavourable comment, principally and predictably in the unionist newspapers. The *Irish Independent* reprinted several articles from English newspapers, and also letters from its own readers representing various points of view. The English *Evening Standard* wrote:

> King Edward, remembering the depth and the strength of a loyal devotion with which his people regard him, may bear with some equanimity the loss of Mr. Kelly's support. His stupid insult comes at an apt time to remind us of the sea of hate and fanatical disloyalty into which the present Government seems determined to plunge an essential part of the United Kingdom.[4]

---

[3] Quoted in the *Irish Independent*, 24 September 1906
[4] Ibid. 26 September 1906

Three days later, the same newspaper printed a selection of readers' letters commenting on the same event, some favourable to Kelly's action and some not. One from a reader in Newry, who signed himself 'Another Northern Nationalist' wrote:

> He has shown the world that the old fighting spirit of Irish Nationality is still alive. Incidents like last Monday's are very refreshing in these dark days. If we had less Union Jack 'Nationalists' and more of Alderman Kelly's stamp, we would soon see the end of foreign domination over Ireland.

These incidents also provoked a certain amount of unpleasant exchanges within the Council. A Councillor named Vance, who espoused unionist views and had a penchant for attacking nationalists whenever he had the opportunity, made a series of vituperative remarks about certain councillors, referring to Councillor Sherlock as the bantam cock of the Corporation, who always crowed high. This led to further insults, lying was alleged, and another councillor, P.T. Daly, called Vance an ignorant little pig.[5]

The following day, Vance tried to introduce a motion to the effect that 'Alderman Kelly, in cutting down the Union Jack from the Corporation's SS. *Shamrock* unknown to and without the sanction of its owners, brought discredit not only to himself, and on the citizens generally, he be and he is, hereby censured'.[6] Alderman Coffey, who happened to be acting in the stead of Lord Mayor Nannetti, ruled the motion out of order. He admitted that he himself was an extreme nationalist, and appealed to his colleagues' loyalty. He approved, he said, of Alderman Kelly's action in cutting down the flag, but rightly or wrongly, his decision was that the matter was out of order. There were bursts of applause and the meeting ended with the gallery singing *God Save Ireland*.[7]

The unpleasantness within the Council occasioned by these incidents was reported in the *London Evening Standard*, which commented that the exhibition of rowdiness and political rancour was more than usually discreditable.

> If the representative citizens of Dublin find it relieved their feelings to call each other dirty pigs and liars, it is not our business to suggest that politer arguments might be equally exasperating and more to the point ... What we have is a right to protest against the deliberate way in which the Corporation has made itself a party to an affront on the flag of the United Kingdom. A motion of censure against Alderman Kelly for pulling down the Union Jack on board the Corporation's steamer, Shamrock, was received with howls and could not even be discussed... It must surely be obvious, even to the intelligence of Dublin irreconcilables, that unless the sympathy of some parties or party in this half of the United Kingdom can be obtained, their aspirations are not very likely to be fulfilled, even to a limited extent. We have yet to learn that English Home Rulers can look quietly on while Irishmen of the most objectionable sort, offer insults to symbols which are respected

---

5 *Irish Independent*, 9 October 1906
6 *Minutes of Dublin City Council*, 8 October 1906, p. 420, DCA
7 *Irish Independent*, 9 October 1906

everywhere throughout the British Empire, save in places where men like Aldermen Kelly and Coffey can get a hearing… But Mr. Vance scored a triumph worthy of his great namesake, by continuing to talk and the meeting had to break up amid loud singing of 'God Save Ireland' from the gallery. It seems quite an appropriate sentiment.[8]

From America came the following letter from the County Dublin Association of Boston, endorsing Kelly's action:

> Resolved that We, the members of the County Dublin Association of Boston, although having had to leave Dublin through causes brought about by Alien Rule, still take a lively interest in all that appertains to be the National, Commercial and Social well-being of our native County and City. We, also believing with our illustrious co-patriot, Theobald Wolfe Tone, that the source of all our country's misfortunes are to be found in the connection with England, do hereby endorse the action of Alderman Kelly, of the Dublin City Corporation, on Monday September 24th 1906, in cutting down the Union Jack of England, which floated over the said Corporation's steam vessel 'Shamrock', while on the trip to the Pigeon House, and we furthermore desire to express our appreciation of the action of Aldermen Kelly, Coffey, Cole and Farrell and Councillors Reynolds, Daly, J.J. Kelly, Vaughan, T. Rooney, J.J. Ryan, P.J. Rooney, Kavanagh and Parkinson in refusing to honour the toast of 'The King' at the luncheon which followed. Signed on behalf of the County Dublin Association of Boston: Charles F. Forrester, President, Peter A. Conroy, Vice-President and John Byrne, Secretary.

A motion to insert this letter in the Council minutes was proposed and carried, 31 voting for and 5 against.[9]

A satirical magazine called *The Lepracaun,* which was published during this period, captures very well the unpleasant atmosphere existing within the Council, and while lampooning with clever cartoons and sharp descriptions of the various personalities involved, managed to raise serious social issues at the same time.

Meanwhile, parallelling his national political activities, Kelly continued to be very active on the various Council committees to which he had been elected. As Chairman of the Public Libraries Committee, he was vigorously pursuing the possibility of opening additional libraries within the city, a policy which he had followed assiduously since he had been first elected to the Corporation. In the same capacity, he was also involved with Hugh Lane's proposal to establish a Municipal Art Gallery in Dublin, for which Lane had generously offered a magnificent collection of paintings to the city. Lane had first sought the Corporation's support for this project as far back as 1903. In 1905, the Municipal Council authorised the Estates and Finance Committee to provide the sum of £500 per annum (€60,000 at 2005 prices)[10] to maintain the Municipal Gallery and for the hiring and maintenance of a temporary premises to exhibit Lane's collection.

---

[8] *London Evening Standard,* 9 October 1906
[9] *Minutes of Dublin City Council,* 1906, pps. 54, 55, DCA

Given an uninterested chairman in this pivotal position, the project could have been halted there and then due to lack of interest and funds. But Kelly was the right man in the right place at this time, and saw clearly what a huge benefit the gallery would be for Dublin. The Public Libraries' Committee under his chairmanship accepted responsibility for the development on condition that the £500 allowed for the gallery did not come out of its budget, as obviously the work of the development and maintenance of the city libraries had to continue. During 1906, therefore, plans for the gallery were going ahead and, complementing the Council's work, a committee was established to gather subscriptions from like-minded supporters and interested members of the public. This committee included many well-known personalities such as Lady Gregory, Douglas Hyde, Emily Lawless, W.B. Yeats, Edith Somerville and George Russell (AE). The Secretary was Sarah Cecilia Harrison, a well-known artist, who later became the first woman councillor in Dublin Corporation, and shared Kelly's interest in the welfare of Dublin's poor. She was a stalwart supporter of the gallery project from its inception, and was a close friend of Hugh Lane. Her brother was Henry Harrison MP, a close associate of Parnell, whose biography he afterwards wrote. A lifelong friendship developed between Miss Harrison and Kelly, and a search then started for suitable temporary premises in which to house the Gallery. Alderman Cotton, on behalf of the Libraries Committee, had undertaken personally to make funds available for the rent until such time as the Corporation grant came through; other expenses had been met by the money contributed by private subscribers. Kelly's role in the history of securing a gallery for the Hugh Lane collection will be discussed in Chapter Six.

But to return to Home Rule: on 7 October 1906, John Redmond gave a speech in Athlone saying that he and his colleagues in the party were most anxious to support the Government scheme when the time came. He took the opportunity of reminding the Government that the Irish were unchanged and unchanging and that nothing except a free parliament, with an executive responsible to it, could ever settle the Irish question.[11]

At the annual meeting of the General Council of County Councils which took place on 18 October, the national demand for Home Rule was reiterated in a strong resolution in its favour, as follows: 'That the Irish people are a free people with a natural right to govern themselves; and that no Parliament is competent to make laws for Ireland except an Irish Parliament, sitting in Ireland, and that the claim of any other body of men to make laws for or to govern Ireland is illegal, unconstitutional and intolerable to the people of Ireland.' Kelly, in seconding this motion, said that they had had enough conferences on the matter and that he feared that some of their MPs were not properly watching the interests of the country. The result of these conferences, he said, was like giving a child 'a ha'porth of sweets to prevent it crying'. This drew laughter from the audience although a Mr. O'Neill said it would be unfortunate if the resolution was

---

[10] See footnote 4, Chapter 1, for calculation methodology.
[11] *Irish Independent*, 8 October 1906

thought to imply a vote of no confidence in the Irish Parliamentary Party. Copies of the resolution were sent to all the county councils and to the Prime Minister.[12]

In a speech delivered on 19 October 1906 by Walter Long, the increasing unease being felt by the unionists was given full expression. Long was the recently elected leader of the Unionist Party and was an MP for Dublin, even though he was not Irish. He declared that for many years the people of Ireland had believed that Home Rule was a nightmare of the past, but the measure which was now contemplated was an even greater danger than the old scheme defeated twenty years before. They were told that Home Rule was not now a possible policy, but that there was to be something else called 'devolution', which would be an instalment in the direction of the larger policy. It was Long's view that this new scheme, like the old, meant ruin to Ireland, ruin to every loyalist and Protestant in Ireland, and a bitter and irretrievable blow to the strength of the United Kingdom.

A meeting of the Orange Order was held in Dublin's Rotunda on 6 November 1906, and passed a resolution 'in opposition to Home Rule, or any tampering with the legislative Union, whether called Co-ordination, Devolution or Separation and to protest against the abrogation of the laws of the realm by an irresponsible civil servant'. (Presumably this referred to Sir Antony MacDonnell). The Round Room of the Rotunda was liberally decorated with loyal mottoes and banners of the familiar type for the occasion, and a fife and drum band played from the gallery. The Chairman, Rev. J.E. Moffatt, M.D., Grand Master of Dublin City, presided. He said they were there to assert their rights and liberties which were threatened by the so-called Liberal Government.[13]

The unionists need not have worried. The Liberal Irish Council Bill, as it was now called, was finally introduced in the House of Commons on 7 May 1907, by the new Chief Secretary, Augustine Birrell, who had replaced Chief Secretary Bryce. It was a poor substitute for Home Rule, and fell far short of satisfying the ambitions of nationalists. It proposed, as had been predicted, the devolution of certain local authority functions to Ireland, such as policing and agriculture. Birrell admitted that it was merely intended to control the administration of certain departments. Approximately 80 or 90 delegates, of whom three-quarters would be elected while the remainder would be chosen by the British authorities, were to manage the new body. The last word would lie with the Lord Lieutenant who could refer any matter he chose to the King. This only served to confirm what nationalists had expected all along. Redmond supported the Bill at the beginning, but by the time the National Convention of the United Irish League met in Dublin on 21 May 1907, he had changed his mind and denounced it roundly, thus removing all chance of a successful outcome. The Catholic Church also came out against it, and the *Freeman's Journal*, normally regarded as favouring the Irish Party, also found fault

---

[12] *Irish Independent,* 20 October 1906
[13] Ibid. 7 November 1906

with it. Ironically, Patrick Pearse was one of those who was willing to give the Bill a chance. Another was Mrs. Alice Stopford Green, the well-known nationalist and historian, who believed that it would 'become one bit of standing ground on which Irishmen shall be able in their own country to begin to fight out their own salvation'. She gave full credit to Sir Antony MacDonnell, whom she regarded as 'the biggest Sinn Féiner of them all'.[14] In September 1907, Redmond held a meeting of the Parliamentary Party in the Mansion House in Dublin, presumably in order to clarify his and the party's position and to deal with the criticism which was coming from various sources regarding party policies. Admission was by ticket only, and security was very tight. A considerable number of those who actually held tickets were unable to gain admission, including a large number of the clergy, as well as members of the National Foresters' organisation dressed in Robert Emmet costumes. All those forced to remain outside were caught in a downpour of rain. Among them was a large number of Sinn Féin party supporters, who held a meeting of their own in the forecourt of the Mansion House.

Inside, speeches were given by Lord Mayor Nannetti, who stated that Dublin was nationalist to the core, and claimed that the Parliamentary Party had achieved great reforms for the country under the leadership of Mr. Redmond. This was greeted with loud applause. But a voice called out: 'This is not a public meeting – it's packed'. Cheers and uproar followed. Redmond ignored the remark. The Lord Mayor cautioned those who wished to speak that this was a meeting of the Irish Parliamentary Party, and that anyone who thought otherwise had no right to be there. Joseph Devlin, MP for Belfast, gave an impassioned speech proclaiming the achievements of the party, and pointing out that the Sinn Féin Party in civic and national affairs in Dublin had the field all to themselves. He demanded to know what industries had the Sinn Féiners of Dublin established in the city? What had these men who criticised the Parliamentary Party done to uplift Dublin? What intellectual or educational development had they caused to take place? Various other party speakers, including Timothy Harrington, also addressed the meeting. Harrington appealed for unity. He said that the name of Sinn Féin was being used as a motto by a party fighting to weaken the ranks of those who were struggling against the common enemy. The other speakers included David Sheehy, Stephen Gwynn, and T.M. Kettle, all party MPs, all making the point that Home Rule could only be won by argument and action in the House of Commons. Redmond finally spoke, and stressed that the Act of Union had no binding, moral or legal force for the Party. 'Resistance to the Act of Union will always remain for us, so long as that Act lasts, a sacred duty and the methods of resistance will remain for us merely a matter of expediency.' He attempted to explain the genesis of what he called the recent Irish Council Bill, and said that the Government had made a fatal mistake when they had introduced it. 'Supported by yourself', shouted another voice, producing cries of 'hear hear' which Redmond again ignored.[15]

---

[14] Quoted in Richard Davis. *Arthur Griffith and Non-Violent Sinn Féin*, Anvil Books, Dublin 1974, p. 41
[15] *Irish Independent*, 5 September, 1907

HOME RULE AT THE MANSION HOUSE.

OLD LADY : "Oh, Johnny, darlin', for the Lord Mayor's sake, come in before yer bet ; that's Fighting Tom, the boy that cut down the flag at the party but ate the lunch. Shure, it's meself that has the trouble with him at the Hill beyant ; that's the raison I had to get polis to protect you agin them Shin Shiners."

Mr. Redmond held his Home Rule Meeting in the Mansion House, Sept. 4th, under police protection, and Alderman Kelly held a Sinn Fein Meeting outside, under the broad canopy of Heaven.

John Redmond held a Home Rule meeting under police protection at the Mansion House on 4 September 1907 while Alderman Tom Kelly held a Sinn Féin meeting outside. Cartoon by Fitzpatrick from The Lepracaun, *September 1907. Courtesy National Library of Ireland.*

Meanwhile, outside the Mansion House, the crowd had grown to between one thousand and one thousand five hundred people, most of them Sinn Féiners, who proceeded to hold their own meeting. Mr. O'Beirne, Secretary of the National Council, protested against their exclusion and the method by which it had been sought to represent the voice of Dublin favouring the Parliamentary Party. Cheers greeted this speech, at which point the police attempted to intervene. Loud cries of 'Stand your ground' were heard, and in the face of the determined attitude of the crowd, the police desisted and the meeting proceeded. Alderman Kelly proposed a resolution expressing loss of confidence in the Irish Parliamentary Party, which was received with loud applause. Councillor Daly seconded the resolution, and said that their friends inside (i.e., the Parliamentary Party) had had to secure the services of the police to enable them to hold their meeting. He himself had come there that night to criticise the party in the words used by Alderman Kelly, and claimed that those who had applied for tickets had had to declare that they were in favour of parliamentarianism before they received them. Councillor T.J. Sheehan protested against the exclusion of himself and his colleagues of the Municipal Council from what he described as the 'so-called Nationalist gathering' assembled inside that night. Then the Sinn Féin Party and their supporters formed into processional order, and marched down Dawson Street towards O'Connell Street singing nationalist songs. They encountered the police along the way and there was a scrimmage. Some people received minor injuries and some arrests were made, before the crowd finally dispersed.[16]

Griffith, sensing the trouble in the Parliamentary Party, prepared to exploit the possibilities of a rift. He knew that certain younger members of the party were displeased with the leadership, and were planning to mount a challenge to Redmond's authority. Among them was Charles Dolan, a young idealistic MP from North Leitrim who was unhappy with party policies. At a meeting of the United Irish League, he proposed that the party members should withdraw from Westminster, 'to work in Ireland for the industrial, agrarian and linguistic betterment of Ireland, while demonstrating a defiant hostility to all English influence in our internal affairs'. He had the support of five others, but the motion had been defeated. Dolan resigned from the Parliamentary Party, but delayed resigning his seat until he was finally forced to do so by the party in June 1907.[17]

Dolan described his experience in the House of Commons in the following terms:

> I found that English and Scottish members took no interest in the affairs of Ireland, that the speeches of Irish members were addressed to empty benches, and that we never received anything from the Government except assurances that were hypocritical and promises that never led to anything. The day of Parnell, Davitt and the Land League is

---

[16] *Irish Independent,* 5 September 1907
[17] Davis, Richard. *Arthur Griffith and Non-Violent Sinn Féin*, Anvil Books, Dublin, 1974, pp. 43-46

over and the voice of Ireland is drowned amid the cries of contending English factions. The Irish members are helpless in the House of Commons, outnumbered six to one and the proper place for the representatives to meet is in Dublin, not London. The true field of action is in Ireland, not England, and it is only by our efforts that Ireland can be raised to a position of prosperity and started on the path of national development, and in appealing to Englishmen we are wasting our energies and demoralising our people.[18]

One can only admire Dolan's convictions and the price he was prepared to pay.

At the same time, Sir Thomas Esmonde, also a Parliamentary Party MP, Senior Party Whip and Chairman of the General Council of County Councils, had independently resigned his Westminster seat, in the belief that Home Rule would never be granted to Ireland. He proposed to work for the repeal of the Act of Union. On 29 July 1907, the Parliamentary Party met in Committee Room 16 in the House of Commons, to discuss the resignations of Esmonde and Dolan. They resolved that, as Dolan had publicly repudiated the policy of the party and publicly declined to act with the party in the promotion of their policy, they were calling on him in accordance with the terms of the party pledge to resign his seat forthwith. They recorded their satisfaction with the fact that Esmonde, unlike Dolan, had at least taken steps to resign as they were finding Dolan far more difficult to handle. He was a relatively new member of the party, and was viewed with derision for having the temerity to criticise established party policies, while not having even the decency to resign.

On 8 December, 1907, Kelly addressed a meeting of Sinn Féin in the Fitzwilliam Ward of Sinn Féin and stated that while, at that moment, they did not advocate physical force, at the same time it would be wrong to repudiate it entirely, as it was their hope some day to drive the English out of Ireland. Sinn Féin policy at present did not mean revolution, but it meant something better than parliamentarianism. It meant first self-respect and self-reliance, and it meant they could accomplish many things in their own country, if they set about doing them in the proper way.[19] It is interesting to speculate whether this was an off-the-cuff comment, or if there had been some discussion at party level as to whether physical force might be considered in the future should circumstances warrant. It is known that Griffith was a member of the IRB, but in 1910 he asked to be allowed to resign. He subsequently joined the Volunteers in 1913. Kelly was never a member of either organisation, so far as is known.

Out of all this turbulence emerged what was called the first national Sinn Féin election. Dolan resigned his seat, and in the ensuing by-election, went forward for his constituency of North Leitrim as a Sinn Féin candidate. Griffith, despite serious misgivings, decided that Sinn Féin had no option but to fight for Dolan's seat. The Sinn Féin Party was going from strength to strength, but this was the first time it had taken on a challenge outside Dublin. Its policy of expansion had succeeded in establishing branch-

---

[18] Quoted in Hogan, David. A Forgotten Sinn Féin Election, *Sunday Press,* 14 October 1956
[19] *Irish Independent,* 9 December 1907

es throughout the country, from 21 branches in 1906 to 57 in 1907 and 115 in 1908. But Dublin was where its influence was strongest. The municipal elections of January 1908 brought the Sinn Féin Party encouraging results. They polled an impressive 6,751 votes, against the Parliamentary Party candidates who won 6,933. Alderman Kelly topped the poll in his own ward, and as Walter Cole had failed to get re-elected, Kelly became the leader of Sinn Féin within the Corporation.[20]

The polling date for the North Leitrim election was fixed for 21 February 1908. Leitrim was a poor county. Its land was poor, the people were disadvantaged and had no knowledge of any political party other than the Parliamentary Party. Griffith fought the campaign through the columns of *Sinn Féin* which was now the title of his newspaper.[21] Appealing for support in fighting the Leitrim election, both in the paper and through a series of meetings up and down the country, he had managed to raise a total of £771. The Sinn Féin Party founded a small local newspaper called the *Leitrim Guardian* to publicise Dolan's campaign, on which it spent £250 and which was used to raise the profile of Sinn Féin. The rest of the money went on travel and expenses. Interestingly, one of Sinn Féin's most stalwart supporters during the campaign was Seán MacDermott, later one of the signatories of the 1916 Proclamation.

The Parliamentary Party had plenty of financial resources and party workers and Redmond declared that they were not going to yield to a mushroom growth of nobodies without a determined struggle. The campaign proved to be a very rough, even dirty fight, in the tradition of Irish electioneering during the Parnell split and, in more recent times in the Fianna Fáil-Blueshirt confrontations. Sinn Féin reports naturally concentrated on the indignities suffered by its own activists, emphasising the activities of the Ancient Order of Hibernians who apparently drafted men into Leitrim from Belfast to break up meetings and intimidate Sinn Féin supporters. This association was supposed to be apolitical but in fact sided with the Parliamentary Party. In the lead up to polling day, there was a series of very ugly incidents at the public meetings. On 14 February, 1908, the Glenkeen Band, which was supporting Dolan, drowned out a meeting of the supporters of F.E. Meehan (the Irish Parliamentary Party candidate) at Kiltyclogher, and was rewarded by having its big drum destroyed. The Sinn Féin Party's only car was wrecked. The worst occurrence happened at Drumkeerin, where Anna Parnell and George Gavan Duffy, who were campaigning for Dolan, were pelted with missiles while attempting to address a meeting. Miss Parnell had a pail of water emptied over her head, and had the box pulled out from beneath her feet as she was speaking. On 19 February, Kelly and other Sinn Féin Party workers who had travelled to Leitrim to canvass for Dolan, were assailed with mud and eggs at Kinlough, and the police had to be called in to keep the two groups apart. Kelly pleaded that Sinn Féin only wanted a fair

---

[20] Ó Luing. *Art Ó Gríofa*, p. 167

[21] A libel action had been taken by a priest in Co. Limerick against the *United Irishman* in 1906. The priest won, and was awarded £300 in damages. Griffith closed the paper down, allowing the title to lapse, and the priest never got a penny. Griffith started it up again within three weeks, renaming it *Sinn Féin.*

A SURE THING.

"It's picking up money backin' this yere pup."

ALL BROKE UP.

"He'd a won de money if it hadn't been for de odder dog."

Mr. Dolan stated that he attributed the result partly to the misrepresentations indulged in by the Parliamentary Party. Generally speaking he considered the result satisfactory for a first attempt.

Charles Dolan, the Sinn Féin candidate in the North Leitrim by-election of February 1908, was supported by Tom Kelly, Seán T. O'Kelly and Arthur Griffith. This cartoon shows them going to North Leitrim with confidence and returning to Dublin after Dolan's defeat, battered and bruised.
Cartoon by Fitzpatrick from The Lepracaun, *March 1908. Courtesy National Library of Ireland*

hearing, and he was told in no uncertain terms to 'get to hell back to York Street'. Griffith published an account of the electioneering methods used by the Parliamentary Party during the campaign, which included payment for free drink and bribes to roughs. He wrote that 'armed with knuckledusters, life-preservers, revolvers and spiked clubs, these blackguards range through Manorhamilton, attacking isolated supporters of Sinn Féin and securing the protection of sympathetic constabularymen when danger threatened themselves'.[22] Meehan won the by-election by a majority of 3,103 votes to Sinn Féin's 1,157, but in fact it was a creditable result for the fledgling Sinn Féin Party, which had been virtually unknown in the area at the start of the campaign.

As far back as the end of July of the previous year, the *Daily Telegraph* of 29 July 1907 (and quoted in the *Irish Independent)*, had carried an article entitled 'The Sinn Féin Policy' which stated:

---

[22] *Sinn Féin*, 29 February 1908

There can be no doubt that the Sinn Féin Party is gaining ground in Ireland, especially amongst the more intelligent and better educated classes. The secession of a man like Sir Thomas Esmonde means more than the average Englishman can understand. Sinn Féin has ideals though they may not be such as can command the sympathy of Englishmen. With regard to its ultimate aims – the restoration of Grattan's Parliament or the erection of an independent Irish Republic – we, as Unionists, can only say we shall combat them as strongly as we did the policy of Mr. Parnell. But at least it may be admitted that Sinn Féin fights with clean weapons; it appeals to what it believes to be the spirit of Nationalism, and does not seek to win independence by robbing the rich or trampling upon the poor.

This must be regarded as a significant acknowledgement of the impact of Sinn Féin policies on a hostile British press.

Griffith declared afterwards:

We have given Ireland what she never had since the Union – a rallying base. Ten years ago, when we set out to do this, we had nothing to sustain us but faith in our countrymen. Our faith has been justified. We were madmen and fools to the political politicians who have been killing our country body and soul for generations. To-day in the teeth of the wealth (of the Parliamentary Party), their Press, their organisation and their friends in Dublin Castle, we have rallied three-fourths of the young men of Ireland and one-third of the national electorate of Ireland to our side. Ten years more and five-sixths of Ireland, Catholic and Protestant, will be banded together in national brotherhood. The Leitrim Election is the Declaration of Independence. The men of future generations will date Ireland's insurrection from the day when 1,200 Irishmen in the poorest and most remote county in Ireland voted for Sinn Féin. [23]

Ten years later, the results of the General Election of 1918 would justify Griffith's claim.

[23] *Sinn Féin*, 29 February 1908

Chapter Six: Dublin 1908 – 1910

These years saw the continuation of Kelly's involvement in many aspects of the Corporation's work. He was still Chairman of the Public Libraries' Committee, while T.W. Lyster of the National Library was Deputy Chairman. The main work of the committee in these years was the development of additional sites for public libraries, including most notably the library at Great Brunswick, now Pearse Street. Also at this time, Kelly was working very hard to identify a site for the new gallery which would be acceptable to Hugh Lane. As an interim measure, Clonmell House, a fine old building in Harcourt Street had been retained as a temporary premises. For this purpose, Kelly had proposed a motion through the Corporation requesting sanction of the £100 per annum agreed for the rent of Clonmell House. He added his hope that 'one room would be reserved in the gallery, even a small one, for the historic side of the city', doubtless reflecting his own interest in the history of Dublin. Interestingly, this motion had been put and carried with only one dissenting voice.[1]

The formal opening of the Harcourt Street Gallery took place on 20 January 1908, presided over by Lord Mayor Nannetti. The invitation to the opening was sent in Kelly's name, as Chairman of the Public Libraries' Committee, and was printed in both Irish and English. Lane wrote the prefatory note to the catalogue, outlining the Gallery's history, and laying down the conditions governing his own gifts. He stated that he was prepared to hand over his collection of pictures and drawings of the British School, and Rodin's masterpiece, *The Age of Bronze,* unconditionally, and also the group of portraits of contemporary Irish men and women. He made it clear that he would add a further significant number of paintings when the promised permanent building would be built on a suitable site. The house in Harcourt Street had been completely redecorated in a fitting manner, and the characteristic eighteenth-century ornamentation of walls and ceilings had been carefully preserved. The opening was an occasion of much interest and the rooms were thronged with important guests. The Catholic Archbishop of Dublin, Dr. William Walsh, was there, as was the incoming Lord Mayor, Alderman Cotton, and Sir Charles Cameron, Chief Medical Officer of the City and many other civic dignitaries. Kelly paid tribute to Lane and also to the financial assistance provided on a personal basis by Alderman Cotton out of his own pocket. Richard Caulfeild Orpen, brother of the artist William Orpen, and Honorary Secretary of the new gallery, read the report of the committee which outlined its history since Lane had first proposed it in 1902. In the *Daily Mail* of the following day, 21 January 1908, there was a full description of the opening:

---

[1] *Sinn Féin,* 29 February 1908

Alderman Kelly, who presided, is one of the Sinn Féin Leaders. From the same platform in perfect harmony could be heard Lord Drogheda (a Conservative Irish Peer), the Lord Mayor Alderman Cotton, a nationalist and a Labourite; Dr. Mahaffy, one of the shining lights of the Protestant Church, and Fr. Finlay, of the Society of Jesus.

In the political climate of the time, it was amazing that a group of people with such diverse views had been able to set aside their differences and present a united front in the matter of the provision of a Gallery of Modern Art for Dublin.

J.M. Synge described the Gallery in the *Manchester Guardian* on 24 January 1908:

This Gallery will impress everyone who visits it, but for those who live in Dublin, it will be peculiarly valuable. Perhaps no-one but Dublin men who have lived abroad can quite realize the strange thrill it gave me to turn in from Harcourt Street – where I passed by from school long ago – and found myself among Monets and Manets and Renoirs – things I connect so directly with the life of Paris. The morning of my first visit was brilliantly sunny, and this magnificent house with the clear light in the windows, brought back I do not know how, the whole feeling I had so often in the Louvre and a few other galleries abroad, but which does not come to one in the rather stiff galleries one is used to in England and Ireland. When one thinks that this collection will now be open to all Dublin people, and that the young men of talent, the writers as well as the painters, will be able to make themselves familiar with all these independent and vigorous works, it is hard to say how much is owed to Mr. Hugh Lane, Alderman Kelly and the Corporation of Dublin, and the artists and others who have carried through this undertaking with such complete success.

Sadly, however, financial problems very quickly began to cause difficulties. The City Treasurer, Edmond W. Eyre, advised on 21 January 1908 that he expected the Finance Committee to take action so that no further payments would be authorised for maintenance and staff at the new gallery. Henry Dixon, a prominent member of the Libraries' Committee, stated that serious retrenchment efforts had already been made, and that the purchase of new books had been banned, and because electricity had had to be paid for out of the budget, he felt that the public should be aware that the libraries were being kept open during daylight hours only, in an effort to economise on the use of electric light. On 22 January, Kelly found it necessary to clarify the financial situation in the public press, but stated that the gallery would not be closed even for one hour. There is a letter from the City Treasurer, Eyre,[2] regarding the financial difficulties being experienced by the Libraries' Committee and the very real possibility that the libraries could be closed due to lack of money to pay salaries. He himself offered to pay these expenses in order to keep the libraries open. Eyre's letter was inserted in the minutes of the Council meeting held on 10 February, without comment, no doubt as a reminder of what was a unique and generous offer.

---

2 *Minutes of Dublin City Council*, p. 93, 10 February 1908, DCA

On 10 February 1908, Dublin Corporation decided unanimously to confer the freedom of the city on Hugh Lane in recognition of his successful efforts to establish a municipal art gallery. It is interesting to recall that at this particular time, while Kelly was battling to keep the gallery and the public libraries open, he was involved in the election campaign to obtain Charles Dolan's seat for Sinn Féin in North Leitrim. The date on which he was attacked by rowdies in Leitrim was 19 February, and the election itself took place on 21 February 1908. This pattern of events indicates the kind of problems with which public figures had to deal in this period.

By 24 February, the newspapers reported that the libraries had been hit with a crisis. They had been closed, it was hoped temporarily, as there were no further funds to pay the running costs. The general public was furious at the closure, particularly as there would be no money to reopen them until the beginning of the new financial year on 1 April. However, the gallery remained open thanks to a few supporters who advanced the necessary money for the time being. It continued to acquire paintings and its fame spread. Many descriptions appeared in newspapers and art journals throughout the British Isles, and further afield in France and in the United States. All stressed the value and importance of the pictures gathered by Lane. In the first six months of its existence, it had attracted 88,772 visitors. The *Irish Times* on 29 September 1908 wrote:

> We have all good reason to be proud of the Municipal Art Gallery. Established only a few months ago by the great enterprise and enthusiasm of Mr. Lane, it has already more than justified its existence. The opening ceremony was in its way one of the most remarkable events in the annals of the city. It provided a platform on which Irishmen of all political parties and all social grades met for the common purpose of promoting a truly national object. The Corporation has taken a consistent interest in the Gallery and has helped in many substantial ways. Leading Irish Unionists have been among Mr. Lane's most generous supporters and, led by Alderman Kelly, the Sinn Féin Party gave the Gallery its most cordial blessing. We were indeed slow to realise our good fortune. The surprise and delight of educated foreign visitors and of the great art critics of Europe, have convinced us by this time that in our Municipal Gallery we possess something which gives a new distinction to Dublin in the eyes of the world.

These were not good years for the Sinn Féin Party, which saw a decline in its fortunes. Edward Martyn resigned as president of Sinn Féin after the North Leitrim election. John Sweetman was chosen in his stead, and Griffith and Bulmer Hobson were elected as vice presidents. Griffith decided to launch a daily newspaper, as he felt that it would be the best means of expanding the organisation. The new paper started with about £4,000 (€470,000 at 2005 prices)[3] in funds, but its circulation was poor. There were always financial problems, and the staff frequently wondered if their weekly salaries would be paid. It was an evening paper, and perhaps it might have had a better chance of success had it been published in the morning. Griffith did everything himself, editing, writing and even wheeling in trucks of paper for the machine room when neces-

---

[3] See footnote 4, Chapter 1, for calculation methodology.

sary.[4] However, money to keep the paper going was only possible through donations from generous patrons, and the *Sinn Féin Daily* was finally abandoned after six months.

However, there were other matters claiming the Sinn Féin leader's attention. A paragraph in Padraic Colum's biography of Griffith sums up what his thinking was in 1908. His efforts at that time were directed at trying to achieve a consensus between Catholic, Protestant Episcopalian and Presbyterian, workman and employer, artisan and farmer, landowner and tenant, the industrial north and the agricultural south.

> The Union was hateful to him because it destroyed the consensus that the Parliament was working towards. and put a great deal of the apparatus for reconciliation beyond the reach of the Irish people. The educational system which in other countries would bring young people of different creeds and classes together, in Ireland, through the stratification of interests, gave no such benefit.[5]

A burning issue was the introduction of the Irish Universities Bill of 1908. It was a matter of intense interest to the Catholic population of Ireland, and to the Gaelic League, whose leaders Douglas Hyde and Eoin MacNeill, were seeking a place for the Irish language in any new arrangement for the universities. This Bill proposed the creation of a national university of Ireland, with colleges in Dublin, Cork and Galway. It also recognised the role of Maynooth College in preparing students for degrees within the remit of the national university. There was a great deal of hostility in certain quarters to the teaching of Irish within the university system. The case for doing so was stated by Eoin MacNeill, who claimed that the basis of higher education in Ireland should be distinctively Irish, and therefore, knowledge of Irish should be required at matriculation. However, the bishops disagreed. Griffith sided with Hyde and MacNeill, and said that it was his belief that, if Irish were lost, something would be lost that could never be restored. Despite the opposition of many political leaders and the Catholic hierarchy, the county councils, who were sponsoring scholarships for the new universities, decided to support the argument for Irish as a compulsory subject for matriculation.

Griffith, in summing up the struggle, claimed it as a victory for Irish-Ireland over the British government-appointed senate of the National University. It was fought with the daily press of Ireland actively or passively hostile, and it was won in the teeth of influences which seemed impossible to overcome. The deciding factor was the money of the county councils; they held the purse, and the people said 'No essential Irish – no ratepayers' money'. Thus, recognition for the position of Irish was won.[6]

Within the Corporation, the issues continually under discussion were those of the housing of the working classes, and unemployment. A Distress Committee had been formed in November 1906 to help Dublin's unemployed, with four representatives

---

4 Ó Luing, *Art Ó Gríofa*, p. 183
5 Colum, Padraic. *Arthur Griffith*, p. 95, Browne & Nolan Ltd., 1959
6 *Sinn Féin,* 31 December 1910

from each of the Dublin Poor Law Unions, north and south, and twelve representatives from the Municipal Council. Labour yards were set up to promote basic skills for both men and women, in order to qualify them for jobs, instead of giving them charity. The work of this committee became well known for the impartiality of its administration and for its policy of preserving the self-respect of the labourers for whom it was finding work of public utility. Money was badly needed to keep this effort going, because of the never-ceasing demands for assistance. The Council made reference to a statement by the Prime Minister that consideration would be given to any representation regarding unemployment from local authorities in Ireland. Therefore, the Corporation of Dublin now requested the Government to take steps to deal with this issue, by special grant to the Dublin Distress Committee to enable the Corporation to undertake public works by borrowing money without interest.[7]

A deputation from the Trades' Council was received by the Estates and Finance Committee of the Corporation. It deplored the position in which many citizens were placed through lack of employment.[8] They pleaded with the Council to devise some method to create work opportunities, but there was a great shortage of money and all the current grants had been pledged, so the Corporation could only anticipate the revenues for the following year by a temporary advance through a bank overdraft, or by raising a substantial public loan. The Trades' Council deputation stressed that time was of the essence, because every hour was an age to a man with a hungry wife and children.

Lord Aberdeen, the Lord Lieutenant, and his wife were both very concerned about the conditions of the families of the unemployed and had worked hard with various charities to try to improve matters. Lady Aberdeen was particularly distressed about the prevalence of tuberculosis in the working-class community. Their efforts were not always appreciated by nationalists, but in fairness to them both, they were always very anxious for the health and welfare of the Dublin poor.

However, some of the Sinn Féin policies were now starting to bear fruit. For instance, an important advance was made in the area of social equality with the introduction of competitive entry into local government and other public services. Tributes were paid in *Sinn Féin* to Kelly's work in improving the system of competitive examinations which was largely substituted for the old system of patronage, which had made it impossible for any young man to secure a position in the municipal service on his own merits. Walter Cole wrote: 'The splendid boon for, possibly, the child of the poorest man in Dublin won by Alderman Kelly would be shorn of its greatest value were it to deny continuous progress to the successful competitions for clerkships and similar posts.'[9]

---

[7] *Minutes of Dublin City Council,* 1908, p. 550
[8] *Dublin Corporation Reports,* Vol. 2 , pp. 761-764, 1908, DCA
[9] *Sinn Féin,* 16 January 1909

The question of the overtaxation of Ireland under the Union was also another very contentious issue, and had been for a number of years. Griffith had continually reminded his readers how unjust the system was, as did D.P. Moran in the *Leader*. Redmond had raised this issue in an important debate in the House of Commons on 1 May 1906. At that time it was claimed that Ireland was overtaxed by two and three quarter millions. The Chancellor of the Exchequer had assured him that the Treasury was not hostile to Irish schemes, though he had admitted that Ireland had a real grievance, which was going to be investigated over the coming months to see how far it was possible to adjust the inequitable financial arrangements between the two countries. Opposition speakers, A.J. Balfour and Joseph Chamberlain, contended that it was not proven that in the matter of taxation Ireland was a pecuniary loser. The current position in 1906 was that the total revenue for the year under investigation was seven and a half million pounds (€900 million at 2005 prices). The direct effect of that on Ireland was that the people were forced against their will to bear an excessive share of the enormous cost of the armaments of the Empire. Redmond had also referred to the fact that no money had been forthcoming from the Treasury for educational purposes. He particularly mentioned grants for erecting and repairing national schools. He had also raised the issues of evicted tenants and the teaching of Irish. In reply, H. H. Asquith (then Chancellor) expressed his earnest desire to take action to remedy the situation. He was not aware, he said, of any hostility to Ireland in the Treasury. He felt that in educational matters Ireland had a real grievance, and he would see that Irish funds were not encroached upon. He intended going most carefully into Irish finances, and hoped Mr. Redmond would be content with that assurance.[10]

In an attempt to cope with the industrial unrest of which there was much, both in Dublin and Belfast, *Sinn Féin* published information regarding the successful Council of Prudent Men which had been established in France in the 1840s as an endeavour to minimise difficulties in the workplace. This concept seemed to offer a logical way of resolving industrial disputes, operating as a mediating power between employers and employees. It aimed to be fraternal and conciliatory and was founded on a strong sense of justice between master and man. As a result, a large proportion of cases were settled in private court without expense and without publicity. *Sinn Féin* commented that such a system would seem to have a lot to offer to strike-ridden Ireland.[11] Archbishop William Walsh was another who had realised the advantage of some form of conciliation mechanism and had participated in efforts to achieve such a system as early as the last decades of the nineteenth century. He had offered his services in the selection of arbitrators during a builders labourers' strike in 1890, and was well known for his beliefs in the efficacy of conciliation boards as a means of averting strikes. He saw the need to preserve the dignity of the workers, and was aware of the need for unions as a haven to shelter them from the power of their masters. Archbishop Walsh was also a keen promoter of Irish-manufactured goods, realising their potential for reducing unemployment.

---

[10] *Irish Independent,* 2 May 1906
[11] *Sinn Féin,* 24 July 1909

The campaign to promote indigenous industries continued, which, in turn, helped to stimulate employment. The *Irish Independent* of 3 May 1906 carried an advertisement for a furniture shop at 46 Camden Street called Sinn Féin Ltd., advising customers that it was the only Irish firm in the trade, and offering prices at 20% discount. In later years, there was a dairy in York Street known as the Sinn Féin Dairy. There is no evidence to suggest that any copyright existed regarding the use of the Sinn Féin title!

As a result of an increased interest in purchasing home-produced goods, achieved to a large extent by the continuous encouragement by Griffith and Moran in their respective newspapers, Aonach na Nodlag, a Christmas fair selling only Irish goods, was initiated in December 1907 by Kelly and others and was a great success. It survived as an annual event up until 1919, when it was closed down on the orders of the military. It took place in the Rotunda, and its activities were vividly described in the columns of *Sinn Féin*. For instance, in 1912, an art exhibition was run in tandem with the Aonach. Under the heading 'The Fifth Aonach', it announced that Alderman Kelly, one of the vice presidents of Sinn Féin, would formally declare the fifth Aonach open in the Rotunda that night. 'In the Aonach you may purchase a suite of furniture, a ton of coals, clothes to cover yourself, things to eat, and a picture – all without leaving the building… The Aonach Committee has catered for the music-loving, by providing music in every room; for dancers a capacious dancing hall, where native dances will be tripped to excellent music; refreshments for everyone, and Edison's wonderful Kinemetoscope to while an hour away in harmless amusement.'[12] A typical advertisement for the Aonach would include a recommendation to Irish people to keep their money in their own country at Christmas, claiming that 90% of the public's Christmas requirements were now available on the Irish market, manufactured by Irish firms. An additional million pounds would be retained in the country and would contribute to the sustenance of 20,000 families, and keep 80,000 Irish people supported in their jobs at home. Surely this was an issue on which unionists, parliamentarians and Sinn Féiners could agree, and was a huge improvement on the situation which had existed back in 1903, when the little Workmen's Industrial Association had started up.

The campaign for the encouragement of Irish industries was one issue on which Griffith and Moran saw eye to eye. But they were frequently poles apart, and Moran was often cuttingly scathing about the Sinn Féin movement, and about the analogy used by Griffith of Ireland's situation *vis-à-vis* the position of Hungary in the Austro-Hungarian Empire when she refused to sit in the Austrian Parliament and demanded her own parliamentary institutions. Moran frequently referred to the Sinn Féin Party as the 'Green Hungarian Band', and had a powerful line in invective when he chose to mock aspects of their policies. He firmly believed that Home Rule would come through the Irish Parliamentary Party.

---

12 *Sinn Féin,* 7 December 1912

The prospects of achieving Home Rule brightened considerably in 1910. Asquith, by now Prime Minister, and his Chancellor, Lloyd George, wanted to enact a highly radical budget involving a range of social benefits to be paid for out of increased taxes. The Tory-dominated House of Lords rejected these proposals. A general election followed in February which left the Liberals and Tories with almost equal numbers and the balance of power effectively in the hands of the Irish. It seemed the ideal moment to press for Home Rule. A Home Rule Bill, however, would run up against the same problem as the budget: implacable opposition from the Lords.

The answer to the budget issue, as seen in Britain, was to remove the absolute veto which the Lords at that time could exercise over legislation sent forward from the Commons. As it happened, removal of the veto would also suit the Irish by removing the Lords' ability to prevent Home Rule ever being put on the statute book. In these circumstances the advantage for the Irish lay in supporting the budget and the related case for diminishing the power of the House of Lords. When the veto had been removed would be the time to demand Home Rule as forcefully as they could, using the balance of power to threaten the Liberals with defeat if they failed to act. After a further general election in December, the Lords yielded and the absolute veto was abolished: a bill twice rejected by the Lords could now become law if passed for a third time by the Commons. Home Rule accordingly assumed the centre of the stage.

The strategy of supporting the Liberal government, without forcing it into a corner on Home Rule until the circumstances were right, made sense in terms of parliamentary tactics. But this could not readily be understood in Ireland where nationalists expected the party to bring pressure for Home Rule to bear on the Liberals once the Irish had the chance of doing so. The Parliamentary Party therefore seemed to be stalling in the tension-filled year of 1910 between the two elections. This roused strong suspicions within Sinn Féin, for whom Redmond's rhetoric protesting the need for Home Rule was not matched by vigorous action at Westminster.

Meanwhile, in Dublin, the election of a new Lord Mayor in February 1910 resulted in the choice of Michael Doyle, who replaced the outgoing Mayor, Alderman Coffey. There was a mixed reaction to the tributes paid to Lord Mayor Coffey at the end of his term. Councillor Cosgrave opposed the motion of thanks to him. He criticised Coffey's lack of attendance at Council meetings, and the Old Age Committee meetings. Cosgrave also claimed that he and his nationalist colleagues did not receive the consideration they were entitled to at Coffey's hands. Councillor Patrick O'Carroll, another nationalist, claimed that Alderman Coffey, while in the Chair, had acted with partisanship and bigotry. Councillor McCarthy said that Alderman Coffey's year of office was marked by some disgraceful scenes, the blame for which lay on his shoulders. He had insulted the minority of the Council, and they of the minority would be '18-carat hypocrites' if they did not protest. Alderman Coffey had shown his 'impartiality' by trying to crush the side that differed from him. He had ruled out a motion to reduce the Lord Mayor's salary. A resolution on the budget from the Sinn Féin Party was also ruled out. Kelly said that his party had justified every step it took, but they had been treated like

THE "COFFEE COOLER."

THE LORD MAYOR ELECT—"It's a tough job for the pay, as much as they talk about making a bit."
THE TOWN CLERK—"Don't be afraid, Willie. I know every one of their movements. You're not the first Trainer I
saved ; bedad, 'tis meself that knows how to manage them."

The Lord Mayor-elect, Alderman William Coffey, a noted teetotaller, will be in opposition to the licensed vintners,
the Unionist Party and Sinn Féin, but will be supported by the Town Clerk, Henry Campbell. Tom Kelly is fea-
tured as the Sinn Féin tiger. Cartoon by Fitzpatrick from The Lepracaun, *February 1909.*
Courtesy National Library of Ireland

'a parcel of dogs'. Councillor Cosgrave's motion of censure was tabled and carried by
thirty-seven votes to seven. In acknowledging the vote, Alderman Coffey (who was a
publican) said he chiefly owed his election to the Chair to the licensed trade. It seems
the publicans still ruled in 1910. *The Lepracaun* continued to satirize the Council members mercilessly and the cartoons from this period provide a running commentary on
the topical issues of the day.

The *Irish Independent* on 2 April 1910 published an analysis on the latest emigration
figures just released for 1909, which gave a sad picture of the drain from the land. A
total of nearly 30,000 had emigrated during that year, an increase of over 5,000 on the
previous year, and comprised 6.7% of the population, 8.8% of whom were destined for
Great Britain and 76% for the USA. Other destinations were given as colonies or foreign countries. The highest rate of emigration was from Kerry and the lowest from
Dublin. Fourteen thousand were male, and listed as labourers, while 12,000 were
female and described as servants. Both categories gave their age as fifteen and upwards.

In Dublin, on 4 April 1910, the budget was discussed at a meeting of the Corporation,
and while there were protests from two visitors sitting in the gallery which resulted in

their being forcibly removed, there was an air of resignation as to its implications for Ireland. Councillor Cosgrave made the point that Ireland was overtaxed already and that Mr. Redmond was supporting the weak and invertebrate Liberals and a Prime Minister who had no sense of honour, and who had misled the Irish people by his promises.

On 18 April, there was a guillotine debate in the House of Commons relating to the budget in line with its tactical policy. The Parliamentary Party supported the motion, and it was passed by a majority of eighty-three votes. Asquith claimed that the budget proposals were identical to those of the previous year and had been approved of by the then House of Commons. No concessions were offered to the Irish members. Redmond's tactics brought on his head the fury of the maverick independent nationalist MPs, William O'Brien and Timothy Healy, whose vituperation was much reported.

King Edward VII died in May 1910, and was succeeded by George V. A motion of condolence to the new King, George V, was proposed by the Lord Mayor of Dublin, Councillor Doyle, and was seconded by the High Sheriff, J.P. Brindley. The motion was carried by thirty-two votes for and seven against. The latter included Kelly, Cosgrave, and O'Carroll. Griffith analysed the issue of the King's death, and asked what, if anything it meant for Ireland.

> Let us ask those who can think – whether they be for or against us politically – what interest it is to Ireland that a George succeeds an Edward, or an Edward succeeds a George? The face beneath the crown changes, but the crown does not change. Whoever its wearer be, it stands today for the government of Ireland by foreigners.

> George the First, vile was reckoned
> Viler still was George the Second.
> And what mortal ever heard
> Any good of George the Third?
> When to Hades the Fourth descended
> Heaven be praised, the Georges ended.[13]

But, as we know, they did not.

With the advent of the new monarch, the issue of the Coronation Oath was raised again. King Edward had always had a horror of certain parts of the oath. He considered it to be a grievous vexation to the Catholic subjects of the King.[14] It was also very offensive to the Catholics of Ireland, and was made much of by Kelly, in his speech regarding the 'infamous oath of an infamous King' at the time of Edward VII's proposed visit

---

[13] Signed W.D. *Sinn Féin*, 12 May 1910
[14] *Irish Independent*. 12 May 1910

to Ireland in 1903. A motion was moved by the Lord Mayor in the Corporation, seconded by Alderman McWalter as follows: 'That the Corporation of Dublin demands that the following declaration from the Coronation Oath, which is intolerably offensive to at least twelve million of persons in these realms, should be deleted therefrom'. The offending extract read:

> I do solemnly and sincerely, in the presence of God, profess, testify and declare that I do believe that in the Sacrament of the Lord's Supper, there is no transubstantiation of the elements of Bread and Wine into the Body and Blood of Christ at or after the Consecration thereof by any person whatever; and that any Invocation or Adoration of the Virgin Mary or any other Saint, and the sacrifice of the Mass, as they are now used in the Church of Rome are Superstitious and Idolatrous.

The Corporation's motion that this offensive section of the oath be deleted was proposed and declared carried unanimously. Prior to the meeting, six members declared they would not be supporting the oath motion, and decided to absent themselves, in order to avoid contentious arguments.[15]

The *Irish Independent* of 12 May 1910 claimed that there was a great deal of sorrow in Ireland at the death of Edward VII, 'bridging over every political and religious animosity. The reign of King George will be a glorious reign, indeed, if it sees Ireland no longer the Poland of the British Empire'. The article refers to an unusual sense of loss at the death of the King, and that he was greatly mourned and thought to have been much concerned with Home Rule. With regard to the oath, it was felt that concessions could be made to the new spirit in the land without compromising on their convictions. Any barrier between the King and his Irish subjects throughout the empire was to be deplored. The Archbishop of Dublin, Dr. William Walsh, wrote to the Administrator of the Pro-Cathedral to ask that a special Solemn Votive Mass be held on the day of the King's funeral in view of his peacemaking efforts as a well-wisher of Ireland, and an earnest worker in the cause of international peace. Had the King lived, he would have looked upon the day that he opened our Parliament House in College Green as one of the happiest days of his life, for it was a well-known fact that he was fully in sympathy with Mr. Gladstone in his Home Rule Bill.[16]

On 20 May, the day of the King's funeral, the centre pages of the *Irish Independent* were outlined in thick black borders, and carried full details of all the services by all denominations held throughout Ireland to mourn his passing. The Solemn Votive Mass in the Pro-Cathedral was sung under the direction of Mr. Vincent O'Brien, who also played Beethoven's Funeral March on the organ. The Archbishop, Dr. Walsh, occupied the throne. Many could not gain admittance and waited on the street where it rained incessantly. The Lord Mayor attended the Mass for the late King and was criticised for so doing. He later wrote to the effect that common decency and sympathy at the death of

---

[15] *Minutes of Dublin City Council,* 1910, pp. 262/263, DCA
[16] *Irish Independent,* 16 May 1910

the King must not be confounded with flunkeyism indulged in by others.[17] Some nationalists had problems with this memorial service for the King, and had painted the name of Terence Bellew MacManus, a Young Irelander, on the steps of the Pro-Cathedral, a reminder of the fact that his remains had been refused entry into any church in the time of Cardinal Cullen.

Within the Corporation, there was a long discussion on how the matter of the oath would be handled. Some felt the full oath should go. Asquith had condemned it, and now that religious persecution – at all events in Ireland – had passed away, the offensive portion of the oath should no longer remain. Dr. McWalter said that the onus was on the Parliament to remove it. He felt that a petition should be presented at the Bar of the House of Commons to that effect. Alderman Kelly spoke and declared that all the Irish MPs had to say to the Liberals was: 'If you don't alter the terms of the Oath, we will kick you out.'[18]

A public meeting in Beresford Place was called by Sinn Féin about the alleged misrepresentation of the Lord Mayor and the Corporation regarding the feelings of Irishmen on the demise of the British sovereign. On the platform were Arthur Griffith, W.T. Cosgrave, Major John McBride, Francis Sheehy-Skeffington and Thomas Kelly. Griffith proposed the resolution: 'That in the opinion of this meeting, Irish Nationalists cannot identify themselves in a public representative capacity with any act or expression of loyalty to the Head of the British Government.' He said it was a resolution on which all sections of nationalists could unite. Francis Sheehy-Skeffington seconded the resolution and said that he wished to thank the National Council under whose auspices the meeting was called, for giving all sections an opportunity of recording their protest against the orgy of flunkeyism in Dublin and throughout the country within the last fortnight. The Sinn Féin members in the Corporation had protested against it, and so had Thomas Kettle and others. This speech gave rise to cheers. W.T. Cosgrave also supported the resolution. Kelly addressed the meeting and referred to the statement that was being spread throughout Ireland that the late English king was a friend of the Catholics. King Edward, he said, was no more a friend of the Roman Catholics than he was of the Mohammedans. He referred to the problems of emigration, and the necessity to campaign against enlistment. Countess Markiewicz also spoke, making the point that Sinn Féin was the one political organisation in Ireland which permitted women to work on terms of full equality with men. She appealed for all to exert themselves to prevent emigration and help the anti-enlistment movement.[19]

On 28 June, 1910, Asquith introduced a bill to alter the oath. He recited its history. It had come into existence in 1678, as a result of the Papish Plot, the aim of which was to preclude Catholics from sitting in either of the Houses of Parliament. Asquith declared that Edward VII had found it repugnant. He read out an alternative formula,

---

[17] *Irish Independent,* 23 May 1910
[18] Ibid. 26 May 1910
[19] *Sinn Féin,* 4 June 1910

which excluded all offensive references to Catholics. It seemed to be acceptable. There was a protest from Captain Craig, speaking on behalf of the Protestants of Ulster (where the majority of the population was Catholic) who said they took a different view of the matter. However, the House divided and voted by 383 votes to 42 to introduce the bill.

The bishops of Ireland, meeting in Maynooth, had recorded a protest against the preservation of an outworn and useless formula which continued to outrage Catholic sensibilities. Similar expressions of opinion had been voiced by Protestant churchmen and nonconformists. At the same meeting, the matter of grants-in-aid for secondary education, which in Ireland amounted to £2.18/-. per student as compared to over £5 per pupil in England, was also discussed. 'The Treasury, which for years maintained the unfair discrimination against Irish Secondary Education, will not be moved to greater generosity by an exposure of the injustice. The demand for redress should be taken up in Parliament with the united strength of the Irish representation, said the bishops.'[20]

In June 1910, the formal opening of the Sinn Féin Bank took place in the impressive new premises acquired by the party at No. 6 Harcourt Street. Its full title was the Sinn Féin Co-operative Peoples' Bank Ltd., and it had been set up in 1909 by the National Council of Sinn Féin to carry on the business of Banker and Bill Discounter, to assist in the development of Irish industries, and to promote popular credit in the towns of Ireland. It was governed by a committee of management, which included George W. Russell (A.E.), Arthur Griffith and P.T. Daly, Town Councillor, and Kelly who acted as treasurer. It was run as a co-operative bank, based on European examples, specifically on the Popular Bank of Milan. Griffith reported on this venture enthusiastically in the columns of *Sinn Féin*.[21] He stated that co-operative banks created a new class of business, because people were brought within reach of banking facilities, with whom ordinary banks would not be able to deal. They operated cheaply as the administrators gave their services on a voluntary basis, and the members took a greater interest in the business over which they had complete control. The office hours included a late night opening on two nights per week, and operated initially from offices at 11 Lower O'Connell Street, but subsequently moved to No. 6 Harcourt Street in June 1910.[22]

No. 6 Harcourt Street from now on became the centre for all Sinn Féin meetings and social occasions. The new building was one of the splendid mansions erected in pre-Union times, in the most fashionable part of Dublin. The reading and recreation rooms were open every night, and the nucleus of a library was set up. Various social activities took place over the ensuing months, such an 'enjoyable Siamsa', (gathering), at which visitors from England, America and the Argentine attended in mid-September. A series of lectures began on 12 October, when Griffith gave a lecture on 'Withdrawal from

---

[20] *Irish Independent*, 22 June 1910
[21] *Sinn Féin*, 2 January 1909
[22] John H. Newman, later Cardinal, had rooms here while he was negotiating the establishment of the Catholic University. Nowadays it is the head office of Conradh na Gaeilge

Westminster'. Others on similar themes were to follow.[23] In a tribute to Kelly at the time of his death by Roddy the Rover in the *Irish Press*, he described how, at the opening of the new premises, Kelly had climbed up on the roof to hoist the flag of Ireland to a mast in the height of a thunderstorm. 'Who knows' he said, 'but we might be under fire in this fortress yet. A few years more, and Kelly was under fire, and the flag he raised flew over a land at war.'

While continuing to function as the headquarters of the Sinn Féin Bank, No 6 Harcourt Street was an important location in the sphere of national politics. It was from these headquarters of the nationalist movement that what became known as the Sinn Féin election of 1918 was planned and executed. The meticulous plans drawn up for this election resulted in the amazing victory which spelt the end of the Irish Parliamentary Party.

[23] *Sinn Féin*, 8 October 1910

Chapter Seven: The Pursuit of Home Rule

In April of 1911 Asquith spoke in the House of Commons and made it clear that all who had voted for him were aware that not only were they voting for a change in relations between the Commons and the Lords, but also that Home Rule for Ireland would be carried in the lifetime of the current Parliament. However, the Unionists continued their fierce resistance and warned of dire consequences if the Prime Minister continued to pursue this course.[1] Inter alia, they pointed out that there would be many deserters from the Liberal Party itself if he persisted. Discussions dragged on and, in June, Redmond stated that the House of Lords had ever been the arch-enemy of Irish reform, but there was now a law passing through Parliament which would curb the power of the Lords and strengthen the authority of the people. 'When this measure takes its place on the Statute Book, it will be no longer possible for an obsolete hierarchy to thwart the public and make representative government a sham.'[2]

Griffith's attitude at this time was to give Redmond's party the right of way. He felt that what that party would get from the Liberal government would not be a national settlement but might be used to advance a national settlement. This was to be his attitude also when he put his name to the Treaty in 1921. However, in 1911, when he decided to give Redmond his head, he realised that progress could only be achieved little by little. He also saw clearly that Ireland without a legislature empowered to collect taxes, would be an Ireland governed in its industry, trade and commerce by England. He stated that the power that could levy and collect the bulk of the taxes was the power which ruled.[3]

In England and in Ireland, 1911 was a year of great industrial turmoil, which had been slowly festering over the preceding years as the distance between wages and prices widened. The Irish Transport and General Workers' Union had been established in Dublin by James Larkin in 1908, and the demand was growing for better pay for the working classes. The dockers', seamen's and railway workers' strikes in Britain drew in the Irish workers also, with consequent hardship for all those involved. Within the Corporation there was ongoing concern over the industrial unrest and the disastrous effect it was having on the everyday life of the workers. Most of them were hardly able to survive the hardship of their existing conditions. The Corporation itself was very short of funds and had little to offer in terms of additional work for the unemployed.

[1] *Irish Independent*, 21 April 1911
[2] Ibid, 5 June 1911
[3] Colum, Padraic. *Arthur Griffith*, p. 102, Browne & Nolan Ltd., 1959

Alderman McWalter proposed a motion to the effect that as over 15,000 people in Dublin were receiving Union relief, and that about 25,000 others were suffering from hunger and cold, practically the only members of the poorer classes who were able to survive, were those who were in jails, lunatic asylums or workhouses. He stated it would be necessary to cut down the expenses of the Corporation of Dublin. He recommended that the salaries of all officials in receipt of between £200 and £300 be reduced by 10%, those with £300 to £400 a year by 15% and those over £400 a year by 20%.[4] A motion to reduce the salary of the Lord Mayor was also proposed.

The major issue of housing now assumed an even greater significance. A proposal by Councillor Byrne, and seconded by Councillor Ryan to establish a committee to provide decent dwellings at moderate rents for the Dublin working-class population was proposed and carried.[5] The fact that housing had no special status of its own had been deplored by the Council many times, so this was a welcome step forward. Kelly himself later recalled its formation:

> Housing is a subject on which I propose to say little here, lest I may be tempted to say too much. I had in my youth plenty of personal experience of the problems which are the matter of housing reform. I was early convinced that the Corporation Improvements' Committee was inadequate to deal with so large a problem as housing and proposed a special housing committee. It required some formalities, but at length, in the year 1912, the Committee which is now so well known came into being.[6]

In June of 1910, an inquiry had opened regarding the clearance of the slums in the Cook Street area which had been declared unfit for human habitation by the Medical Officer for Health, Sir Charles Cameron. The Corporation sought a loan of £18,000 (€2.1 million at 2005 prices)[7] to acquire the whole area, clear it, and erect proper housing on the site. Alderman Kelly at the time said that the only solution was to clear the area, and the parish priest of the nearby Franciscan church, and the rector of St. Audoen's both supported the scheme.[8] In addition to clearing such sites, the Corporation was called on in these years to deal with incidents of houses collapsing, sometimes causing grave injuries and even loss of life, as happened in 1904 when a wall had given way at St. Augustine Street and John's Lane. In April 1911, two houses had collapsed in South King Street, leaving only one wall standing, but miraculously no one was either killed or injured. Unfortunately, it was not always the case that the collapse of tenements left their inhabitants unscathed, but it was not until a major tragedy occurred in 1913, when two houses in Church Street fell down killing seven people, that public awareness became acute, and an inquiry into public housing was instituted. As a result of the heightened publicity caused by this sad event, the Council decided to

---

4 *Dublin Corporation Reports,* 1911, Vol. 1, pp. 272/273, DCA
5 *Minutes of Dublin City Council,* 1911, p. 292, DCA
6 Kelly. *Capuchin Annual,* 1942, p. 597
7 See footnote 4, Chapter 1, for calculation methodology
8 *Irish Independent,* 15 June 1910

send two of its members, O'Beirne and Travers, to visit Birmingham to inspect the type of working-class housing under construction in that city, and to assess its possible application to similar building projects in Dublin. Travers was an associate of the Institute of Sanitary Engineers. They produced a detailed report on the types of houses being built there, and described such issues as proper planning and open spaces, and made valuable comparisons with the needs of Dublin.[9]

It was not the most auspicious of times to be seeking money for the Lane gallery. The chairman and secretary of the Committee, John Mulligan, and Richard Caulfeild Orpen, wrote to the newspapers outlining the danger to the survival of the gallery, because the introduction of a half-penny rate under the Public Libraries' Act was being blocked with all other government measures by the opposition Conservative and Unionist Party in Parliament, not on its merits but as a matter of parliamentary tactics. The writers pointed out that the gallery had the support of all parties and was an institution of true public utility, and of rare cultural value, appreciated by all classes of citizens, who were now merely asking for funds for its maintenance.[10] The Municipal Gallery was not the only institution affected by the blockage of funds. The Public Libraries' Committee had passed through a severe crisis due to lack of money, thus impeding the completion of the new library at Brunswick Street. Matters such as the gallery and the public libraries, while very important as issues, were difficult to deal with when unemployment, industrial unrest and housing had to be given priority. Opponents of the gallery project were not shy about attacking its champions on these grounds. The most vociferous of these was William Martin Murphy, the proprietor of the *Irish Independent*. He said that many people in Dublin felt that in a city with 20,000 families living in tenement rooms, with the highest death rate of any city in the United Kingdom, and with the rates of more than ten shillings in the pound, improved houses and sanitary conditions were a more pressing obligation on the community than providing river palaces for French art. This latter reference was to an ongoing dispute over the site of the new gallery, for which one of the proposals being seriously considered was to build the gallery on the site of the Ha'penny Bridge straddling the Liffey.[11]

Another Royal Visit

In July 1911, King George V and Queen Mary were planning to visit Dublin. Once again, the matter of an official address to the royal couple became a burning issue for nationalists. Recalling the Corporation's stance at the time of Edward VII's visit in 1903, Griffith argued that a good deal of bad feeling would be avoided if no attempt were made to induce Dublin Corporation to depart from the dignified and politically proper attitude it had then assumed. He claimed that an address of welcome to the British monarch from an Irish public body would be an endorsement of the right of a

[9] *Dublin Corporation Reports,* 1911, Vol. 1, p. 555, DCA
[10] *Irish Independent,* 21 April 1911
[11] Carden, Sheila. 'Alderman Tom Kelly and the Municipal Gallery' in *Dublin Historical Record,* Vol. LIV, No. 2, 2001, pp. 116-138

British government to rule the country. Kelly proposed a resolution calling on all nationalists in Dublin to demand that councillors, who had been elected as supporters of the principle of self-government, must attend any meeting of the Corporation where a motion might be passed to present an address from the municipality, and to vote for its rejection. Furthermore, Kelly wanted a committee created to ensure that the nationalist position would not be misrepresented. The O'Rahilly seconded the motion, and a committee was formed to deal with the issue.[12]

The usual pantomime took place within the Corporation. Councillor Ireland proposed that the Corporation of Dublin should present an address of welcome to 'His Most Gracious Majesty, King George the Fifth and Her Most Gracious Majesty the Queen, on their approaching visit to the City; and that the Town Clerk take all necessary steps to have the same drafted and presented in a becoming and fitting manner, worthy of this ancient and second City in the Empire.'[13] The matter was efficiently dealt with at a subsequent council meeting, when it was moved by Councillor Briscoe and seconded by Councillor Mahon that while Ireland was still deprived of her parliament, the Council should proceed to the next business. This motion was proposed and carried by 42 votes to 9.[14] There is an interesting letter inserted in the minutes from a Mr. J.F. Kerrigan, of Herbert Park, Ballsbridge, forwarding a copy of a resolution passed at a public meeting held in Ringsend on 9 April 1911, congratulating the Corporation on its decision not to present an address of welcome to the King and Queen. However, this was not the end of the matter. The Paving Committee of the Corporation voted independently to accord a welcome and granted the use of the streets for a welcome display. All the street decorations were ordered from England. Alderman Farrell, then Lord Mayor, voted in favour of an address even though he claimed he was against it, stating that he had nothing personal against the King. Alderman Cotton said that he well knew the views of Mr. John Redmond, and that the latter and the members of the Irish Parliamentary Party would be ashamed if the Corporation did not give permission for an address of welcome. The Castle was placed under police protection to prevent those entering who were known to be opposed to the visit. On 22 June 1911, the day of George V's coronation, a vast meeting of 30,000 nationalists congregated at Beresford Place to protest against the King's visit, and was addressed by The O'Rahilly, Laurence Ginnell, Griffith, Cathal Brugha, Kelly, James Connolly, and Countess Markiewicz. Yeates, the opticians at the corner of Nassau and Grafton Streets, had, on the exterior of their premises, a permanent advertising exhibition of two giant spectacle lenses. For the royal visit, they had inserted in each a portrait of King George and Queen Mary. Helena Molony, a member of Inghinidhe na hÉireann (Daughters of Ireland), was arrested and given a choice of a fine of forty shillings, or one month's imprisonment, as a result of throwing a stone at the portraits. She chose the latter, and so could be regarded as the first woman of her generation to be jailed in Ireland's cause.[15] However, she spent only a few days in jail as, much to her annoyance, an anonymous person paid the

12 *Sinn Féin*, 25 March 1911
13 *Dublin Corporation Reports*, Vol. 1, 1911, p. 763, DCA
14 *Minutes of Dublin City Council*, 1911, p. 244, DCA

fine, and she was thus released. This person turned out to be Anna Parnell, who considered that Helena Molony was more valuable out of jail than in.

The date of the royal visit was 8 July 1911. There were demonstrations outside the City Hall, in which the police become involved, and some disturbances occurred. At a special meeting of the Corporation, a motion moved by Alderman Kelly and seconded by Councillor O'Neill directed the Town Clerk to apply to the police authorities for a public inquiry into the conduct of the police at the City Hall on 5 July. This proposal was carried with only two members dissenting, one of whom was Alderman Farrell, the Lord Mayor.[16] A letter of apology was subsequently received from Dublin Castle apologising if any member of the Council had been inconvenienced, but pointing out that the police action had been necessary because of the number of disorderly persons who had congregated outside the City Hall on that date. The attitude adopted by Lord Mayor Farrell, who voted for an official welcome, and Alderman Cotton, who supported him, encapsulates the difficulties some nationalists had in dealing with the attitude of Sinn Féin members within the Corporation. Those members of the Corporation who supported John Redmond and his Home Rule policy thought that the King was entitled to a public welcome, an attitude not shared by the Sinn Féin members. Alderman Cotton, for instance, who was a generous contributor to the fund for the Municipal Art Gallery and who realised its importance for the city, now strongly supported an official welcome for the King.

The continuous industrial problems surfaced again when a major strike of railway workers commenced in the autumn of 1911. A motion was put to the Council meeting on 26 September, proposed by Alderman Murray and seconded by Councillor Sherlock, appealing to the directors of the Irish Railways to reinstate all the employees who had participated in the present strike, and begged them to receive a deputation from the Council to discuss the matter. The motion was tabled and carried. On the suggestion of Alderman Kelly, it was agreed that Aldermen Bergin, Corrigan, Bewley and Flanagan, and Councillors Ireland, O'Neill, and Sherlock should form the deputation and to act as a conciliation board for all current disputes.[17]

In a debate on housing, Alderman McWalter spoke to the effect that the issue of housing for the working classes could not be dealt with until the Rathmines and Pembroke districts were made to bear their proper burden of the cost, and that steps should be taken to find the necessary means of amalgamating those townships within the Corporation's remit.[18] Councillor Sherlock proposed an amendment that in the best

---

[15] Van Voris, Jacqueline. *Constance de Markievicz*, University of Massaachusetts Press 1967, pp. 84-85

[16] *Minutes of Dublin City Council*, 1 September 1911, p. 421, DCA

[17] Ibid. 1911, pp. 453-454, DCA

[18] The townships were developing suburbs on the fringes of the city, beyond the jurisdiction of the Corporation, and thus were responsible for their own arrangements for the management of roads, water, lighting etc. The areas of Rathmines and Pembroke, which were developed in the mid-nineteenth century, managed to hold on to their independence until 1930, when they were finally assimilated into the city. (Ó Maitiú, Séamas *Dublin's Suburban Towns 1834-1930*, Four Courts Press, 2003, pp. 214-216)

interests of public welfare, the existing unnatural division between the Council Borough of Dublin and the townships should cease, and that the control of the areas named be vested in a Council of Greater Dublin, and that a special committee be appointed to consider the terms which the Corporation would be prepared to offer as an inducement for amalgamation.[19] As the Corporation saw it, the townships would be potentially a source of revenue to deal with the housing problem, and would help pay for the clearances necessary in order to rebuild modest housing estates for the city. Naturally, the attitude within the townships was that they would like to keep their own revenue from rates for the maintenance and improvement of their particular areas, and were anxious to retain their existing separate status.

The unveiling of the long-awaited monument to Parnell, in O'Connell Street, designed by the Dublin-born American sculptor, Augustus St. Gaudens, took place on 1 October 1911. All Corporation members were invited. The Lord Mayor decreed that the Corporation would attend in state (i.e. in their robes). Sadly, Parnell's sister, Anna Parnell, had died a few days previously, and John Howard Parnell (her brother) was not able to attend the unveiling ceremony for that reason. At a Council meeting held on 26 September 1911, Alderman Kelly proposed a motion of sympathy to the relatives of the late Anna Parnell. On the same date, a motion was proposed to the effect that the name of Great Britain Street be changed to Parnell Street. It was claimed that this proposal had the support of the residents.[20]

The first day of December 1911 saw the new library at Great Brunswick Street (now Pearse Street) opened to the public, four years after building had commenced. Kelly had been chairman of the Public Libraries Committee when plans for this new city library had commenced, and, given his interest in providing educational facilities for the underprivileged, it can be assumed that this project was very close to his heart. Its dignified appearance and magnificent reading room made it a landmark building, and added greatly to the public amenities of the city. The fact that the library was built at all in those stringent times, when civic budgets were severely cut, was something of a miracle, and the authorities owed a lot to the generosity of the Carnegie Trust which contributed a sum of £28,000 (€3.2 million at 2005 prices)[21] towards the library services in Ireland at the time.

Unrest in Ulster

By 1911, a large cloud was looming over Ulster where the Unionists had become more and more uneasy about the impending Home Rule. They felt deeply threatened and their unease was being whipped up by the various powerful figures emerging as leaders of the anti-Home Rule movement. As a result of the industrial unrest and consequent

---

[19] *Minutes of Dublin City Council,* 1911, p. 293. DCA
[20] Ibid. 1911, p. 452
[21] See footnote 4, Chapter 1, for calculation methodology

strikes, a strong anti-Catholic feeling was being fomented, and Catholic workers in the docks were being attacked on a regular basis, making it impossible for them to turn up for work. In September 1911, 50,000 (by some accounts 100,000) Orangemen demonstrated at the home of James Craig, one of the most prominent of their leaders. The charismatic Edward Carson addressed them, and stated that the morning Home Rule became a reality they themselves must become responsible for the government of the Protestant province of Ulster. His resolution that they would 'defeat what they believed to be the most nefarious conspiracy that had ever been hatched against a free people' was hugely acclaimed.[22] Two days later, four hundred delegates from the Orange lodges, unionist clubs and the unionist councils resolved to take immediate steps towards framing the constitution of a provisional government, to come into being when a Home Rule bill was passed and to be in force until Ulster should again resume, unimpaired, her citizenship in the United Kingdom.

For Carson to call Ulster 'Protestant' was, in fact, inaccurate, as the Catholic population slightly outnumbered the Protestants. The Northern Unionists had a powerful ally in Westminster in the person of Bonar Law, the new leader of the Conservative Party. Law, who was a Scots Presbyterian with connections in Ulster, claimed to speak for seventy members of the party. At the back of all the bluster lay a resolution that Ulster would not in any circumstances consent to be ruled by a largely Catholic parliament.

A most unexpected ally for Home Rule now emerged in the person of Winston Churchill. His father, Lord Randolph Churchill, in 1886, had sided with the Unionists against Gladstone's proposals for Home Rule, and had coined the slogan 'Ulster Will Fight and Ulster will be right'. However, his son, having crossed the floor of the House to join the Liberal Party, now offered to address a Home Rule meeting in the Ulster Hall in the company of Redmond and Devlin, the very place in which his father had first uttered this famous cry. Chief Secretary Birrell, having been informed that there was every danger of a riot if this plan went ahead, managed to get Churchill to agree to a change of venue. Birrell was convinced that Churchill and the other speakers would have been in physical danger had the original plan been carried through. However, the feeling generated against Home Rule ensured that by the end of September 1911, arrangements had been put in place for a provisional government for Ulster in the event of the Home Rule Bill being passed.

Birrell spoke about Ireland in Ilfracombe on 19 October, stating that the government scheme envisaged setting up a parliament consisting of two chambers and an executive. This Irish parliament would have control over purely Irish concerns but would be subordinate to the imperial parliament. The bill, he expected, would be introduced the following March. After studying Ireland for many years, Birrell said his overall impression was how, after all the fighting and revolution, and confiscation and menace, after all the Penal Laws and famines and tithe wars and Coercion Acts, after the destruction of

---

[22] Macardle, Dorothy. *The Irish Republic,* Corgi, pp. 72-73

native industries and the yearly drain on the population of emigration, there were still in Ireland four and a half million people, and the majority of them still adhered to their old religion. Such tenacity of faith was, he believed, almost unexampled in the history of the whole world.[23]

At the beginning of 1912, the Home Rule plan showed every sign of coming to fruition. Redmond was convinced that the time had come for the Irish Parliamentary Party, holding as they did the balance of power in Westminster. Griffith and Sinn Féin were allowing the Parliamentary Party a clear field to deliver on Home Rule, as a basis for the genuine independence that was to follow. The bill, having been fought over every inch of the way, finally reached the Lords in January. Here it was rejected, and now, under the new system, had to be dealt with under the provisions of the Parliament Act. Carson, speaking in the House of Commons, used the opportunity to propose that Ulster would be excluded from its scope. At the beginning of April, the provisions of the forthcoming Home Rule bill were made public. These specified that there would be two chambers of parliament in Dublin and about forty Irish MPs at Westminster. Ireland would pay no direct contribution to the imperial revenue. Customs, and probably excise duties, would remain under imperial control, with local power to vary duties. Taxation would be consonant with the social system of the United Kingdom. Old age pensions and land purchase would remain as imperial responsibilities. Ireland would have no power to impose duties on British goods. Redmond, leaving for London on 4 April said, 'The glass is rising'. Asked whether that was a political message, he said that it was.[24]

Nearer home, once again industrial issues were to the fore and great concern was being expressed within the Corporation regarding the several strikes now taking place in Dublin. In January 1912, Kelly proposed that the Conciliation Committee recently appointed by the Council be convened to consider the effect of the bakers' strike. A.R. Barlas, secretary of the Local Government Board, wrote to the South Dublin Union saying that, owing to the dispute in the coal trade, about 170 workmen and boys employed in the bottle works in Ringsend had been let go. As a knock-on effect, a considerable number of coal carters and others had also lost their employment. Exceptional distress was being caused by the same strike in Relief District No. 1 of the South Dublin Union, where nearly 2,000 men were idle, most of them with large families.[25] The strikes continued for several months. In April 1912, a fund was inaugurated in Dublin for the immediate relief of the distress suffered by Dublin workers, who had been thrown out of work as a result of the miners' strike in Great Britain.[26] In a ballot announced on 4 April, the majority of the British workers voted against a resumption of work. By the end of May, a transport workers' strike had begun in England, bringing the port of London to a standstill.[27]

23 *Irish Independent*, 20 October 1911
24 Ibid, 4 April 1912
25 *Minutes of Dublin City Council*, 1912, pp. 256-260, DCA
26 *Irish Independent*, 5 April 1912
27 Ibid. 28 May 1912

The proposal to establish a housing committee in the City Council was gathering momentum. On 15 April 1912, a resolution was moved by Councillor Cosgrave, and seconded by Councillor Cogan, that in order to give effect to the resolution of the Council in the matter of forming a housing committee, a committee to consist of twenty members, one from each ward, would assume all duties and functions now discharged by the Estates and Finance and Improvements Committees, and that the City Treasurer would act as its secretary. The motion was tabled, and with the addition of an amendment to propose Patrick Tobin, secretary of the Paving and Improvements Committees, to act as secretary, instead of the City Treasurer, the motion was carried, twenty-four votes for and seventeen against.[28]

This resolution was shortly followed by another proposal to the effect that the housing committee would be a permanent committee of the Council, that its twenty members would be selected by the Council at the quarterly meeting in January of each year, that it would have charge of all matters relating to the selection of sites for artisans' and labourers' dwellings, for their maintenance and letting and would deal with unhealthy areas, obstructive buildings and reconstruction schemes under the Housing of the Working Classes' Acts.[29]

The first meeting of the new housing committee did not take place until 14 January 1913. The members appointed were seven aldermen and thirteen councillors, who included those who had been most vociferous regarding housing matters such as Councillors Partridge, Cosgrave and Miss Harrison. Councillor C.J Murray was appointed chairman, and Kelly vice-chairman. It was ordered that the Borough Surveyor's department, the Public Health Committee and the City Architect's Office be represented at all meetings. A résumé of the work in hand was delivered to the members by the joint secretaries, E.W. Eyre and Patrick Tobin. These included developments at Cook Street, Lisburn and Lurgan Streets, and certain developments in the Trinity Ward, Beresford and Church Streets. They considered the question of converting all unsanitary tenements into self-contained flats, by remodelling them and installing modern sanitary accommodation. Consideration was also given to the clearing of various sites for redevelopment throughout the city, including the Ormond Market area, the area of Tenters' Lane/Weavers' Square which became known as Fairbrothers' Fields, Marino and other areas.

Joseph Devlin of the United Irish League announced a national convention, to be held in the Round Room of the Mansion House on 23 April 1912, to consider the Home Rule bill about to be introduced in the House of Commons. Corporation delegates were invited, but the Corporation seemed to be divided on whether it should be represented or not. Kelly proposed that a special meeting of the Council be convened to consider the bill, and that in the meantime no action should be taken. This proposal

28 *Minutes of Dublin City Council*, 1912, p. 274, DCA
29 Ibid, 1912, p. 522

was defeated, and it was decided that two Corporation delegates should attend the meeting.[30]

Meanwhile, in London, Asquith received a deputation from the Belfast Chamber of Commerce who expressed their concerns regarding the Home Rule bill. This deputation included the president of the Linen Merchants' Association, and representatives of the Flax Spinners' Association and the Power Loom manufacturers, among others. They explained that the Belfast Chamber numbered upwards of 400 members, and was a non-political organisation of businessmen. They had examined the bill carefully, and had come to the conclusion that under the current rule of the imperial parliament they obtained benefits which would never be secured under an Irish government. They asked that they might not be deprived of their liberties, by being placed under the control of a local parliament dominated by men animated by widely different ideals. The deputation also claimed that they would suffer because of their lack of knowledge of the Irish language. Asquith thanked them and told them he felt their fears were groundless, but that he would bear them in mind. The deputation was subsequently received by Bonar Law, the leader of the Unionist Party, who expressed his sympathy with them, and said he entirely concurred with their views against Home Rule from a commercial point of view.[31]

Asquith in Dublin

In July 1912, Prime Minister Asquith and his wife were planning to visit Dublin. This visit seemed to have been proposed by Asquith's chief whip, the Master of Elibank Lord Murray, who had discussed the idea with Redmond who responded enthusiastically. Dublin worked itself up into a frenzy of excitement as plans were made to welcome the couple. The occasion became a great demonstration of public goodwill towards a head of government who had undertaken the task of conferring self-government on Ireland. The Asquith party sailed into Kingstown (now Dún Laoghaire) on 18 July 1912. They were greeted by Redmond, Dillon, Devlin, and the parish priest of Kingstown, together with a crowd of 10,000 people, several bands and a choir two hundred strong. A certain priest, carried away by the enthusiasm of the moment, called for cheers for 'The Liberator'. The Prime Minister's party then travelled into Westland Row by train. A large procession of members of public bodies had assembled at the Mansion House in carriages, and proceeded down to the station to greet the visitors. They were accompanied by a guard of honour of the Irish National Foresters, and Ireland's Own Band. The Lord Mayor, Lorcan Sherlock, and Miss Sarah Harrison, (Dublin's first woman councillor and famous artist) received them, wearing their robes of office. A brilliant torchlight display greeted the carriages when they emerged from the station. In the first carriage were the Prime Minister and Mrs. Asquith, together with John Redmond, followed by a second carriage with the Misses Asquith, the Chief Secretary Birrell, Messrs.

---

30 *Minutes of Dublin City Council*, 1912, pp. 263-264, DCA
31 *Irish Independent*, 11 July 1912

Dillon and Devlin. The crowds showed remarkable enthusiasm, unanimity and good order. Four hundred policemen regulated the traffic during the procession from Westland Row to the Gresham Hotel. At College Green, the procession halted and the band played *The Memory of the Dead,* the vast crowd joining in. Mr. Asquith rose in his carriage and bowed towards the old Parliament House in College Green in homage to Grattan. The greatest number of people was in O'Connell Street, and as the Premier passed the O'Connell Monument, he again bowed in silent homage to the figure of the illustrious Irishman. Outside the Gresham Hotel, the chorus of *A Nation Once Again* was taken up by thousands. A wonderful scene ensued of cheering crowds and crashing bands, and hundreds of people shouted to them from windows and housetops, waving handkerchiefs and green flags. The illuminations at the various statues along the way, those of Sir John Gray, Fr. Mathew, and the newly unveiled Parnell Monument, all added to the scene, as did the Foresters and the Ancient Order of Hibernians, with their bright sashes and waving white plumes. The party entered the Gresham hotel, and Mrs. Asquith emerged on the balcony raising a glass to toast the crowd. She was followed by her husband and Redmond, who both made short speeches. Redmond welcomed Asquith with enthusiasm and gratitude, saying that the Prime Minister had come on a mission of peace, justice and liberty. Asquith's short speech was full of promise for the future of Ireland and definite on the commitment of the Liberals and the democracy of England to secure the speedy and complete settlement of the Irish cause. He referred to Grattan and Parnell, and said that the Irish people were about to reap the fruit of their labours. The Lord Mayor also delivered a speech of welcome. The party then travelled on to the Chief Secretary's Lodge in the Phoenix Park, where they stayed for the duration of their visit.[32]

The *Daily Chronicle* carried an account of the Asquiths' arrival:

> There were men in the great assembly of greeting who had watched the long agony of the famine, who had fought with O'Connell for Repeal, who had been out in the hillsides in '67, who had fought with Davitt and the Land League, who had seen the bright promise of Parnell fade into bitter disappointment... Mr. Asquith has brought a message of peace and reconciliation and the response has been instantaneous and overwhelming.[33]

The visit was marred by the fact that Asquith had been followed from England by some suffragettes who tried to use his visit to advance their cause. During the procession from Westland Row to the Gresham, one of them approached the carriage and threw a hatchet at him, missing him, but hitting Redmond on the side of his head – it was only a slight graze, which was dealt with quickly, and had no ill-effects. The other incident was potentially more serious. A big meeting had been scheduled for the Theatre Royal at which both Redmond and Asquith were scheduled to speak. On the night the Asquiths arrived in Dublin, staff closing down the night's entertainment in the Theatre Royal, caught a young woman in the act of setting fire to curtains in a box, while others were

---

[32] *Irish Independent,* 20 July 1912
[33] Quoted in the *Irish Independent,* 19 July 1912

seen behaving suspiciously with a canister in the same area. The fire, which was starting to blaze both in the box and on a carpet nearby, was extinguished efficiently by the staff, and the young woman admitted that their intention had been to burn down the theatre to prevent Asquith from appearing there. She was arrested by the police and appeared in court, together with the woman who threw the hatchet. Both were given sentences of five years' penal servitude.

Unperturbed by the suffragettes, the Prime Minister's visit continued. The next day he was addressed by the Ulster Liberals, who assured him that Protestants were by no means unanimously opposed to Home Rule. The Theatre Royal meeting went ahead as scheduled with representatives present from local authorities throughout the country, including Lord Mayor Sherlock of Dublin. On his return to England, Asquith remarked that no description could do justice to the welcome he had received from the Irish people in their ancient and historic capital.

Concurrent with these proceedings, the Irish Women's Franchise League held a meeting in Beresford Place. The Irish suffragettes made it clear that they had no connection whatsoever with those suffragettes from England who had tried to set fire to the Theatre Royal, and had caused the incident with the hatchet. At the same time, there was also a Sinn Féin Party meeting in Foster Place, from which a telegram was sent to Redmond in the Theatre Royal, protesting against the proposal that under Home Rule Irish taxes would be collected by the imperial parliament. Both these gatherings received scant coverage in the newspapers, filled as they were with all the exciting details of the Prime Minister's visit.

Eamonn Ceannt (later a signatory of the 1916 Proclamation), signing himself Honorary Organising Secretary of the Sinn Féin Party, complained to the *Irish Independent* regarding the meagre coverage in that paper of their meeting in Foster Place. He claimed that there was double the number of people at it than at Redmond's meeting in the Theatre Royal, and that a resolution had been passed to the effect that the gathering of Irish taxes should be in the hands of an Irish government. The *Independent* subsequently rejected his complaint.

Meanwhile, the march of the Ulster opponents of Home Rule continued unabated. A monster meeting took place at Blenheim Palace on 27 July, chaired by the Duke of Marlborough. The estimated attendance was 30,000, and the principal speakers were Bonar Law, Edward Carson and F.E. Smith. Law, referring to Asquith's visit to Dublin, said he had touched the lowest depths of humiliation when he accepted the welcome of the Lord Mayor and Corporation of Dublin, awarded to him as the obedient tool of the Nationalist Party, when the same Corporation had refused to offer an address to the sovereign, whose first minister he was.

In the House of Commons, Birrell reported that since 2 July there had been eighty assaults on workmen in the Belfast shipyards or nearby. Extra military and police forces were dispatched to protect workers terrorised by these outrages. Devlin spoke in the same debate and observed that when he had made the House aware a few nights previously of the brutal assaults which were taking place, there had been cheers from the opposition benches. O'Grady, another MP, asked Birrell if there was any knowledge of the fact that the foremen of Messrs. Workman and Clark Shipyards, had taken around books to the benches of the men and asked them were they prepared to join Orange clubs, and every man who did not sign was marked down for ill-treatment. O'Grady asked Birrell if he could find out on whose instructions the foremen had acted.

In Dublin, Lord Mayor Sherlock appealed for funds to alleviate the distress in Belfast, consequent on the brutal intimidation which was preventing thousands of workmen from going to their work. He hoped that the response would indicate fully the feeling of general repugnance existing in Dublin against the methods of reckless political leaders, 'which have brought about the present conditions of things in the industrial capital of the country'.[34]

On 27 August 1912, the *Irish Independent* reported that the Ulster Loyalist propaganda was damaging Belfast business very seriously by the sense of insecurity which it was creating, and that businessmen were becoming alarmed at the possible consequences of its continuance on the prosperity of the city... 'If it continues it will bring about a transference of business operations from Belfast to other and more law-abiding towns in Ireland. Some firms are already considering this. If one of them were to take action there would be an end to the whole Carson movement.'

There then occurred a further series of demonstrations by the Ulster Loyalists, culminating in the decision to draw up a covenant to be signed by all opponents of Home Rule. The day appointed for 'Ulster Day' when the covenant was to be signed by all, was 28 September 1912. The wording was couched in inflammatory terms, stressing that all were convinced in their consciences that Home Rule would be disastrous to the material well-being of Ulster and would subvert their religious and civil freedom. Thus, they were pledging themselves to band together to defeat the Home Rule conspiracy being forced upon them by Parliament. Four hundred and seventy thousand covenant forms were prepared and were signed in towns right across Ulster, and in cities such as London, Glasgow, and Liverpool, while in Dublin two thousand people appended their signatures. However, Asquith continued on his Home Rule course, even though his own position was becoming increasingly perilous. On 1 January 1913, Carson, with the support of Bonar Law, moved that Ulster be excluded from the terms of the Home Rule Act. The debates continued until finally, at the end of January 1913, the Home Rule Bill was passed in the House of Commons and sent to the Lords, who defeated it by 326 votes to 69. By this time, it was clear that the only possible solution to the intransigence of the Unionists was to exclude Ulster from any arrangement that Asquith might reach regarding the grant of Home Rule, even in its proposed limited form. The Ulster Volunteers became known as the Ulster Volunteer Force in January 1913, and

---

about the same time began to import arms from England. The fires that had been ignited were burning too fiercely to be extinguished. The political arguments dragged on and on, through 1913 and into 1914. Eventually, Redmond had to admit that there was no other way out than to agree on a form of partition. By the time the Bill was finally ratified in September 1914, the First World War had started.

Chapter Eight: The 1913 Strike and the Formation of the Irish Volunteers

The early years of the century had been marked by many major industrial disputes in Dublin. In addition, there was a large number of strikes in Britain, notably those organised by the seamen's and the dockers' unions. They had had serious knock-on effects for the port workers in Dublin and Belfast in 1911 and 1912. In Dublin in 1913, the employees of the coal merchants, the iron foundries and Jacob's biscuit factory all went on strike. As previously mentioned, Griffith, through the columns of *Sinn Féin,* had consistently advocated the formation of labour conciliation boards based on the French model, in an attempt to create a just forum in which the workers could have confidence. The Lord Mayor of the time, Lorcan Sherlock, actively supported this plan, and it had the approval of Archbishop William Walsh, Catholic Archbishop of Dublin.

In the Corporation, following Sinn Féin Party policy, Alderman Kelly put forward a motion, seconded by Councillor Beattie, to set up a conciliation board, to which all labour disputes could be referred. This board should comprise the Lord Mayor, the presidents of the Chamber of Commerce, the Port and Docks Board, the Mercantile Association, the Institute of Architects and Engineers, the Institute of Bankers, three members of the Labour Party, and three members to be chosen from Dublin Corporation. The motion was tabled and carried.[1]

Reaction to the proposal was positive. The minutes record that the Chamber of Commerce wrote to the Council conveying approbation of the plan 'in the hope that it might lead to and promote good feeling between employers and employed and to lessen the waste and suffering arising from strikes and labour disputes.'[2] The Dublin Trades Council wrote, on 23 April 1913, agreeing to appoint representatives to the Conciliation Board provided the workers were guaranteed equal representation with the employers, and other bodies concerned. Kelly proposed that this letter be inserted in the minutes of the Council.[3]

A further letter was sent from the Chamber of Commerce to the Lord Mayor, stating that it had nominated four members of the Chamber to attend an informal conference, with four members of the Dublin Trades Council, to discuss the possibility of establish-

---

[1] *Minutes of Dublin City Council,* 1913, p. 130, DCA
[2] Ibid, 1913, p. 237/238
[3] Ibid 1913, p. 298

ing the Conciliation Board. Mention was also made of such conciliation councils in England and the good work done by such bodies in avoiding dislocation of trade caused by strikes and other industrial disputes.[4]

It was proposed that every trade should have its own conciliation committee formed of equal numbers of employers and employed. If the Trade Committee could not settle disputes locally, the issue could be submitted to the Conciliation Board. It was believed that in most instances such disputes could be settled by amicable discussion between men practically acquainted with the trades, without outside interference. Procedures to be followed in the event of a strike were also drawn up.[5]

The leader of the striking workers, James Larkin, General Secretary of the Irish Transport and General Workers' Union, was willing to entertain the idea of a conciliation board, as was also James Connolly, the organiser of the Union in Belfast. However, when the representatives of the employers and the workers met, this plan fell apart, broken by the refusal of the employers to reinstate all the strikers. The general malaise reached a climax on 26 August 1913 when the tram drivers went out on strike. After a week of street gatherings and riots, Larkin called a public meeting of workers and supporters in O'Connell Street on 31 August, and, despite the efforts of the police to prevent him from doing so, succeeded in addressing the crowds from the window of the Imperial Hotel. He referred to a 'lockout' of the men who had been 'tyrannically treated' by William Martin Murphy, the chairman of the Dublin Tramway Company, and the spokesman for the employers. The police baton-charged the crowd, killing three people and injuring an estimated four hundred, within minutes. Larkin was arrested.

Prior to this meeting, the military authorities had arranged to draft 313 members of the RIC into the city in order to supplement what they considered to be an inadequate number of DMP men to contain the industrial riots which were likely to occur. The distinction between the two was that the RIC, which did not usually operate in Dublin, was armed, while the DMP was not.[6]

Larkin's meeting sparked off smaller outbursts of violence in other parts of the city, causing injuries to many inoffensive citizens. In some instances, the police entered houses and attacked their inhabitants for no reason whatever. This eruption of strikes, rioting and violence stemmed directly from the conditions under which many people lived – the abject poverty, the bad quality of their housing and their inability to provide for their families in any adequate way.

In Dublin Corporation, on 1 September 1913, a motion was moved by the Lord Mayor, Lorcan Sherlock, and seconded by Kelly, to the effect that the Council demanded an immediate public inquiry into the conduct of the police, as over 400 people had

---

4 *Minutes of Dublin City Council*, 1913, p. 297, DCA
5 Ibid, 1913, p. 328
6 Yeates, Pádraig, *Lockout*, Gill & Macmillan, Dublin 2000, p. 61

been injured in the city during the previous two days, and the injuries in some cases had resulted in loss of life. The question was raised as to who had been responsible for giving such an instruction to the police. Copies of the Corporation's resolution were immediately forwarded to the Lord Lieutenant, to the Chief Secretary for Ireland, and to the Chief Commissioner of Police. Furthermore, the Council instructed the law agent to attend the inquest on James Nolan to be held that day, and to take all necessary steps to secure a full report of all evidence tendered. An addendum to the motion was moved by Alderman Dr. McWalter, and seconded by Councillor O'Hanlon, that in the opinion of the Corporation the peace of Dublin would be best served by the withdrawal of the extra police and military from the streets.[7] Alderman Dr. James McWalter, a respected public representative greatly concerned about the conditions of the working classes, described how his own surgery was filled with inoffensive citizens who had been assaulted without provocation while going peacefully about their business. Other councillors, who had personally experienced the consequences of the police behaviour, supported him.

Kelly also spoke vehemently about the conduct of the police. He had witnessed the gratuitous violence at first hand, and was shocked by what he saw. He proposed a motion, passed by the Council, that a peace committee be convened to arbitrate between the Tramways Company and the Irish Transport and General Workers' Union. This peace committee consisted of, among others, the Lord Mayor, Kelly himself, Councillors Harrison, Corrigan, O'Neill and Mr. Scully, the High Sheriff – twelve in all. The law agent was further instructed to take all necessary steps to secure justice for any citizen injured by the police during the previous two days.[8] In the usually restrained Corporation reports and Council Minutes, the expressions of indignation expressed by the officials and councillors about the conduct of the police are exceptional.

On 7 October, A.E. (George Russell) addressed an open letter to the Masters (i.e., the employers) of Dublin. He warned them, the aristocracy of industry in Dublin, that they had tended to grow blind in long authority, and that their every action was being considered and judged day by day by those who had the power 'to shake or overturn the whole Social Order, and whose relentlessness in poverty to-day was making our industrial civilisation stir like a quaking bog'. He indicted them for allowing the poor to be herded together in certain parts of the city, and criticised them for their insolence and ignorance of the rights conceded to workers universally in the modern world. He finally warned them that democratic power would wrest from them the control of industry. This letter was published in the newspapers on 7 October 1913.[9]

Complaints from the councillors were expressed many times at their meetings over the ensuing months. Another reference to the conduct of the police on 'Bloody Sunday', as

---

[7] *Minutes of Dublin City Council,* 1 September 1913, pp. 440/441, DCA
[8] Ibid, 1 September 1913, p. 440
[9] Quoted in *1913 Jim Larkin and the Dublin Lockout,* Dublin 1964, pp. 55-57

it came to be known, was recorded in the minutes at a meeting of the Council held on 20 October 1913. Councillor Miss Harrison proposed a motion regarding the serious damage done by the police to persons and property at Corporation Dwellings, Corporation Place, when an unwarranted violent baton charge was made against inoffensive people. She demanded that the Council seek compensation from the Government for the injured persons, as well as payment for the property destroyed. She added that it was important that the citizens should have full knowledge of the views and actions of their representatives, and, to this end, proposed that unrestricted access be given to the public to attend their ordinary meetings. This motion was ruled out of order; yet it was felt at the time to be important enough to be included in the official minutes of the Council and indicates the level of concern and strength of feeling amongst some of the councillors at that time.[10]

Following the subsequent inquest on two of the victims, James Nolan and John Byrne, alleged to have died as a result of injuries sustained in the baton charge, Thomas F. Burke, attending the inquests on behalf of the Municipal Council, stated that he was unable to secure the services of any person to take a verbatim report of the proceedings. He offered instead the account printed in the *Freeman's Journal*, on 2 September 1913, as an accurate report of the evidence given. It includes a very long account of conflicting evidence and the verdicts subsequently arrived at by the juries, which were that both men had been struck, Nolan by a baton blow causing fracture of the skull and compression of the brain, and Byrne by a blow which had caused a depressed fracture of the skull and haemorrhage into the cranial cavity. There was no direct evidence to show who had administered the blows. Burke's report was circulated to all interested parties, by direction of the Lord Mayor.[11] The Corporation's law agent, Ignatius J. Rice, however, stated that the Corporation had no power to take legal action to secure justice for any citizen injured in the streets by the police.[12]

Further details of the street disturbances are recorded in the Council minutes when a motion proposed by the Labour councillor, William Partridge and seconded by Councillor Brohoon, condemned the action of the authorities in drafting members of the RIC into the city during the lockout. They were let loose on the streets without identification numbers, and concealed by their uniforms committed assaults on innocent defenceless persons with impunity. Partridge and Brohoon demanded that in future no constable be allowed to do duty in Dublin without having an identification number clearly displayed, and requested that copies of their resolution be forwarded to the Lord Lieutenant and the commissioners. The majority of the councillors considered a watered-down version of Partridge's motion more suitable, and Councillor Richardson supplied a less vehement proposal more to their liking, which was proposed

---

10 *Minutes Dublin City Council,* 20 October 1913, p. 499, DCA
11 *Dublin Corporation Reports,* Vol. 3, 1913, p. 773, DCA
12 *Minutes of Dublin City Council,* 1913, p. 534, DCA
13 Ibid, 1914, p. 71

and carried, by 24 to 16, to the effect that the Council suggested to the authorities the advisability of having all on-duty RIC men numbered as were members of the DMP.[13]

Partridge then proposed another motion, seconded by Miss Harrison, demanding that an impartial commission be appointed under statute to inquire into the charges made against the authorities of Dublin Castle. These charges included the outrageous misconduct of the police, and their connection with the employers who locked out their workers. However, the motion was defeated by 23 votes to 14. Kelly voted in favour.[14] The consequences of the lockout became more evident as the months went by. A letter was received by the Council from Charles Verschoyle, Superintendent of the Artisans' Dwellings Department of the Corporation at Benburb St., dated 17 February 1914, regarding arrears in payments of rents. He stated that arrears had risen to an abnormal extent owing to the labour troubles and that he was 'at his wits' end' and lived in hope that the troubles would end, as he did not like putting the people on the street or into workhouses. As time went by with no sign of a settlement, and the arrears crept up, he proceeded to serve some notices to quit. He felt that this would focus attention on the state of affairs and hoped that the Corporation would step in and relieve him of the responsibility. The Lord Mayor reported that he had made arrangements with the City Treasurer that no proceedings be initiated until the strike had ended. The Committee issued instructions to withhold all proceedings until further notice. Mr. Verschoyle indicated that he would endeavour to collect arrears, but pointed out how difficult this would be as unemployment was so high and great numbers of people had had to dispose of their little properties, including household goods, which left them worse off than they had been at the start of the labour troubles.[15]

In a similar vein, Alderman Dr. McWalter referred to two citizens of Dublin who had died of pneumonia due to exposure after eviction from their tenement rooms, and called on the Local Government Board to initiate an inquiry into their deaths. He demanded to know what steps were being taken by the Poor Law Authorities to offer relief to these men and their families, and what provision existed, outside the workhouse, to prevent death from exposure, in view of the fact that about 3,000 notices to quit were being issued in Dublin each week.[16]

The Chief Secretary, Birrell, informed the Prime Minister that he had decided to hold a public inquiry into the events of Bloody Sunday. He felt that Home Rule was of little consequence to the average Dublin worker, and he quoted Larkin's saying that 'Home Rule does not put a loaf of bread into anybody's pocket.'[17] The report of the official inquiry turned out to be substantially a whitewash of the police activities, and the strike did not end until early 1914. Larkin advised the workers to end it at a meet-

---

[14] *Minutes of Dublin City Council,* 1914, pp. 71-72
[15] *Dublin Corporation Reports,* 1914, Vol. 1, p. 851, DCA
[16] Ibid, 1914, Vol. 1, p. 966
[17] O'Broin, Leon, *The Chief Secretary,* Chatto & Windus, London 1969, p. 75

ing on 18 January 1914, when they could no longer hold out against the misery and the effects of starvation on their unfortunate families. Those who had jobs to which they could return capitulated to the inevitable and trickled back to the workplace.

On the political front in the winter of 1913, there was a coming together of nationalists of diverse views which resulted in the formation of an organisation which became known as the Irish Volunteers. Its inaugural meeting was held in the Rotunda in Dublin on 25 November 1913 at which Eoin MacNeill became Chairman. MacNeill, in his inaugural speech, acknowledged the influence of the Ulster Volunteers, arguing that if it was the right of the people of Ulster to decide their own future, by implication it was the right of those in the Rotunda that night to decide theirs.

Four thousand men enrolled at that meeting, including Griffith who had been a member of the IRB, Patrick Pearse and Éamon de Valera. The new organisation was impressed by the drilling and arming methods of the Ulster Volunteers, from whom they felt lessons could be learnt. The secret Irish Republican Brotherhood quickly assumed control of this new movement.

Kelly did not join. He was upset when he heard the news of the formation of the Irish Volunteers. He foresaw the desertion of No. 6 Harcourt Street, and the ensuing financial difficulties, and felt,

> it would mean the end of Sinn Féin, as we knew it… I had no intention of being present… But on the day before it, I got a letter which was so worded that I felt I should be doing the national cause a disservice if I were absent. I went. It was a great meeting. I was down as one of the speakers. My few words were not reported. I said: I came here to ask you to do something I am not going to do myself – to join the Volunteers. Be very careful of the leaders you choose. From to-night Ireland will take her place as a military nation.[18]

Though Kelly and his fellow councillor, Seán T. O'Kelly, both attended this inaugural meeting of the Volunteers, Sinn Féin, as a party, was not officially represented, and none of its members was appointed to the provisional committee of the new movement. Its stated aims were to obtain the rights and the freedom to which Ireland was entitled as a nation, extending to the use of force if necessary; and that its obligations were Ireland's protection and defence. Any Irishman, whatever his religion or politics, was welcome to join in the Irish Volunteer movement in pursuit of these aims, and it was understood that it was to be an armed movement.[19] Griffith had addressed this issue many times in the columns of *Sinn Féin*, emphasising the necessity of being able to handle arms, and had taken part in drilling activities in Croydon Park himself. He considered that the Irish Volunteer movement would be of great use as a means of inculcating the spirit of nationalism in the people, but he did not envisage using these

---

[18] Kelly, Tom, 'I Remember', *Capuchin Annual*, 1942, p. 599
[19] Quoted in Ó Luing, *Art Ó Gríofa*, p. 237

skills against the might of England. However, it had been part of Sinn Féin's policy that it was necessary for every Irishman to have the ability to use arms since a motion to this effect had been proposed by Eamonn Ceannt and adopted at a meeting of the National Council on 20 January 1913. Griffith praised the aims of the Volunteers and wrote that it was the duty of every able man to bear arms in defence of his country, whatever might happen, and that the Volunteer movement was the vehicle for this.[20] By early 1914, Griffith was convinced that Ireland was going to get some form of Home Rule, and while not satisfied with what was proposed, he felt that some advantage could be gained upon which to build for the future.

By the end of 1914, an estimated 10,000 people had joined the Volunteers, many of whom were Irish Parliamentary Party supporters. Prominent Volunteer members included Bulmer Hobson who was elected secretary, Roger Casement who became treasurer, Thomas MacDonagh, Seán MacDermott, Joseph Mary Plunkett, and Patrick Pearse. From the beginning, Redmond was uneasy about this new movement, and, wishing to control it, nominated twenty-five representatives of his own party to its provisional committee. The committee reluctantly agreed to Redmond's proposal, fearing a split within the nationalists if his request were to be refused.

An immediate problem arose for both the Ulster and the Irish Volunteers, when a proclamation from the British government decreed that no arms or ammunition could be imported into Ireland. The Ulstermen had been bringing arms in large quantities over the previous year, and the new Irish Volunteers intended to follow their example. Neither group took any notice of the proclamation, however, and continued to parade and drill at weekends. They were ignored by the authorities in both Belfast and Dublin. On 24 April 1914, a large consignment of arms, purchased in Germany by the Ulster Volunteers, was landed at Larne. Soon after, rifles and ammunition, purchased by Darrell Figgis and Erskine Childers in Hamburg for the Irish Volunteers, were landed at Howth on 26 July. The Volunteers were out on their usual manoeuvres when the news broke that the cargo had arrived. Men rushed to the quayside at Howth to receive their guns, and proudly marched back to Dublin with them on their shoulders. News of the landing had also reached Dublin Castle, and the marchers encountered a force of police at Bachelor's Walk, on the north quays. A detachment of the King's Own Scottish Borderers arrived to support the police, opened fire on the crowd and killed three people, leaving some forty others wounded. Coming so soon after the Bloody Sunday encounters, it was an unfortunate repetition of state aggression. Asquith regarded the calling out of the military as most improper, an act that converted a minor incident into a massacre.[21]

In March 1914, the date for the passing of the Home Rule Bill was at hand, but, in order to appease the Unionists, an accompanying amending bill was announced, which

---

[20] Quoted in Ó Luing, *Art Ó Gríofa*, p. 238

[21] Ó Broin, Leon, *The Chief Secretary*, Chatto & Windus, London 1969, pp. 102-105

proposed the exclusion of Ulster on a temporary basis from the scope of the legislation. Redmond's acceptance of Asquith's partition plan to deal with Ulster's intransigence disappointed many nationalists. The possibility of partition had the effect of increasing the membership of the Irish Volunteers, which now numbered some 70,000, according to police estimates.[22]

Kelly outlined his own attitude to the proposed Home Rule Bill, referring back to his youth when Gladstone's bill was introduced in 1886:

> I often stood at Grattan's statue on evenings in that year and listened to the conversation of the knots of men who used to foregather there, discussing the absorbing topic of the day, and someone more in the know than the rest, would point to the centre door (of the old Parliament House) and say: That is the door that Mr. Parnell will go in through. Ah, me, what a disappointment and what a change! Then Home Rule meant some recognition of Ireland as a Nation; Home Rule to-day means Ireland a parish, and no matter how fainting we may be with hunger, we shall not give our birthright for this miserable mess of pottage.[23]

King George V intervened at this point. He called a conference to discuss the partition issue and to try to get agreement on the area to be excluded from the scope of the Home Rule Bill. Those participating were Prime Minister Asquith and his Chancellor of the Exchequer, Lloyd George, two representatives of the Unionist Party, Redmond and Dillon representing the Irish Parliamentary Party, and two of the Ulster extremists, Carson and Craig. No agreement had been reached when, on 4 August 1914, the United Kingdom declared war on Germany. The implementation of Home Rule, to which the royal assent had been given, was postponed until the end of the war.

On the outbreak of the war, Redmond at once threw himself into the recruitment of Irishmen for the British army. He felt that it was a matter of honour for him to do so, as Britain was about to grant Home Rule to Ireland. He was perhaps influenced by Mrs. Asquith (no doubt inspired by her husband) who told him that he had the opportunity of his life to set an example to the Carsonites, were he to offer all his soldiers to the Government. She felt that it might strengthen the claim of Ireland upon the gratitude of the British people.[24]

Redmond made a major speech at Woodenbridge, Co. Wicklow, on 20 September, and said that Ireland would be forever disgraced if young men did not volunteer for service in the British Army immediately in such a worthy cause. Young men throughout the country, including many Volunteers, responded to his call, but a minority of the Volunteers rejected it and, led by MacNeill, formed a breakaway group opposed to enlistment in the army. Griffith argued that only an Irish government could commit

---

[22] McArdle, *The Irish Republic*, p. 101
[23] *Sinn Féin,* 22 February 1913
[24] Asquith, Margot, *Autobiography,* Methuen, London 1962, pp. 84 -85

Ireland to involvement in a foreign war. The minority retained the name the Irish Volunteers while those who stayed with Redmond became the National Volunteers. The former numbered some 11,000, the latter about 170,000. Recruitment to the British army continued with some 4,000 men a month estimated to be joining by early 1915. Redmond requested that the National Volunteers, having joined the British army, be given a separate status with an Irish identity but this request was ignored, and the National Volunteers were absorbed into British divisions with no national identity. The Ulster Volunteers were allowed to form their own divisions, to carry their own colours and serve under their own officers.

The attitude of the British authorities towards Ireland, coming to the end of 1914, was that they had to become more tolerant towards manifestations of nationalism, such as, in particular, seditious newspapers, of which there were quite a few, and also the marching and drilling of the Volunteers (both Irish and National) and the Citizen Army through the streets of Dublin. Birrell had always been sensitive to the feelings of Irish Catholics, and had worked hard to cultivate as good an atmosphere as possible between the British government and Ireland. He was genuine in this, and in 1914 had an additional reason to follow his instinct in order to secure a good flow of volunteers for the British forces in their hour of need. He seemed unaware that there was a new breed of young Irish nationalists on the scene who were scornful of Home Rule and who dreamt of a rebellion.

In October 1914, Birrell's new Under Secretary, Sir Matthew Nathan, took up office. Initially, he went along, for the most part, with Birrell's thinking, but he became more uneasy as the months went by, and the flow of inflammatory speeches at meetings and in the small nationalist papers kept increasing. Nathan determined to deal with this development as best he could by planning, in co-operation with Redmond and Dillon, for the arrival of Home Rule. He analysed the significant organisations, including the Ulster Volunteers, now numbering some 84,000 men; the Irish and National Volunteers, Sinn Féin, the IRB and Fianna Éireann. He also assembled information on individual public figures whom he considered to be potentially troublesome, and his list included Roger Casement, Bulmer Hobson, Thomas Clarke, Major John McBride, Thomas Kelly, Arthur Griffith, Francis Sheehy-Skeffington and Countess Markiewicz.[25]

The British authorities were apprehensive that the Germans might attempt to invade Ireland, and a close watch was being kept particularly on Roger Casement, who according to their sources was conspiring with the Germans. The suppression of what they considered to be seditious newspapers was under active consideration. If they were suppressed, this action could have had a detrimental effect on recruitment, and their owners might be regarded as martyrs. This was the view of the Irish Parliamentary Party, which was supposed to be in tune with Irish opinion and on whose advice the Castle

---

25 Ó Broin, *Dublin Castle and the 1916 Rising,* Sidgwick & Jackson, 1966, pp. 24 -25

authorities tended to rely. Nathan was so uneasy about the effects these newspapers were having by spreading disaffection that he finally decided to suppress them. These included the *Irish Volunteer, Ireland* and *Irish Freedom.* Griffith's paper *Sinn Féin* was suppressed at the end of 1914. He replaced it with another, *Éire,* which was also suppressed, and then *Scissors and Paste,* which managed to survive for about two months. With the closure of all three of his papers, Griffith then entered into collaboration with the IRB to produce *Nationality,* for which he worked in collaboration with Seán MacDermott. From Liberty Hall, James Connolly was publishing the *Worker's Republic* which openly advocated an insurrection. In passing, it is interesting to note that in the lifetime of the *Spark* (another short-lived nationalist paper which was published between 7 February and 22 April 1915) it ran a poll asking the question: 'Who is the Irish Nationalist whom Dublin wishes most to honour?' Griffith came out on top, followed by Eoin MacNeill, Thomas Kelly, Fr. Fitzgerald (a Franciscan priest) and Patrick Pearse.[26]

Asquith formed a coalition with the Tories in May of 1915 as the war began to take its terrible toll. This new administration included men with very critical attitudes to Irish nationalism such as F.E. Smith, Bonar Law and Carson. In Ireland, the appointment of the latter was seen as a 'reward' for their defiance on the Ulster question. To nationalists, the composition of this government was signalling the death of Home Rule. Birrell wrote an analysis of the current state of Ireland for cabinet consideration. From his sources, he felt that the loyalty of the Ulster Volunteers could be trusted for the duration of the war, while the National Volunteers comprising about 170,000 men equipped with only 10,000 out-of-date rifles, did not amount to much. The Irish Volunteers, or Sinn Féiners as he called them, numbering about 12,000 did not represent a fighting force. He felt that the Parliamentary Party did not display the slightest sign of sedition or opposition to the war.[27] There was reason to believe that Dillon was not happy with Redmond's recruitment fervour as expressed at the meeting in Woodenbridge, nor did he agree with the suppression of nationalist newspapers.

All during this period the Volunteers were marching with their arms, and the Citizen Army, led by James Connolly and Countess Markievicz, were engaged in similar manoeuvres. Even so, Birrell continued to believe that the situation was not serious, despite Nathan's unease and his wish to take some action to stop what seemed to be a steady erosion in the significance of the Parliamentary Party and the National Volunteers. However, nothing was done. The possibility of conscription in Ireland was now a serious threat. It was causing huge resentment and unease throughout the country, and many young priests, with nationalist inclinations, were urging their congregations to be ready to resist it.

Dr. William Walsh, Archbishop of Dublin, was very critical of Redmond's action, and refused to co-operate with the military in the matter of recruitment. He rejected a

---

26 Quoted in Ó Luing, *Art Ó Gríofa,* p. 261
27 Ó Broin, *The Chief Secretary,* pp. 118-119

request from the military to hang recruiting posters on the railings of the Dublin churches, and also a request from the authorities who, without having prior permission, publicly announced a parade service at the Pro-Cathedral on Easter Sunday 1915.[28]

A letter in the Corporation minutes recorded the formation of a national committee against conscription, and referred to a conference held on 20 July, attended by representatives from the principal National, Industrial and Labour bodies, presided over by Alderman Laurence O'Neill.[29] Messages of support had come from various parish priests, the mayor of Waterford, members of the GAA, Laurence Ginnell M.P., and others. Resolutions against conscription were passed at this conference, and the letter signed by T. Kelly, Hon. Secretary, concluded with the words: 'There is no use in shutting our eyes to the danger, or drawing other conclusions – we are faced with the attempt to exterminate the remnant of our young and vigorous manhood, and we must resist it.' The resolution proposed by Kelly, and passed was simply worded and read as follows: 'That we declare we will not have Conscription.' A further motion was proposed that a national committee be formed to publicise the resolution against conscription. Alderman O'Neill was appointed as the Municipal Council's delegate.

The recruitment campaign continued to remain top priority with the British authorities. But the Sinn Féin movement was consolidating, and developments such as the imprisonment and banishing of members to England for activities such as drilling and seditious speeches were causing resentment and were seen to be provocative acts. Then in August 1915, the funeral of O'Donovan Rossa, organised by the Irish Volunteers, acted as a catalyst. The Volunteers appreciated only too well what an opportunity was being created for them with the return of the body of the old Fenian from the United States for burial in Dublin, and they were determined to make the most of it. The coffin lay in state for several days in the City Hall, and subsequently in the Pro-Cathedral, attended by Volunteers in green uniforms. On 1 August, the coffin was brought to Glasnevin cemetery for burial followed by thousands of mourners, many of them in uniform. The National Volunteers and the Irish Volunteers marched together, the only occasion ever on which they did so. The affair was a masterpiece of stage management, and Patrick Pearse was chosen to deliver the eulogy at the graveside.

Pearse had risen from obscurity to a senior position in the nationalist movement, a fact which went apparently unnoticed by the authorities. He had been instructed by Tom Clarke, who had been imprisoned for so long in Portland prison, to 'make it [the oration] as hot as hell', and to throw all discretion to the winds.[30] At the graveside of this Fenian hero, Pearse delivered a powerful speech in both Irish and English, evoking images of the hardship and degradation endured by generations of Irishmen, and with resonances of historic rebels, such as Mitchel and Tone. Such a powerful speech, and

---

28 Morrissey, Thomas J., SJ, *William J. Walsh, Archbishop of Dublin, 1841-1921*, pp. 272-273
29 *Minutes of Dublin City Council*, 1915, p. 416, 23 July, DCA
30 Quoted in Morrissey, *William J. Walsh, Archbishop of Dublin, 1841-1921*, p. 276

the sight of their very own army in their green uniforms shouldering their guns, was calculated to strengthen the national spirit in the mourning crowds. Nothing like it had been seen on the streets of Dublin since the funeral of Parnell, and the Castle authorities thought it best not to interfere. Padraic Colum quotes a telling reference: 'The Parliamentary Party which had been looked to for three decades had no place in the mighty demonstration.'[31] Kelly was present at the funeral; his special pass to the graveside survives in the custody of the Old Dublin Society.

During the autumn of 1915, the IRB and its small circle of collaborators continued to plan for an insurrection, taking advantage of Britain in her wartime difficulties. The Irish Volunteers continued with their drilling and marching, and the bulk of their membership was unaware of the fact that plans for an insurrection were being actively developed. Neither Eoin MacNeill nor Arthur Griffith was informed of what was afoot. They had to be kept in ignorance because it was realised that neither would agree to an insurrection except for defensive purposes. James Connolly was pursuing his own plans with the Citizen Army. It is generally accepted that Thomas Clarke and Seán Mac Diarmada were the driving forces for a rebellion, and collaborating actively with them were Patrick Pearse, Eamonn Ceannt, Thomas MacDonagh, and Joseph Plunkett. Roger Casement was commissioned to purchase arms in Germany. Groups of nationalists continued to meet, drill and march, and the British authorities on the whole, despite their misgivings, did not take action to curb their activities. They had much to occupy their minds, especially as the war was going very badly, and more and more recruits were needed. There was a growing demand in Britain for conscription to be extended to Ireland. The question was when?

---

[31] Colum, *Arthur Griffith*, p. 137

Chapter Nine: Kelly and the Rising

At the beginning of 1916, the position of the British government was unenviable. It was in serious difficulties because of the war and the lack of manpower to fight it. Its policy on the Irish question was in confusion, as it had to contend with not only the rise of the Volunteers, but also the waves of dissension emanating from the North, through the activities of diehard unionists such as Carson, Bonar Law and Walter Long, which seemed to spell the end of any attempt at Home Rule for the time being. While mindful of having to placate the northern politicians, Asquith was well aware of the pressure being put on Redmond and Dillon, and indeed Birrell, to ensure that the promise of Home Rule, given in previous months, would be fulfilled. Delay meant erosion among the supporters of the Parliamentary Party, who, when progress was not being achieved, were turning towards an alternative. From early in 1916, recruiting meetings were being held by the Irish Volunteers, while rumours of an impending insurrection were circulating freely. These events were all taking place alongside the recruitment drive to attract Irishmen into the ranks of the British army.

Within the Corporation, the year had started with a strong motion objecting emphatically to any attempt by the Government to curtail the funds for education in Ireland, and calling upon the Irish members of Parliament and all public representatives in Ireland to exert their influence to defeat the threatened removal of funds from the promotion of the Irish language and other aspects of education in Ireland. The Council also strongly endorsed the declaration from the Irish Parliamentary Party against conscription, expressing its conviction that any attempt to enforce it would be against the will of the majority of people and would meet with vigorous resistance.[1]

It was decided that copies of this resolution would be sent to Redmond, Carson, Ginnell, and the Prime Minister, Chief Secretary and various local government bodies in Ireland. An amendment was put by Councillor Sherlock to the effect that the Council would congratulate the Irish Party on the success of their efforts against conscription in Ireland, but this was a step too far for many of the councillors, and was rejected by 32 votes to 8. A further amendment was proposed by Alderman Byrne to congratulate the leaders of the differing political parties in the country who had consistently opposed any form of compulsion regarding conscription in Ireland. This proved more attractive and was tabled and carried.[2]

---

[1] *Minutes of Dublin City Council,* 1916, p. 2, DCA
[2] Ibid. p. 31

Meanwhile, the activities of the Irish Volunteers were causing a certain amount of concern in No. 6 Harcourt Street, the headquarters of Sinn Féin. These premises were also being used by the Volunteers for their meetings, and Kelly expressed the conviction of the Sinn Féin members that there was a serious time coming. He referred to the tension that was building up as the weeks went by, and feared that the British government would take the opportunity of the Easter manoeuvres to disarm the Volunteers. It was realised that if this threat were to materialise this provocation could result in bloodshed.[3] The rumours hinted at revolutionary plans in which the Sinn Féin Party was not involved, but which seemed to be confirmed by the constant drilling and marching taking place quite openly in the city, where the Volunteers were regularly carrying out exercises and field manoeuvres. The Citizen Army marched out every night and performed practice seizures of strategic locations such as canal bridges, and one night actually surrounded Dublin Castle. These actions were considered by many to be acts of folly and highly provocative to the military authorities. A major display of military manoeuvres by the Irish Volunteers took place in the city on St. Patrick's Day, 17 March 1916, concluding with a march past in College Green at which their President, Eoin MacNeill, took the salute. This demonstration in the centre of the city was the first time the Irish Volunteers had taken such assertive action in daylight, and the traffic was held up for two hours, while the Volunteers, many of whom carried rifles and bayonets, paraded through the streets. Their numbers were estimated at 2,000, and they were accompanied by pipe bands. Leaflets outlining the objectives of the Irish Volunteer movement were distributed amongst the large crowd of spectators. On 30 March, a public meeting took place in the Mansion House, presided over by Alderman Corrigan, to protest against the deportation to England of certain members of the Irish Volunteers. The principal speaker was Eoin MacNeill, and the following resolution was adopted unanimously: 'This public meeting of Dublin citizens in the Mansion House, Dublin, asks all Irish people to join in opposing the Government's attempt, unanimously condemned by national opinion last year, and now renewed, to send Irishmen into banishment from Ireland.'

Another public meeting was held the following night at Beresford Place, presided over by Kelly, which endorsed the resolution concerning deportation passed the previous night. In view of subsequent events, it is worthy of note that Sheehy-Skeffington was one of the speakers at the Beresford Place meeting. On 9 April a parade of Volunteers took place to protest against the arrest and deportation of Ernest Blythe and Liam Mellowes.[4]

In the House of Commons on 11 April, in response to a parliamentary question, Birrell stated that it would be injudicious to disclose what plans the Government had to counteract the activities of the Irish Volunteers, but he assured the House that they were being closely observed. It is against this background that the effect of the Castle docu-

---

[3] Kelly. 'I Remember' in *Capuchin Annual,* 1942, p. 599
[4] Sinn Féin Rebellion Handbook, Easter 1916, *Irish Times Weekly,* pp. 5-6

ment has to be considered, and it is easy to explain why it was given such credence at the time.[5] While neither the Sinn Féin Party nor the rank and file of the Volunteers knew anything of the planned insurrection by the military council of the Irish Republican Brotherhood, they were aware of the general air of expectation that had permeated the city for many months. MacNeill could have expected to be kept informed, as indeed could Arthur Griffith, but the reality was that only a small handful of men knew that anything was afoot. Kelly describes in his memoirs his accidental meeting with Arthur Griffith on the corner of Abbey Street early in Holy Week. Griffith asked him if he knew anything of a document purporting to have come from Dublin Castle, in which a plan was outlined to intern all known nationalists prior to Easter Week, and to suppress a number of nationalist organisations, as well as ordering the disarming of the Irish Volunteers. This document was understood to have emanated from the Chief Secretary's office, and was signed by the Undersecretary, Sir Matthew Nathan, and the General Officer commanding the forces in Ireland, General Friend. Part of the text ran as follows: 'The following persons are to be placed under arrest: All members of Sinn Féin, the Central Executive Irish Sinn Féin Volunteers, Executive Committee National Volunteers, the Coiste Gnótha of the Gaelic League and others.' Buildings to be taken over included the City Hall, Sinn Féin Headquarters, the Mansion House, and Scoil Éanna. This became known as the Castle Document, and was said to have been smuggled out of the Castle in cipher form by a sympathiser. No newspaper would take the risk of publishing it for fear of suppression, and ways and means had to be sought to bring it before the public. Subsequently, Francis Sheehy-Skeffington approached Kelly with a copy telling him that in his opinion the document should be publicised if bloodshed were to be avoided. It was alleged by Patrick J. Little, the editor of *New Ireland,* that the Government had released it with the intention of provoking armed resistance. He believed the document was genuine and described his own part in trying to bring it before the public, in the course of a long article in *The Capuchin Annual* 1942, entitled, 'A 1916 Document – The Mystery of the Dublin Castle Cypher', which gives its full text.[6]

In any event, Kelly read out the document at a meeting of Dublin Corporation on 19 April 1916, declaring that it was with the object of avoiding the undoubtedly serious consequences of such an inflammatory plan that he did so. It was at once denounced by the British authorities as a fabrication. But in the context of the times, and the fact that so many prominent people had been arrested and deported over the previous few months, it was eminently credible to the nationalist public. An article published in the *Irish Times* on 28 March 1958, by John Brennan (the *nom de plume* of Mrs. Sidney Czira, a sister of Grace Gifford Plunkett) claimed that the reason the document was taken seriously was that it was read out by Alderman Kelly, who was well known for his pacifist views, and who was highly respected for his moral courage and known even to his political opponents as 'Honest Tom'. Little did he know the trouble he was storing

---

[5] Sinn Féin Rebellion Handbook, Easter 1916, *Irish Times Weekly,* p. 6
[8] Little, Patrick, J. 'A 1916 Document', in *Capuchin Annual* 1942, pp. 454-467

up for himself when he did so. It elevated his profile as a troublemaker in the minds of the authorities, and while he always would have been known as a trenchant critic of the British regime, he had consistently eschewed violence. This one action lifted him into an entirely different category, and was probably responsible for his internment a couple of weeks later, and subsequently in 1919. Thomas MacDonagh insisted that the document was genuine, and had been put into their hands by friends in the Castle. This was reported by an informer who said that MacDonagh, on the Wednesday before Easter, also told his men: 'We are not going out on Friday (Good Friday), but we are going on Sunday. Boys, some of us may never come back.'[7] Many people remained undecided about its authenticity, but an account survives of a testimony given by one Eugene Smyth who worked in Dublin Castle and who declared that it was genuine. 'I was in a position to know, at first hand, the entire contents of the suggested plan of operations, and I can definitely confirm the truth of the contents of the document.[8] Leon Ó Broin wrote that it was concocted, probably by Joseph Plunkett, but that it was not directed against the Government but intended to fool MacNeill and to provide justification for the initiative the military council was preparing.[9] MacNeill did, in fact, issue a warning on Spy Wednesday to the Volunteers to be on guard against the Government's plan to suppress them.

James Stephens believed it to be authentic. He wrote of the sensation it caused in Ireland when it was published:

> One remembers today the paper which Alderman Kelly read to the Dublin Corporation, and which purported to be State Instructions, that the Military and Police should raid the Volunteers, and seize their arms and leaders. The Volunteers had sworn they would not permit their arms to be taken from them. The Press, by instruction apparently, repudiated this document, but the Volunteers, with most of the public, believed it to be true, and it is more than likely that the rebellion took place in order to forestall the Government. This is also an explanation of the rebellion and is just as good a one as any other.[10]

Mrs. Czira (pen name John Brennan) got an account from Tom Kelly many years later as to how the document came into his possession. He told her:

> It was given to me by poor Sheehy-Skeffington. Like myself, he was a man of peace, and he asked me to make it public so as to save bloodshed. I was always thankful that by a slip of the tongue I said I got it from Mr. Little, the Editor of *New Ireland,* for if I had mentioned Skeffington's name, I would have blamed myself ever after for his having been murdered. You may remember that the officer who murdered him [referring to Bowen Colthurst] tried to pretend that he found a copy of the document on his person.[11]

---

7   Quoted in Ó Broin. *Dublin Castle and the Rising,* p. 80, London 1970
8   Breatnach, Labhrás. *An Pluincéadach,* Áth Cliath 1971, p. 56
9   Ó Broin. *Dublin Castle and the Rising,* p. 147
10 Stephens, James. *The Insurrection in Dublin,* 3rd edition, Scepter Publications, Dublin 1965, p. 73
11 Brennan, John. *Irish Times,* 28 March 1958

Sheehy-Skeffington wrote about his concern regarding the effect on the Irish people of the action envisaged in the Castle Document, in a letter he sent to the London *New Statesman,* and which was only published on 6 May 1916, after his death. He had viewed the plan with great alarm. He wrote:

> The Volunteers are prepared, if any attempt is made forcibly to disarm them, to resist and to defend their rifles with their lives. If General Friend and his subordinate militarists proceed either to disarm the Volunteers or to raid the Labour Press, it can only be because they want bloodshed – because they want to provoke another '98 and to get an excuse for a machine-gun massacre. Is there in Great Britain enough real sympathy with small nationalities, enough real hatred of militarism, to frustrate this Pogrom Plot of British Militarist Junkerdom? The Irish Citizen Army are prepared to offer similar resistance, not only to disarmament, but to any attack upon the press which turns out the *Workers' Republic* which is printed in Liberty Hall.

To the end of his days, Kelly was unsure of the authenticity of the document. At the time he perceived it as his duty to publicise it, but various versions of its origins appeared with the passing of the years, including the theory that it had been put together by Joseph Plunkett to help fan the flames in support of a rebellion. It succeeded only to a small extent, as support for the subsequent Rising was very limited, and the public, initially, very much resented the problems it brought with it. It was only after the executions, followed by internment on a large scale and the exacerbation of the conscription issue, that public opinion changed. In an article written by Geraldine Plunkett and published in the *Irish Press* on 8 January 1937, about the Castle document, she claimed Kelly told her that he still had in his possession at that time, the original document printed in Larkfield, at Kimmage (home of the Plunkett family) together with the covering letter written by P.J. Little. Unfortunately, these items do not seem to have survived.

Kelly, in his reminiscences concluded: 'As to the genuineness of the document I have grave doubts. I think myself it was part of a move in the military plan – justifiable in war; and it did have the desired effect. But I think it was forged.'[12] Following on the furore caused by his action, he was warned that Bowen-Colthurst (Capt. J.C. Bowen-Colthurst, of Portobello Barracks, the murderer of Sheehy-Skeffington) was looking for him, and he had to leave home and seek refuge elsewhere. Bowen-Colthurst shot four people that week, and Kelly was lucky to have escaped with his life.

If the document itself was a fabrication, it bore a remarkable resemblance to actual contingency plans which had been prepared by the authorities and which were described afterwards by Colonel Edgeworth Johnstone, Chief Commissioner of the Dublin Metropolitan Police. This is what he told the Royal Commission of Inquiry held after the Rising: 'My plan was that the police, assisted by the military if necessary, should simultaneously arrest all leaders, some twenty or thirty, in their homes in the morning,

---

12 Kelly. 'I Remember' in *Capuchin Annual,* 1942, p. 600

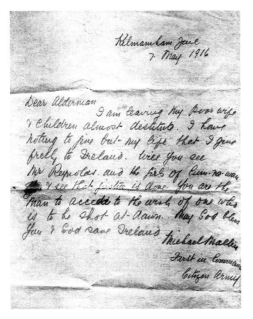

Kilmainham Jail
7 May 1916

Dear Alderman

I am leaving my poor wife & Children almost destitute. I have nothing to give but my life that I gave freely to Ireland. Will you see Mr Reynolds and the first of Cumann-na-mban & see that justice is done. You are the man to accede to the wish of one who is to be shot at dawn. May God bless you & God save Ireland

Michael Mallin
First in Command
Citizen Army

Letter to Alderman Tom Kelly from Michael Mallin, written the day before his execution at Kilmainham Jail for his part in the 1916 Rising. Mallin commanded the garrison at the College of Surgeons with Countess Markiewicz. He was second in command of the Irish Citizen Army after James Connolly but signs himself here as 'First in Command' suggesting that he may have believed (wrongly) that Connolly had already been executed. Private Collection

send them immediately across the Channel, and intern them on the other side… Meanwhile, I considered that after that, a house-to-house search should be carried out, and that all known Sinn Féiners should be disarmed, and all drilling and marching and arming, except with Government permission should be stopped.'[13] Colonel Johnstone added that he had laid the plan before a conference on 9 February 1916 and that it was approved by Mr. Birrell, the Chief Secretary, and that the delay in carrying it out was due to the fact that the troops which would have been needed for the purpose could not then be spared from England. General Maxwell complained afterwards of the most undesirable prominence which was given by the *Evening Mail* to Alderman Kelly's faked document. 'Kelly's speech and the document should never have been published. The publication did a great deal of harm.'[14]

The Rising occurred on Easter Monday, 24 April. The leaders surrendered on 29 April, and were taken to Kilmainham Gaol. Great praise was given in the press to the fearless conduct of the Catholic clergy in ministering to those who were executed, and imprisoned; work very often carried out without any thought of their own personal safety in very dangerous conditions. Archbishop Walsh's own parish saw many local residents taking refuge in the Pro-Cathedral to escape from the danger of fire and collapsing buildings. 'Their terror was evident in their piteous appeals. The fierceness of the fighting in and about Marlborough Street was such that no less than ten civilians were shot dead in the streets.'[15] Many were taken prisoner as the days went by, some of whom were interned in Kilmainham and others at Richmond Barracks. Kelly, for his pains in reading out the Castle document at the Corporation meeting, was amongst the interned. The probable date of his arrest was 4 May, and he was detained initially at Kilmainham. He was absent from Dublin Corporation from mid-April, and was not

---

13 Quoted in Sinn Féin Rebellion Handbook, *Irish Times Weekly*, p. 128
14 *Midleton Papers*, File No. 30/67/31, pp. 1603/7. PRO London
15 Quoted in Morrissey, *William J. Walsh, Archbishop of Dublin, 1841-1921*, p. 288

listed again until 4 September 1916. Later, he was to recount how he was haunted by the sound of the shots from the execution yard in Kilmainham, which he was able to hear from his cell. He was moved from Kilmainham to Richmond Barracks, and is listed as being there on 20 May, which seems to indicate that he spent approximately 17 days in Kilmainham.[16] He was never charged or tried, and was released by 7 June. This imprisonment undoubtedly affected his health. His eldest son, Isaac, was also arrested and sent to Knutsford on 3 May, but was released before the end of the month. A letter survives dated 13 June 1916, written on behalf of the Major General I/C Administration Irish Command, from Headquarters, Parkgate Street, acknowledging a letter from Kelly in respect of the removal of watercolours and other objects, when his house was searched on Sunday 30 April. He expressed regret that the enquiries had not resulted in the discovery of these goods. 'As evidence in the matter is quite insufficient to connect the military with the matter, the military authorities are not able to admit any liability.' Kelly's reply (undated) also survives, part of which runs as follows: 'I have to say that the officer in charge of a party of military who searched this house on Sunday, 30 April, put all the papers found in the bureau in a small trunk and took them away. There can be no doubt about the military taking away the papers, as the same party took my eldest son at the same time, so I am sure the officer will remember. I hope the missing sketches and books will yet be found as I value them very much.'[17]

Richmond was where the courts martial of the leaders of the Rising took place, and many descriptions of it exist. It was constructed in the early nineteenth century, and so named in honour of the Lord Lieutenant, Charles Lennox, Duke of Richmond. The Barracks had two large parade grounds, connected by an archway, over which stood a clock tower. In the early decades of the nineteenth century the living conditions for the soldiers and their families were very bad, but due to a public outcry in England, conditions changed for the better from about 1850 onwards. At that time, the gymnasium was added, which figured so greatly as a reception centre for detainees after the 1916 Rising.[18] With the surrender, the first of the prisoners to arrive there were those from the GPO and the Four Courts, which included most of the leaders, with the exception of Pearse and Connolly. The officials were relying to a great extent on the various spies and informers to identify the prisoners. As soon as they arrived, they were carefully scrutinised by the Detective Branch of the DMP. All of those recognised as prominent in the Rising were detained in the gymnasium, and had to spend the night sleeping as best they could on the floor.

The following day the men were taken out and moved into different areas of the prison, depending on their status. At intervals guards came and went, and they were given sporadic meals of bully beef and hard biscuits. Senator Joseph Connolly described the harshness of the regime in his memoirs. Connolly, a well-known nationalist, had been

---

[16] Sinn Féin Rebellion Handbook, *Irish Times Weekly*, p. 79
[17] *Kelly papers*, Allen Library, Christian Brothers, North King Street, D. 1
[18] Ó Broin, Seosamh. *Inchicore Kilmainham and District*, Dublin 1999, pp. 92, 186-187

arrested in his native Belfast, and was taken with his associates to Dublin by train and thence to Richmond. He describes their arrival in the great square, and he and his comrades were brought, not to the gymnasium, but into another section of the Barracks and into an upstairs room.

> There was neither food nor water and the latrine service was limited to a couple of buckets on the landing which served our room and the room opposite. There was neither blanket nor mattress nor other furnishing in the room, so, as night fell, we just huddled together to try and keep warm. We got through the night somehow, shook ourselves and stood up to greet our first Sunday morning as guests of George V.[19]

Their food, when they eventually got some, consisted of small amounts of bully beef and hard biscuits. Seven or eight of them were transferred to a smaller room identified as L.5, in which they were kept for about a month. Connolly recounts their horror as the news of the courts martial and the executions were related to them by some of the young soldiers who were their guards. He mentions that the food improved after a visit to the Barracks by Prime Minister Asquith, who had come to Dublin on 11 May to see for himself the effects of the Rising.

Count Plunkett was another of those who were imprisoned there. On 1 May, his house was searched and ransacked, and he was arrested and brought first to Ship Street Barracks, and thence to Richmond. His arrest was probably due to the fact that he was the father of Joseph, as he himself did not play any part in the Rising. Some 3,000 prisoners were detained in Richmond. Few had overcoats or jackets, and they had to lie on cold and dirty boards during a spell of wet weather, with insufficient and unsuitable food and restrictions dangerous to health. During the early days of the imprisonment of these men, the courts martial and executions continued unabated. Count Plunkett was brought out one evening for exercise in the Barrack Square, from whence he saw his son, Joseph, in an upper window looking down at him:

> For half an hour father and son looked their hearts to one another, and never saw each other again. The following morning Joseph was executed.[20]

His father got the news from a fellow prisoner. Count Plunkett was detained in a small room on the landing adjacent to L.5, and, except that he had privacy and perhaps a stretcher to lie on, he had no other concessions. He was released early, and his room was then occupied by Kelly.

> Poor Tom, whom everybody loved and respected, suffered untold agonies not indeed at the hands of the enemy, but due to internal digestive trouble. This left him quiet and morose, but always infinitely patient.[21]

---

[19] Gaughan, J. Anthony, ed. *Memoirs of Joseph Connolly*, Irish Academic Press, 1996, pp. 107-109, 112-113

[20] *Dublin Castle Records,* Microfilm Reel 10, Box 23, Colonel Office Class CO 904, TCD

[21] Gaughan. *Memoirs of Joseph Connolly,* pp. 112-113

Right from the beginning, large batches of men were being deported daily to England from Richmond, and gradually the numbers dwindled. Some had been court-martialled and executed. Finally, there were only four prisoners in L.5, while Kelly continued to occupy the little room on the landing. So far as is known, he was detained there until his release in June.

The Supreme Council of the IRB had drawn up a list of persons to form a provisional government in the event of a successful outcome from the Rising.

> The revolutionaries had made some small provision for the day of victory, however unlikely. A provisional civil government, less abhorrent to the people than they were, had been selected – Alderman Tom Kelly, Arthur Griffith, William O'Brien, Mrs. Sheehy-Skeffington and Seán T. O'Kelly (Sinn Féin, Sinn Féin, Labour, Suffragette-socialist and Sinn Féin respectively). It is most unlikely that any of these prominent citizens knew of the august role for which they had been chosen... In case Tom Kelly refused the chair, Seán T. was to direct the civil government.[22]

Kelly's nomination by James Connolly as leader of this proposed provisional government is also mentioned in the biography of Francis Sheehy-Skeffington by Leah Levenson.[23]

On 3 May, Redmond had addressed the House of Commons, stating that the outbreak would appear to be over. He strongly denounced 'this insane movement', and claimed that the overwhelming mass of the Irish people regarded the Rising, as he did, with a feeling of detestation and horror: 'Such a rebellion or outbreak, or call it what you like, has been put down with firmness. I do beg the Government and I speak from the bottom of my heart, and with all earnestness, not to show undue severity to the great masses of those on whose shoulders there lies a guilt far different from that which lies upon the instigators and promoters of the outbreak.'

His close colleague, John Dillon, who had been in Dublin during the events of Easter Week, seemed far more aware of the significance of what had happened, and appreciated the danger in which the Parliamentary Party now stood. Birrell and Nathan had both resigned. Dillon wrote to Redmond in London that his wish was to see the break-up of the Government. He warned of the result of any compromise by the Irish Party. 'Either we must have a Home Rule executive in Ireland, which will act on our advice, or we must go into active opposition.'[24]

Redmond remained convinced by Asquith's reassurances that there would be no further executions, and neither man seemed to know that the military commanded by Sir John Maxwell now held full control. But Dillon was far closer to reality, as he was in daily

22 Quoted in Edwards, Ruth Dudley. *Patrick Pearse, The Triumph of Failure*, p. 276.
23 Levenson, Leah. *With Wooden Sword, A Portrait of Francis Sheehy-Skeffington, Militant Pacificist*, p. 223
24 Quoted in Lyons, F.S.L. *John Dillon*, p. 375

contact with the happenings in Dublin. He wrote in a further letter to Redmond on 6 May, with a suggested draft which he urged Redmond to adopt as Party policy.

> Now that the insurrection has been completely put down, and order restored, we feel bound to protest in the most solemn manner against the large number of military executions of men, many of whom were not prominent leaders of the insurrection. And we solemnly warn the government that very serious mischief has been done by the excessive severities which have followed the suppression of the insurrection, and that any further military executions will have the most far-reaching and disastrous effects on the future peace and loyalty of Ireland.[25]

On 13 May, the Lord Mayor and the City Treasurer called on Archbishop Walsh to obtain his signature to a petition that Alderman Tom Kelly should get a fair and immediate trial. The Archbishop signed this petition.

On 17 May, the Bishop of Limerick, Dr. O'Dwyer, wrote to Sir John Maxwell refusing his request to remove certain priests who had shown sympathy to the insurgents. He told Maxwell that his procedure was 'wantonly cruel and oppressive'. 'You took care that no plea for mercy should interpose on behalf of the poor young fellows who surrendered to you in Dublin. The first intimation which we got of their fate was the announcement that they had been shot in cold blood. Personally, I regard your action with horror, and I believe that it has outraged the conscience of the country. Altogether your regime has been one of the worst and blackest chapters in the history of the misgovernment of this country.'[26] The bishop sent his letter to the newspapers, and its widespread publication acted as a torch to those of previous moderate opinion throughout Ireland, who had become increasingly shocked and horrified at the conduct of the military authorities.

Monsignor Michael Curran, a secretary and friend of Archbishop Walsh, records that on 27 May Mr. Justice Shearman and Sir Mackenzie Chalmers of the Royal Commission of Inquiry visited Archbishop Walsh to find out what in his opinion were the causes of the rebellion. The Archbishop ascribed it to the breakdown of the constitutional movement, and the misplaced hopes of an early delivery of Home Rule by the British Parliament.[27] They also asked about the attitude of the clergy regarding the 'famous Alderman Kelly document'. The Archbishop told them he did not want to publish his views for fear he might destroy any chance of the settlement that was at present being attempted.

John Dillon travelled to London on 10 May to attend a Parliamentary Party meeting. The statement about the Rising was not what he had proposed, but nonetheless a demand for an inquiry as to its causes had been made. Dillon addressed the House of

---

25 Quoted in Lyons, F.S.L. *John Dillon*, p. 378
26 *Cork Examiner*, 27 May 1916
27 Morrissey, *William J. Walsh, Archbishop of Dublin, 1841-1921*, pp. 291- 292

Commons on the following day. He expressed his deep concern about the effect the actions of the military were having on the Party, the fruits of whose labour over the decades were being destroyed. He accused the Government of sanctioning rivers of blood, and asserted that the Prime Minister was not being kept informed by Maxwell of the actions of the military in Dublin, and the number of executions and murders. He cited particularly the murder of Francis Sheehy-Skeffington, which the authorities in Dublin had attempted to hush up, and claimed that nothing but a public inquiry into Bowen-Colthurst and his activities would satisfy the Irish at that point. He demanded that the Prime Minister should stop any further executions. He finished by saying that the Irish Parliamentary Party had been held up to public odium by the insurgents because the Party had supported the Government in the Great War, and claimed that the least the Party was entitled to was every assistance at this time from the members of the House and the Government.[28]

A settlement of the Irish question was now perceived to be vital by the Government. The scale of the carnage in the war was growing, and conscription for Ireland had again been raised at Westminster on 9 May, but was rejected by Asquith as inexpedient. Redmond said it would be insane to try to enforce it, and the proposal was withdrawn. In order to placate Irish-American opinion, Lloyd George was entrusted with finding a solution to the political stalemate, and once more some form of Home Rule was on the agenda, together with the earlier plan of excluding Ulster to make Home Rule palatable to Unionists. On 29 May, Lloyd George sent Carson the proposed wording of a bill to revive the Home Rule Act of 1914, and excluding the six counties in the North for a provisional period of 12 months. In a separate note to Carson, he made it clear that Ulster would not merge with the rest of Ireland at the end of that provisional period. This was a note which Carson treasured.

Meanwhile, in the Corporation a special meeting was called to consider the effects of the Rising. Kelly, Cosgrave and Seán T. O'Kelly were now absent due to imprisonment. A letter from the local government board stated that, in view of the destitution caused by the Rebellion, the Boards of Guardians of the North and South Dublin Unions had applied to the City Council to have the provisions of Section 13 of the Local Government (Ireland) Act 1898 put into force. Until application was made, the guardians had no power to obtain overdrafts for the purpose of relief. A letter from the South Dublin Union, dated 5 May, stated that there was exceptional distress in the electoral divisions of the Union in the city and county of Dublin.

The Lord Mayor (Gallagher) said that the guardians of the Union had satisfied the Council that serious distress existed, and the Council wished to apply to the Local Government Board to make an order authorizing the guardians to administer relief.[29] He had made a report about the effects of the recent insurrection on the finances and

---

28 Lyons, F.S.L. *John Dillon*, p. 382
29 *Minutes of Dublin City Council*, 1916, p. 252, DCA

future of the city, but a bill to meet the emergency had not been well received by the Home Secretary, particularly with regard to the grant of financial facilities to the Corporation. He also referred to the numbers of men, women and boys who had been arrested on suspicion in connection with the insurrection and who were confined in detention camps. Many families who were bereft of husbands and fathers after the Rising were suffering great distress. Alderman Byrne asked that the Government also be urged to grant compensation to those dependants of innocent citizens who had lost their lives during the rebellion.[30]

On resumption of work subsequent to the Rising, within the Corporation itself the city engineer advised that several officials and employees were still missing, although some had been released from detention and had returned to work. Special mention was made of the death of Séan Connolly, a member of staff from the secretary's office who was shot on the first day of the Rising. He was said to have been a young man of excellent abilities, well known for his acting talents, having performed with the Abbey Theatre, When work resumed in the City Hall, the committee room and secretarial offices were found to be in a very disordered condition. All negotiable money and various articles of furniture and stationery had disappeared, including two bicycles. The secretary had satisfied himself that these items were taken during the occupation of the City Hall by the military.[31]

As regards the destruction of property during the Rebellion, a list of ruined buildings was drawn up by the Corporation. As soon as possession was authorised by the military authorities, the work was organised and started by the city engineer, assisted by the fire brigade, the staff of which worked day and night. Some of the ruins were demolished by contractors working for the owners, but the more immediately dangerous structures were dealt with by the Corporation workers themselves. The number of premises involved, exclusive of the GPO, numbered 240. This list included buildings on Upper and Lower Sackville Street, Eden Quay, Cathedral Street, Earl Place, Middle and Lower Abbey Street, Beresford Place, Moore, Henry, North Earl Streets and Sackville Place. The Presbyterian Church and Royal Hibernian Academy both in Lower Abbey Street, were destroyed, as were buildings in Marlborough Street, Harbour Court, Princes Street, North Lotts, Coles Lane, Henry Place, Sampsons Lane, Usher's Quay, Clanwilliam Place and Lower Mount Street.[32]

A town reconstruction exhibition devoted to the subject of the reconstruction of cities and towns destroyed during the war, was being held in Paris at this time. It was suggested that it would be useful for a delegation from the Corporation to visit it, in view of Dublin's pressing housing problems and the unfortunate new and serious problems of reconstruction. A motion to this effect was authorised, and it was agreed that the Lord

---

[30] *Minutes of Dublin City Council,* pp. 300, 301, DCA
[31] *Dublin Corporation Reports,* 1916, Vol. 3, p. 87, DCA
[32] Ibid, 1916, Vol. 2, p. 477-478

Mayor and some colleagues should visit London to see the Prime Minister, and subsequently attend the Paris exhibition.[33]

In a letter sent to the Council from Louis A. Byrne, city coroner, he paid tribute to the great services rendered by the members of the city fire brigade who worked with the ambulances during the insurrection. It stated: 'To my personal knowledge, these gallant fellows worked night and day, and several times under fire, bringing in the wounded (Sinn Féiners, Military and Civilians), and by their care and training saved many a valuable life.'[34]

A sad letter to the city clerk was recorded in the minutes from Sir Thomas Esmonde, an old colleague from the National Council days, dated 11 June 1916, regarding the loss of his son in the Great War, serving on the HMS *Invincible*.

> Dear Campbell, Since my boy's death, I have been too broken to write letters; but I must write to ask you to thank the Municipal Council of Dublin very sincerely for me, for their exceeding kind resolution of sympathy, for which I am most grateful. And will you specially thank the Councillors who were good enough to move and second its adoption. Accept my sincere thanks too for your own kind words, reminiscent of old friendship. Sympathy in a time like this is precious beyond acknowledgement.[35]

The delegation from the housing committee was received by the Prime Minister on 6 July. A number of Irish MPs accompanied them, and they were introduced by John Redmond. They appealed for financial help for two reasons. One was to enable the Corporation to lend money to citizens whose premises had been destroyed, to assist them to rebuild in accordance with the requirements of the Corporation. The other was to enable the Corporation to borrow money for the necessary street widening and improvements, and to purchase, themselves, any sites on which the occupying tenants did not propose to rebuild. The Prime Minister gave them a kindly and appreciative statement of what he considered ought to be done. He said that the case was so exceptional that if a scheme were placed before the Government by the Corporation, after consultation with the Local Government Board, he would be prepared to approach the Treasury with a view to granting them the necessary assistance by way of loan to be repaid to the Treasury, through the Corporation, over a number of years. The deputation was satisfied that their request had been taken seriously. It was a very difficult issue for the Corporation, because long before the Rising, the Council had been assiduously seeking money to rebuild on a very large scale, and here was a demand to the Treasury for urgent funds to make good the damage done to the city by the perpetrators of the Rising, all at a time when there were huge demands for money because of the war.[36] Despite the war, the delegation went on to visit the Paris exhibition.

---

[33] *Minutes of Dublin City Council* 1916, 301-302, DCA
[34] Ibid. pp. 305-306
[35] Ibid. p. 328
[36] Ibid. pp. 339/340

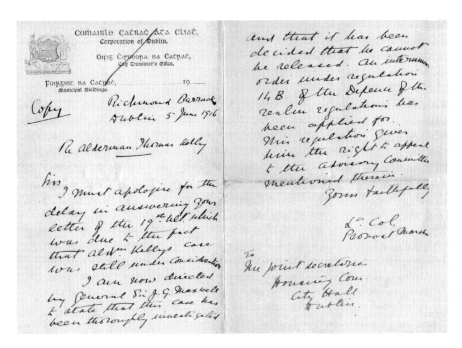

Copy of letter on behalf of General Sir J.G. Maxwell, Commander of the British Forces in Ireland, to the Joint Secretaries of Dublin Corporation Housing Committee, dated 5 June 1916. Alderman Tom Kelly cannot be released from prison, but he does have the right to appeal. (Kelly was released shortly after this letter was received). Private collection

Meanwhile, in order to alleviate the hardship for families left bereft of husbands and fathers after the Rising, three organisations were set up to collect and disperse funds as they became available. The first was the Lord Mayor's fund, reputedly unsympathetic to the Volunteers, which lasted only a month. Secondly, there was the fund started by Mrs. Tom Clarke, which seemingly existed only to help the families and relations of the executed leaders. The third was the National Aid fund for prisoners and Volunteers' dependants, and those who had suffered for their nationalist opinions. Subsequently, Mrs. Clarke's fund and the National Aid fund emerged as a unified organisation under the title of the 'National Aid and Volunteers' Dependent Association'.

There had been much unfavourable comment about the actions of the British government in the American press. Since the Allies wanted America to join in the war which was continuing to go badly, it was particularly important for Lloyd George's government[37] not to alienate the Americans unnecessarily. The British ambassador in Washington, Sir Cecil Spring Rice, had told his government that American attitudes towards Britain had changed for the worse because of recent events in Ireland. An Irish Relief fund had been opened with Dr. Thomas Addis Emmet as president, and several

---

[37] Asquith had resigned in December 1916.

prominent archbishops and bishops were among its patrons. From this fund, $80,000 was sent to Ireland by July, and $50,000 more followed.[38] In the meantime, Lorcan Sherlock approached Archbishop Walsh on 17 June and asked him to be president of the National Aid fund, to which he assented.[39]

The City Council passed a resolution on the killing of innocent civilians in the King Street area, demanding an open inquiry into the matter, and it was subsequently decided to refer this to the House of Commons. Two citizens, Patrick Bealan and James Healy who had been brutally murdered, were mentioned specifically, and the explanation given by the military authorities was considered unsatisfactory. A further motion was put and carried that the Council call on the Government to release immediately all Irish prisoners interned in Great Britain, or grant them a trial by jury.[40]

Another casualty of the Great War was the subject of a motion of condolence, when the Lord Mayor proposed a vote tendering the Council's sympathy to the widow and relatives of the late Lieutenant Tom Kettle of the Dublins in their recent irreparable loss. This was seconded by Councillor J.S. Kelly as follows: 'Ireland has paid another toll in this terrible war by losing one of her most brilliant young intellects. Tom Kettle gave his life for a cause that to him meant Truth and Justice and Humanity, and no greater tribute can be laid on any man's grave.'[41]

Reports were now coming from various quarters complaining of ill-treatment of Irish prisoners held in Britain concerning accommodation, food and, in some cases, solitary confinement of Irish prisoners. Within the Corporation, Alderman Byrne tried to raise this matter specifically in the case of Frongoch, where at the time there were 38 prisoners held in solitary confinement for refusing to inform on comrades. However, the matter was ruled out of order.[42]

Tom Kelly, who had been released from prison in indifferent health in early June, took up his municipal duties once again on 4 September 1916, in time to second a motion moved by Alderman Byrne, urging the Corporation to protest in the most emphatic manner against the callous recklessness with which certain politicians and newspapers were urging conscription for Ireland, utterly regardless of the effect which its application would have on the peace of the country. Byrne's motion, challenging the right of any authority other than an Irish parliament to impose military service compulsorily on Ireland, was proposed and carried.[43]

At this time, it was noted in the Council that Councillors Seán T. O'Kelly, William Partridge, Patrick T. Daly and W.T. Cosgrave were now disqualified, as they had been

38 Quoted in Macardle, *The Irish Republic*, p. 179
39 Morrissey, *Archbishop William Walsh*, p. 293
40 *Minutes of Dublin City Council*, 1916, p. 396, DCA
41 Ibid. p. 414
42 Ibid. p. 428
43 Ibid. p. 44

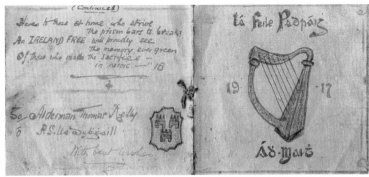

Tom Kelly's inspection of Frongoch on behalf of Dublin Corporation was appreciated by the nationalist prisoners who were held there. This hand made St. Patrick's Day card was sent to him in 1917 by P.S. Ó Dubhgaill and is decorated with the Irish Harp and the Three Castles of Dublin. It contains two poems 'A St. Patrick's Day Toast' and 'Sagart a Rúin' the latter detailing the harsh conditions in Frongoch. Private Collection.

absent from the Council for more than six months due to imprisonment. O'Kelly, writing in Irish from Reading Gaol in a letter dated 29 November 1916, explained why he was not available for Corporation work, but it made no difference. It was ruled that a vacancy be declared in respect of each of the persons mentioned and that co-option would take place the following Monday to fill these vacancies.[44]

Great concern continued to be expressed regarding the fate of the political prisoners. The Council proposed to hold an all-Ireland convention for the purpose of establishing a political prisoners' amnesty association. Copies of the resolution were sent to all public bodies, trade unions, trades' councils and national organisations and representatives were invited.[45] Kelly proposed that three members of the Council be appointed to visit Frongoch camp, and report on the conditions under which hundreds of their

[44] *Minutes of Dublin City Council,* 1916, p. 527
[45] Ibid. p. 447

countrymen were detained there, most of whom were citizens of Dublin. The motion was passed and Kelly, O'Neill and Sherlock were delegated.[46]

The fateful year of 1916 ended with the centre of Dublin in ruins, its citizens in deep distress, its Corporation pleading unsuccessfully for funds with which to rebuild the city, and the threat of conscription looming ever larger. Meanwhile, war was continuing on an unprecedented scale, with catastrophic losses at the battle of the Somme. Great Britain had a new Prime Minister who lacked interest in tackling Irish affairs and the Irish Parliamentary Party was in its death throes.

---

[46] *Minutes of Dublin City Council,* 1916, p. 548, DCA

Chapter Ten: Housing Dublin's Poor

I assert that the main cause of the social evils of Dublin is the dire poverty of the major portion of the working classes, which is the greatest barrier to social progress. It is all very well for those who have never lived in them to hold up their hands in horror of those tall, gaunt, repulsive tenements houses; but those who, like myself, lived in them for years, know that life amongst the poor is only made tolerable by the help which one poor family renders another in times of stress.

(Extract from Kelly's special memorandum in response to Report by Local Government Board on Dublin's housing, issued February 1914)

Arguably, Kelly's most enduring legacy from his long public service career is the influence he had on the development of local authority housing in Dublin. Long before Kelly entered the Corporation, there had been numerous attempts to raise the issue of the terrible conditions in which so many of Dublin's citizens lived. The city's first medical officer of health, Dr. Edward Dillon Mapother (1835-1908) issued a report in 1876 with recommendations regarding some of the worst slum areas.[1] He campaigned for a comprehensive sewerage system and had managed to effect certain improvements. However, the money to carry out these schemes was very restricted and, in order to achieve some progress, the Corporation went into private partnership with the Dublin Artisans' Dwelling Company and other public utility societies in certain instances. During the 1880s, Dr. Charles Cameron, who was Mapother's successor, instituted radical new changes in the matter of inspecting, cleansing and clearing the slums. But the overall situation was slow to improve, and by the time the effects of the new Local Government Act of 1898 became apparent, the matter of Dublin's housing was an issue of primary concern to the newly elected councillors. On 21 August 1899, Alderman Farrell proposed a motion, seconded by Councillor Kelly, saying that the tenement system was unsanitary and unfit for human habitation, and requesting the Public Health Committee to prepare a scheme to deal with the problem. Progress was painfully slow. As previously mentioned, by 1905 the Council had been considering a proposal from Kelly to form a permanent committee to deal with the abolition of the slums.[2] In 1907, a motion was proposed and carried that the Improvements Committee and the Public Health Committee launch a full inquiry and a joint report to the Council, recommending the best means of dealing with the large number of slum buildings which were so prevalent throughout the city. In 1910, a housing committee was formed to administer

---

[1] Corcoran, Michael. *Our Good Health: A History of Dublin's Water and Drainage,* Dublin City Council 2005, pp. 43-44

[2] *Minutes of Dublin City Council,* 1905, p. 484 DCA

housing work which at the time was being carried out by the Estates & Finance Committee and the Improvements Committee.[3] Again in 1911, despite the fact that proposals to establish a housing committee had been discussed many times, it was only after so many years of lobbying and putting pressure on the reluctant Council that on 8 May 1911 the matter was finally resolved with the following motion:

> That the question of the abolition of the slums, in which a very large portion of Dublin's working class population are housed and the substitution therefore of decent dwellings at moderate rent has become so pressing that it is imperative that some decisive steps should be taken to deal with it immediately. With a view to concentrated and sustained effort in this direction this Council shall proceed to appoint a Committee to consist of ten members, which Committee shall be known as the Housing Committee, and shall devote its attention solely to this question whether by the utilisation of the powers which this Council holds or by the encouragement of private enterprise: and that, if necessary a new or varied Standing Order be drafted and presented to the Council to give effect to the terms of this motion.[4]

The results of the census of 1911 had shown that about 63% of the population of the city were working class. Of these, 87,305, or about 45%, were housed in tenements. Ten thousand, six hundred and ninety six families, representing 37,552 persons, were housed in dwellings so decayed as to be on the borderline of unfitness for human habitation. In other words, 17,527 families, consisting of 60,253 persons, or 31%, were in urgent need of sanitary housing accommodation. The point had been made in the reports of the Commissions in 1879 and 1900 that one of the principal causes of the high death rate was bad housing. The full benefit of spending on the care or prevention of tuberculosis could not be achieved until the housing question was fully dealt with. If decent accommodation were provided, much saving might thereby be effected, and with almost certain consequent reductions in crime and sickness.

In 1911, two councillors, Messrs. O'Beirne and Travers, visited Birmingham to inspect working-class schemes. They submitted a very detailed report to the Council on the types of new housing town-planning schemes, and provision of open spaces under development, all of which were relevant to Dublin.

It took until 14 February 1913 before the Council's resolution was put into effect, and the new Housing Committee assembled for its first meeting. It consisted of twenty members, one from each ward. Councillor Charles J. Murray, LLD was elected chairman, while Alderman Kelly, representing the Mansion House Ward, was elected his deputy. It was charged with 'all matters relating to the selection of sites for, and the erection of, Artisans' and Labourers' dwellings, the maintenance and letting of same, and to deal with unhealthy areas, obstructive buildings and re-construction schemes under the Housing of the Working Classes Acts'.

---

3 *Minutes of Dublin City Council,* p. 515
4 Ibid. 1911, p. 292, DCA

Alley off Gardiner's Lane. From Departmental Report into Housing Conditions in City of Dublin. *(HMSO 1914)*

The new Housing Committee on its inception took over several projects which were already in hand from the General Improvements' Committee and had continued their work of clearing and preparation of sites. In the first twelve months of the new committee's existence, plans for the erection of 1,300 new dwellings were put through in four areas of the city, two of which were virgin soil sites, and two slum clearances.

Later in that same year, the collapse of the Church Street houses occurred, causing seven deaths and serious injuries to several of the inhabitants. For years, the pulpit, platform and press had drawn attention to the evil of the slums. Application after application had been made by the Corporation to the Local Government Board and other sources for additional funds and loans. The Church Street tragedy focused public attention on the housing issue, and resulted in the establishment, in October 1913, of an inquiry into the housing of the working classes in the city. This inquiry was instituted by the Local Government Board, and was conducted by four persons nominated by the Board, so, in effect, it was investigating itself. It sat from 18 November 1913, and concluded on 23 December of the same year. It communicated with the Housing Committee and asked for its co-operation in drawing up its report, but the Committee was not impressed by the personnel chosen for this work. The Committee felt that 'men of large experience should have been appointed – either as experts in dealing with social problems or eminent sanitarians' (sic). Only one of them had, in any way, come in contact (and that merely in a remote capacity) with the housing, sanitary and other problems facing the city.[5]

When the inquiry produced its report in February 1914, it contained a detailed account of the existing types of houses in Dublin, and the number of their inhabitants. The report described the dwellings in different categories: those which were structurally sound and capable of being put in good repair; those deemed unfit for human habitation and incapable of being rendered fit; and the remainder, which were so decayed or badly constructed that they were on the borderline. It recognised that closing down tenements would lead to further problems since their inhabitants had nowhere to go while new houses were being built. It described the conditions of the tenements and quoted statistics such as the ratio of privies to individuals in each house, which in many cases

---

5 *Dublin Corporation Reports,* 1914, Vol. 2, pp. 155-156, DCA

was only one for between twenty and forty people. Most of the tenement dwellers survived on a diet of bread and tea. Primary school records showed that school attendance was about 50%. Moreover, the report was very critical of the Corporation. There seemed to be a conflict of interest on the part of some of the councillors, fourteen of whom owned tenement properties. The report was strongly of the opinion that new housing should be constructed on green field sites on the outskirts of the city, a view conflicting with the general policy of the Housing Committee which was that the slums in the centre of Dublin should be first cleared and rebuilt.

Magee's Court, off Charlotte Street. From Departmental Report into Housing Conditions in City of Dublin. (HMSO 1914)

In due course, the Housing Committee issued its own report on the inquiry's findings. It drew attention to the fact that the report had been released to the public nearly two months before it had been given to the Corporation, and without any of the evidence on which it was based, 'thus affording an opportunity to that section of the Press which is uniformly hostile to Dublin Corporation to utilise the intervening period of time in strongly criticising, if not defaming, the administration of our city'. It described the composition of the inquiry's personnel as four officials devoid of any experience of the general administrative work of the Corporation, and, therefore, not in a position to appreciate the improvement schemes carried out in the city in recent years. The Housing Committee considered that they were unfit to take a sympathetic view of the progressive stages of dealing with this great social problem, and the numerous difficulties which lay in the path of the local authority in trying to solve it. In fact, it was evident at the outset that the Committee of Inquiry had set its face against taking any broad or comprehensive view even of the Corporation's activities in other departments of public work and the many schemes for improving the city which had been carried out in recent years, all of which were associated in one way or another with the housing and sanitary conditions as they existed. The Housing Committee drew particular attention to the conduct of C.H. O'Conor, its chairman, whose method of examining and general attitude to Sir Charles Cameron, Chief Medical Officer for Dublin, and the Corporation's chief witness, left much to be desired. The chairman had created a distinctly bad impression on those attending the inquiry, who knew all that Sir Charles had done in his thirty-four years' long and brilliant service as Superintendent Medical Officer of Health, in building up, under tremendous difficul-

6 *Report of Departmental Committee appointed by the Local Government Board for Ireland to inquire into the Housing Conditions of the Working Classes in the City of Dublin, H.M.S.O., London, 1914.*

Dilapidated houses, 30 and 31 Grenville Street.
From Departmental Report into Housing
Conditions in City of Dublin *(HMSO 1914)*

ties, a higher standard of public health administration in the city. In addition, the Town Clerk and the Law Agent had felt compelled to withdraw from the inquiry as a result of O'Conor's attitude. The Committee was happy to note, however, that in a recent debate in the House of Commons on the issue, Augustine Birrell, Chief Secretary for Ireland, who was also President of the Local Government Board, gave full credit to Dublin Corporation for the great municipal undertakings which it had successfully carried out, while at the same time, with its limited resources, providing to a greater extent proportionately for the housing accommodation of the working classes than any other city in the three kingdoms.[7]

The Committee claimed that the housing problem in Dublin at that time was the 'outcrop of generations of vicissitude in the political, manufacturing and social conditions of our people. There was a time when Irish resources alone made Dublin the proudest and most magnificent city in these kingdoms. Much of this glory and opulence had gone, largely accelerated in modern days by the exodus of the wealthier classes to the suburbs. Factories had ceased to exist, and the heritage of decay and ruin had been handed down to the present Corporation to grapple with. The least we should, therefore, expect from any Commission of Inquiry is a broad and generous treatment of the subject, and a just recognition of the efforts of the Corporation in dealing with it'.[8]

The rebuttal by the Housing Committee concluded with the following paragraph:

> We thought this Commission was appointed to take evidence of how much additional housing accommodation was required, and how it was to be obtained. A portion of the report is directed to that consideration, but the best part of it is a general attack on the Corporation of Dublin in its Public Health administration, which was proved to be without foundation by witness after witness. We say the report is discounted, so far as that attack is concerned, by the fact that in no single instance is that testimony of efficiency once referred to.[9]

The rebuttal, signed by the six members of the Housing Committee, was issued on 20 May 1914. By this time, Kelly had become chairman, and the other signatories were

---

[7] *Dublin Corporation Reports*, 1914, Vol. 2, pp. 155-159, DCA
[8] Ibid. 1914, Vol. 2, p. 178
[9] Ibid. 1914, Vol. 2

Charles Murray, vice-chairman, William Cosgrave, Peter O'Reilly, W.J.M. Coulter and Alfred Byrne.

Much information about the state of the city's housing appears in this Local Government Report, in the official response and rebuttal issued by the Housing Committee, and also in Kelly's own special memorandum which was his personal response to the inquiry's report. He drew particular attention to the fact that the majority of houses under consideration were at least 100 or 150 years old. He included the following paragraph:

> I assert that the main cause of the social evils of Dublin is the dire poverty of the major portion of the working classes, which is the greatest barrier to social progress. If work and wages were plentiful and ample, the solution of the housing problem would be simple. It is all very well for those who have never lived in them to hold up their hands in horror of those tall, gaunt, repulsive tenement houses; but those who, like myself, lived in them for years, know that life amongst the poor is only made tolerable by the help which one poor family renders another in time of stress, and until that state of affairs is permanently remedied, many of the social evils, in my judgement, will remain.[10]

The policy being pursued during these years by the Corporation was conservative because of financial constraints, and its main aim was to provide the cheapest and most basic accommodation possible within the city. Some consideration was given to acquiring suburban sites which would have been much cheaper, but the perceived need was to keep the workers in the city centre so as to avoid transport costs, and to enable them to have their midday meal with their families. Kelly was highly critical of the Commissioners' proposal to erect 14,000 cottages on the outskirts of the city as it was unjustifiable to ask the poor casual labourer, who depended for his existence on an odd day's work here and there in the city, to live at a distance from his chances of employment, and thus add to his labour and expense.

Kelly was also critical of the fact that no mention had been made in the Board's Report of the Royal Commission on the Housing of the Working Classes of 1885, which included among its members Cardinal Manning and Edward Dwyer Gray, MP, owner/editor of the *Freeman's Journal.* It was Gray's opinion, at that time, that unless something was done to restore the general prosperity of the country, to relieve it of the steady drain of money by taxation and of population which had been going on for more than three-quarters of a century, there would be no chance of relieving the deplorable condition of the working classes. At that time there were 32,000 families living on one-room tenements, while now (in 1914), there were 20,000 families so housed, which indicated a considerable improvement.

Dr. Charles Cameron, Superintendent Medical Officer for Dublin, had made a submission to the new Committee, setting out his views on the advisability of taking over, on

---

[10] *Dublin Corporation Reports*, 1914, Vol. 2, p. 179

a large scale, houses originally built for single families, and but now occupied as tenements.

> It is melancholy to observe how rapidly fine houses in the north east part of Dublin are becoming ruinous – some have completely disappeared, leaving vacant spaces as depositories for filth. I believe the fine old houses of Dublin could be converted into dwellings superior from a health point of view, to the 'model dwellings' with their small rooms. From an architectural point of view, the prevention of houses in leading streets like Gardiner Street, from becoming dilapidated or absolutely ruinous is desirable. Already many of the houses in that street present a disreputable appearance, owing to broken windows and fanlights, want of paint and broken railings. If the tenement houses in the better streets were in the possession of the Corporation, they would be kept clean and in good repair.[11]

In 1913, a comprehensive report on the progress being achieved in new housing had been drawn up for the Council by the chairman of the Housing Committee, C.J. Murray, giving particulars of housing schemes under construction, e.g., Cook Street (nearing completion), Plunkett Street, Benburb Street, Bow Lane, and others. Some of the sites were cleared by the Corporation and then leased to the Dublin Artisans' Dwellings Company, who erected 216 dwellings on the Cook Street site, and 138 on Plunkett Street. Thirteen acres were being developed in Inchicore comprising 55 two-storey houses containing four rooms, bath and scullery and 165 two-storey houses, containing three rooms, WC and scullery. It was noted that a large proportion of the total expenditure was due to the high prices paid for some of the sites, and that legal and other expenses were also costly. This report was adopted by the Council.[12]

Typical examples of the type of houses being erected were those in the Beresford Street and Church Street schemes. These included 24 four-roomed cottages costing £210 each (€24,000 at 2005 prices),[13] 98 three-roomed costing £190 each, and 34 two-roomed at £134 each. The rents to be charged were seven shillings per week for four-roomed cottages, six shillings and sixpence for three-roomed, and four shillings and sixpence for the two-roomed respectively. The Beresford Street development included a playground with seats, trees, a shelter and sandpit.[12] The number of houses in this particular development was later to be reduced somewhat, in view of a recommendation from Kelly to include small front gardens in the scheme, to prevent 'idlers from squatting on the windowsills, which could be most annoying to the occupants'.[15] This was clearly an issue at the time. By January 1914, schemes also under consideration were 180 dwellings on five and a half acres between Gloucester Street and Summerhill, 1,250 houses on a 50-acre site at Marino and 900 dwellings at Cabra.[16]

---

11   *Dublin Corporation Reports,* 1913, Vol. 1 pp. 1006/1007, DCA
12   Ibid. 1913, Vol. 1 p. 1066-1084
13   See footnote 4, Chapter 1, for calculation methodology.
14   *Dublin Corporation Reports,* 1913, Vol. 1, pp. 1079-1080, DCA
15   Ibid. 1915, Vol. 1, p. 59
16   Ibid. 1914, Vol. 1, p. 63

Elevation by Dublin City Architect Horace O'Rourke, showing the final concept for Marino Housing Estate, 1922.

The Marino site was interesting. As early as 1910, an offer had been made to the Corporation by a Mr. James Walter to sell a large parcel of land of approximately 50 acres at Marino for housing purposes. This site, so close to the city centre, was very attractive, and during this period the concept of the 'garden city' type of development was beginning to reach Ireland, mainly through the influence of a Scottish town planner, Patrick Geddes. Geddes had been greatly taken by garden city ideas coming through from Germany and France, and which were being adopted with enthusiasm in England. In 1911, Lord and Lady Aberdeen, the Viceroy and his wife, who were deeply committed to improving social conditions in Dublin, invited Geddes to bring his Cities and Town Planning Exhibition to the city. Geddes thought Dublin had great potential and was excited by its possibilities for planned development. He organised a series of lectures to complement his exhibition and suggested various innovative ways of dealing with derelict sites. It was the first occasion in modern times that planning had become an issue and the Housing and Town Planning Association of Ireland was formed on 30 September 1911. Bearing in mind the establishment of the Housing Committee, and also the Inquiry into the Housing of the Working Classes, at which Professor Geddes gave evidence, the housing issue was being brought before the attention of the public as never before. The location of new housing in the suburbs was being actively discussed, and a potentially exciting development of ideas was under way.

Marino, on the face of it, appeared to be just the site for a garden city development. The original land purchased from Mr. Walter comprised some 50 acres, and additional land had been acquired from the nearby Christian Brothers, bringing the total site to 96 acres. However, to the Corporation, preoccupied as it was with the necessity of housing as many people as possible as cheaply as possible, the garden city concept seemed wasteful and frivolous. At the initial stages, when the Marino project was first discussed by the Corporation, a proposal for a garden city was greeted with the protest: 'We want no garden city – give us working class dwellings.'[17] And, subsequently, Kelly proposed an amendment that all references to a garden city be replaced by the word 'housing'.

In 1914, a newly formed body called the Citizen's Housing League commissioned Geddes and Raymond Unwin, an associate of Geddes, to draw up a housing plan for Dublin and submit it to the Housing Committee. The League inspected the Housing Committee plans for the various centre-city schemes, and while it came up with valuable and interesting ideas, these were seen generally to be outside the scope of what the Corporation could accomplish on their very limited means. Cold water was poured on the Geddes/Unwin Report by the City Treasurer, Edmund W. Eyre, and, in the absence of the City Architect who was ill, by two members of his staff. In their view, it would considerably reduce the Corporation's ability to provide accommodation for the greater number of the poorest citizens – which at that time was estimated to be 43,366 living in unsanitary, back-to-back houses, the 27,518 houses situated in lightless and airless courtyards, the 42,020 tenements without water supply inside the dwellings and the 58,028 houses with no separate WC. They summarised their findings in relation to the Church Street scheme:

> The proposed arrangement is a typical example of English Garden Suburb Planning and in our opinion thoroughly impracticable within the congested area of a large city… It is a matter for the Housing Committee to decide whether a small number of well-to-do tenants will be provided with ideal suburban surroundings and artistically housed in confined city areas, or whether a large number of poorly-paid workers are to be accommodated in simple self-contained cottages at uniform rents, and under excellent healthy City conditions.[18]

A special subcommittee of the Housing Committee reported on Geddes and Unwin's recommendations. It set out a very comprehensive analysis of their findings under various headings, but in conclusion, the subcommittee felt that Geddes and Unwin had approached the subject purely from a town planning point of view. 'While we accept the paper ideal of garden suburbs, we must from our experience give expression to the opinion that it is impossible for a man earning from 25/- to 30/- per week to pay 6/6d. per week rent and pay tram fares to and from his work'. This subcommittee report was signed by Kelly (chairman), W.T. Cosgrave, P. O'Reillly and W.J.M. Coulter.[19]

However, the times were conspiring to delay the implementation of various schemes, both old and new. Financial stringencies caused by the Great War, and by the uncertainty of Ireland's political future, hampered all but the most urgent development. The Rising in 1916 destroyed Sackville Street (O'Connell Street), which had to be largely rebuilt. Representations were made in the autumn of 1916 to the House of Commons

---

17 Aalen, F.H.A. 'The Working Class Housing Movement in Dublin', 1850-1920, pp. 174-175, in Michael Bannon (ed.) *The Emergence of Irish Planning, 1880-1920,* Turoe Press 1985
18 *Dublin Corporation Reports, Vol.* 1, 1915, pp. 707-753, DCA
19 Ibid. Vol. 1, 1915, pp. 747-753

for financial assistance in repairing the property in the destroyed areas of the city. However, this matter was not going to be easily resolved in the short term.

The elaborate plans for the large Marino site, drawn up by Geddes and Unwin on the garden city principles, were put aside, and were subsequently reissued later, in 1919, in a modified form by the then City Architect, Horace T. O'Rourke. Geddes and Unwin had envisaged 1,100 houses arranged around central allotment areas, and a mixture of small squares, long terraces of single-storey cottages, and some two-storey houses. They advocated a considerable use of trees, grass verges and spacious open playgrounds. They planned to retain Marino House as some kind of community centre. O'Rourke's plans for Marino, which were presented to the Corporation in May 1919, provided for 550 houses and involved the demolition of Marino House. Building did not finally commence until 1924, and by that time, although diluted and changed from Geddes and Unwin's original designs, the plans did include provision for playgrounds and open spaces, but the result was closer to the conservative notions of the Housing Committee.[20]

In 1914, an attempt had been made by Alderman McWalter to deal with the matter of those Corporation councillors who owned neglected tenement property in the city. He proposed a motion to the effect that no official of the Corporation should be allowed to acquire any such properties in the future and that all existing houses be disposed of by those concerned, and, furthermore, that those owning them should have to declare their interest in the event of a salary increase being considered. This does not seem to have been a popular move, and the motion was postponed.[21]

McWalter, seconded by Councillor Harrison, further moved that since it was impossible to place the burden of providing proper housing accommodation for the poorer classes in Dublin on the local rates, it was the duty of the imperial exchequer to provide funds for this purpose, inasmuch as the unduly large proportion of poor and helpless people in Dublin arose from the emigration of five million strong and healthy persons from Ireland because of iniquitous laws. This motion was carried.[22]

Meanwhile, during 1914, schemes had been brought forward for two particularly bad areas known as Spitalfields in the Francis Street and Meath Street area, and Glorneys Buildings in Gardiner Street/Gloucester Place and Rutland Street. These schemes were very significant, and they were approved.[23] Two other major developments were dealt with at the same time. One encompassed 22 acres named Fairbrothers' Fields which was situated south-west of the Coombe and provided an opportunity of developing proper access to the Dolphin's Barn/Rialto area of the city. The other development was on

---

[20] Miller, M. 'Raymond Unwin and the Planning of Dublin', pp. 270-274 in Michael Bannon (ed.) *The Emergence of Irish Planning, 1880-1920*, Turoe Press 1985
[21] *Minutes of Dublin City Council,*1914, p. 70, DCA
[22] Ibid. 1914, p. 74
[23] Ibid. 1914, pp. 100-101

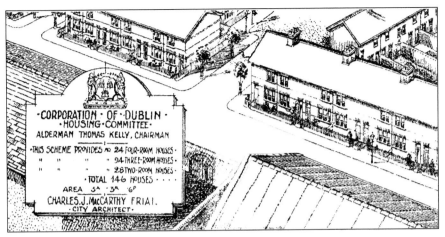

Bird's eye view of Church Street Housing Scheme, 1914. Designed by Dublin City Architect Charles J. McCarthy. Approved by Dublin Corporation Housing Committee under Alderman Thomas Kelly, Chairman.

some 10 acres at Mount Brown at Kilmainham, known as the McCaffrey estate, which provided space for the construction of 240 dwellings.

During these years, it had been a continuous battle for the Corporation to obtain financial support from the Government. On 19 June 1914 the Lord Mayor proposed a motion, seconded by Alderman Byrne, that a deputation representing the Lord Mayor, aldermen and burgesses of Dublin meet the Prime Minister, Chancellor of the Exchequer, Mr. Redmond and the Irish members of Parliament, to request a large measure of state aid for properly housing the working classes. In view of the amount being paid by the citizens into the imperial exchequer for this purpose, the deputation was to point out that Dublin had done more than any other Corporation in similar circumstances. The motion was carried by 41 to 1.[24]

Alderman McWalter brought forward an interesting motion, seconded by Councillor Fox, containing a list of proposals to be submitted to the first session of the Irish parliament: to provide rebates of rates in certain circumstances; to simplify the powers compelling landlords to keep tenements in a proper state; to provide food for necessitous school children, and a daily supply of free milk for families in which there was an infant under six months old. The motion was carried: such was the simple faith in the imminent arrival of Home Rule. The range of issues, as evidenced in the many proposals recorded in the reports and minutes of Dublin Corporation, in which McWalter took an interest, suggests he was among the more imaginative and sympathetic individuals in the Council at this time.[25]

---

[24] *Minutes of Dublin City Council,* 1914, p. 298, DCA
[25] Ibid. 1914, p. 367

A further development of interest was that for the Ormond Market area, a site situated in the city centre, on the north side of the Liffey, for which the construction of 155 dwellings was proposed. It was felt that the central granite-paved portion of the market could be utilised as a playground, and it was planned to include a sandpit and swings, and that the central area would be marked with a fountain with a suitable inscription. The planting of some shrubs and trees was also mentioned.[26] Could this be a little bit of garden city influence creeping in? However, by the end of the year, the Corporation had decided to make the Ormond Market site available to Archbishop Walsh for the erection of a new Catholic cathedral.[27] This suggestion had come from the Geddes and Unwin Report. The Archbishop had had this idea in mind for some time, but in March 1915, he wrote to the Corporation to the effect that he was finding it impossible to pursue the matter because the cost of dealing with the full acquisition of the site and settling with its many inhabitants was proving prohibitive. He now regarded the acquisition of a suitable site for a cathedral for Dublin to be out of the question.[28] The Housing Committee then resumed proceedings to carry out their original housing scheme. There is mention of one Peter Kearns, known as the 'King of Ormond Market' and the difficulties the Corporation had in dealing with him when trying to get possession of the site.

In March 1916 came a proposal to improve the North Lotts area. This was a bad district, bounded by Sheriff Street, Guild Street, Lower Mayor Street and Commons Street. In his motion proposing the scheme, Kelly described the area as having many houses, yards, courts and laneways unfit for human habitation, and said that the narrowness, bad arrangements and bad condition of the streets and houses, and the want of light, ventilation, proper conveniences and the general sanitary defects made it injurious to the health of the tenants. The local parish priest, Fr. James Brady, of St. Laurence O'Toole's church, Seville Place, wrote to the Corporation in support of the improvement scheme, and described why it was necessary:

> The Newfoundland Street Site is about half the size of the newly reclaimed area at Fairview. According to your report, it contains 378 houses, with 2,182 dwellers. Most of these houses have only a ground floor, and the tradition is that they were run up in a hurry soon after the reclamation of the land about the middle of the eighteenth century. Now, what must have been the nature of the soil on which these dwellings were originally constructed? Probably of the worst slime of the *then* dirty City. The tenement houses elsewhere condemned have at least this advantage – they are off the ground, and air and light can enter through their once stately doors and windows. Here you have probably the best air in the City, but no openings to admit it to the lives of the people. We are practically between two seas – an ideal site for workers' dwellings on a large scale – abundance of employment close by, the best class of the working community anxious to live here. Why not let them? The conditions of life here at present for such a deserving class can only be realised by one who lives on the spot and comes into daily contact with

26 *Dublin Corporation Reports*, 1914, Vol. 1, pp. 818-819, DCA
27 *Minutes of Dublin City Council*, 1914, pp. 512-515, DCA
28 *Dublin Corporation Reports*, 1915, Vol. 1, pp. 686-687, DCA

them. Indeed, I can hardly describe them as decent, and I venture to think that but for the healthy and cleanly habits of the majority of the population of the area, they would have been long since closed as unfit for human habitation. Everything that the good taste and industry of the inhabitants could do to patch up their dwellings and make them tidy and respectable has been done, yet they can only be described as 'whited sepulchres'. [29]

Kelly's motion in relation to this scheme was proposed and carried.

It can fairly be said that the Committee as a whole got through an amazing amount of complex work, and displayed great energy and skill in achieving so much during the first years of its existence. Tributes were paid to both Murray and Kelly, and it is extraordinary to recall that so many other issues also occupied their time, considering the momentous political events which were gradually emerging on the national stage. At the final meeting of the Committee for the year 1914-1915, the Lord Mayor (Sherlock) proposed a vote of thanks to Kelly, which was seconded by Sir Joseph Downes, expressing the Committee members' appreciation of the great efforts made by Kelly in tackling the housing problem, and tendering their best thanks for the extraordinary devotion with which he had applied himself to its consideration. They expressed the hope that he would be elected chairman for the coming year.[30] Kelly was re-elected as chairman for 1915, as was Councillor Briscoe as his deputy.

The year of 1915 brought with it a great threat to the immediate future of the building trade, as a result of the industrial unrest. A case for improving the situation was made by the two joint secretaries of the Housing Committee to the Local Government Board, dated 24 March 1915, in view of the pressing need to deal with the housing issue and the urgency of providing employment for the numerous idle artisans and labourers associated with the building trade. Private building enterprise in the city was practically at a standstill. It was essential that the Local Government Board should give favourable consideration to the several housing schemes shortly to be submitted to them.[31]

On 30 April, Kelly made a special plea for money for the scheme on the Ormond Market site, which had been acquired and cleared. It had been depopulated by its clearance, and the poor who were evicted from it had been hoping for an early reinstatement in healthy dwellings on the site where they were formerly housed.[32] A reply from the City Treasurer, Mr. Eyre, said that the Treasury Commissioner would be unable to make any further advances for housing loans until the war was over. The Commissioner suggested that an appeal should be made directly to the Treasury for money for this important scheme.[33] The Housing Committee regarded it as a very serious matter for the

29 *Minutes of Dublin City Council,* 1916, pp. 149-150, DCA
30 *Dublin Corporation Reports,* 1915, Vol. 2, p.143, DCA
31 Ibid. 1915, Vol. 2, p. 143
32 Ibid. 1915, Vol. 2, p. 535
33 Ibid. 1915, Vol.2, pp. 536-537

future of housing in Dublin, and one which was paralysing efforts to bring about an improvement in the housing conditions. Kelly, in closing the Committee's report, recommended that the site be developed in sections until a more favourable monetary position came about. The Housing Committee was authorised to include in the following year's estimates a sum of £8,000 (€806,000 at 2005 prices) to enable a portion of the site to be developed.

By 21 May, Kelly in his capacity as chairman had written to the joint secretaries of the Housing Committee, P. Tobin and E.W. Eyre, to say that the Committee had not heard from the Local Government Board, and that unless funds were provided for the completion of schemes at Inchicore, Blackhall Place, Beresford Street and in the Trinity Ward, all further building work by the Corporation would have to be suspended. This would be most unfortunate in view of the pressing problem and the dearth of employment in the building trade owing to the war. He drew attention to the fact that countless millions were being spent on the prosecution of a war to which Dublin alone had sent some 14,000 to fight the empire's battle. He demanded to know if they were on their return to find the empire's gratitude in the refusal of the Government to remove their families from the horrors of life in the dilapidated tenements into comfortable homes.

Attention was now drawn to the fact that the price of housing materials was bound to increase, because large portions of France and Belgium and other places would require rebuilding after the War. Furthermore it was becoming more difficult than ever to obtain access to money. The Local Government Board wrote again to the Council on 23 September 1915, refusing all further loans.[34]

In the course of a discussion in Westminster on the report of the Departmental Committee, even the opponents of the Corporation of Dublin were obliged to admit that the housing conditions were intolerable, and that it was impossible for the Corporation to improve matters without financial assistance from the Government. The bitterest critic could not help expressing the view that the conditions in Dublin were the worst of all the big cities in the three kingdoms. They asserted that the single-room tenements (of which there was a preponderance in Dublin) were the greatest abomination and source of crime imaginable and that state aid was absolutely necessary to enable the Corporation to rehouse the people turned out of the slums, at rents within the reach of the poorer classes. Sir Robert Cecil did not spare the Corporation from the gravest charges of maladministration (charges which were completely disproved), but also had to admit that it was incredible at this period of the world's history that such a state of things as obtained in Dublin could exist. The Chief Secretary, Birrell, rejected the criticism of the Corporation stating that it had carried out so much for the benefit of the community that it was not a body to be spoken of in the way Sir Robert Cecil had done. He demanded to know what the Parliament was going to do to remedy the

---

[34] *Dublin Corporation Reports,* 1915, Vol. 3, pp. 108-109

situation. He advocated that an immediate grant of public money be made to the City Council to clear away the slums and erect this much-needed housing accommodation. He said that it was impossible to understand how the Local Government Board had failed to understand the pressing urgency of this question or could dismiss in such a flippant manner the application of the Corporation. He stated that the report could not be allowed to rest.[35]

It subsequently emerged, through correspondence between the Housing Committee and the Local Government Board, that the Board had not applied to the Treasury at all for additional funds for housing, and then had tried to justify its lack of action by saying that the date for granting such funds had now passed. In other words, it had been advised in time by the Corporation, but had failed to contact the Treasury. This correspondence was quite contentious.

The Corporation had been severely criticised for not buying ground outside the confines of the city for housing. Considerations of convenience to sources of employment and means of transit had been carefully taken into account, as no business community would build dwellings for the workers on sites far removed from the places where they earned their living. Were its operations unhampered by the decrees of a government department and existing conditions with regard to finance, the Council would be able to provide houses for a larger number of workers, not far removed from their places of employment. At that time, September 1915, there were 15 cleared sites being built on by the Corporation, on approximately 84 acres in different parts of the city.

A special meeting of the Corporation was held on 25 October 1915, at which it was claimed that the report on public housing by the Departmental Committee had been utilised for slandering the administration of the city. It concluded that the Local Government Board had forfeited whatever confidence it should have commanded. There followed a resolution from the Council declaring its lack of confidence in the Board.[36] Kelly stated that the Board was a nominated semi-judicial body, which frequently held inquiries into the management of representative local authorities. It was now time for some higher authority to hold an inquiry into how the Local Government Board conducted its own business. Municipalities across the water, such as Edinburgh and Glasgow, could shape their own destinies without being hampered and impeded by well-paid inactivity or stupid and harassing interference on the part of government departments.[37]

Councillor P.T. Daly proposed that copies of the correspondence between the Council and the Board be sent to the members of Parliament for Dublin City and County, as well as to John Redmond, William O'Brien, and Sir Edward Carson as leaders of various sections of Irish political opinion in the House of Commons, with a view to find-

35 *Dublin Corporation Reports,* 1915, Vol. 3, pp. 117-118, DCA
36 Ibid. 1915, Vol. 3, p. 123
37 Ibid. 1915, Vol. 3, p. 490A

ing out what amount of money had been passed or spent on housing schemes in Britain.[38] The Ormond Market development was finally sanctioned by letter from the Local Government Board in a letter dated 1 December 1915.

Early in 1916, the Housing Committee urged that, as the installation of electricity in the Beresford and Church Street schemes had not been budgeted for, it would now be prudent to include it so that the houses could be wired as the building progressed. Kelly, in his capacity as chairman, recommended this strongly, in order to avoid costly work later. In the matter of the Ormond Market scheme, it was stipulated that all work must be done by local labour as a condition of the contract, and that only trade union labour could be employed.

The Spitalfields site was again referred to on 14 January 1916. Kelly stated that the Corporation was irretrievably committed to the purchase of the site prior to the suspension of the government loans, as the Local Government Board had sanctioned a loan of £7,000. The site was in an exceedingly unsanitary quarter, and Kelly recommended that the sum of £8,000, which had been obtained as a loan for portion of the Ormond Market site, should now be switched to Spitalfields. This would enable them to deal with approximately one-third of the area. He wished to recommend formally that Report No. 211 of 1915 be altered accordingly, and a special meeting of the Council was convened for 8 March 1916 to adopt his recommendation.[39]

The proposal for the improvement scheme of the North Lotts area was put forward by C.J. McCarthy, the City Architect, early in 1916. This site, of approximately 15 acres, was in close proximity to the quays, an area bounded on the north by Sherriff Street, on the east by Guild Street, and on the south and west by Lower Mayor and Commons Streets. Beautifully designed plans were included with this application, together with suggestions for two children's playgrounds. The proposal was for a grand total of 537 houses, of two-, three- and four-roomed dwellings, the work to be carried out in three phases.[40]

The site was very old and the houses unsanitary, and they were certified by Sir Charles Cameron as unfit for human habitation. A description of the area given in Charles Haliday's *Scandinavian Kingdom of Dublin,* is quoted in the proposal, which states that North Lotts derives its name from the fact that in 1717 the Corporation distributed amongst themselves the land reclaimed by the building of the North Wall by drawing lots. In Brooking's Map of Dublin, 1728, also quoted, these areas were still represented as being covered by the tide. The Housing Committee report of 21 January 1916, signed by Kelly, stated that the Council had carefully considered the Medical Officer's report regarding the narrowness, claustrophobic atmosphere, bad arrangements and condition, general sanitary defects and evils connected with these houses, for which the

[38] *Dublin Corporation Reports,* 1915, Vol. 3, p. 517, DCA
[39] Ibid. 1916, Vol. 1, pp. 303-304
[40] Ibid. 1916, Vol. 1, pp. 318-329

City Architect had prepared a plan for 564 houses and playgrounds. The preparation of this report did not commit the Council to an obligation to proceed with the scheme immediately, but at such time as more favourable conditions were likely to arise in the money market.

In April 1916, the Rising put a stop to all this work. It had a devastating effect on housing budgets, because the reconstruction of the buildings in the centre of the city had to have priority. There was a lot of destruction also in other areas of the city, and this factor exacerbated the overall situation and made the lot of the working-class population more miserable than ever. As previously mentioned, on 3 May Kelly was arrested, because of his action in reading the Castle document within the Corporation. His experiences, first of all in Kilmainham and subsequently in Richmond Barracks, took their toll, and he did not reappear in the Corporation until the beginning of September 1916. Others were not so lucky. Councillors Seán T. O'Kelly, William Partridge, P.T. Daly, and W.T. Cosgrave were deported and imprisoned in England. Because they were missing from the Council meetings for over six months, they were disqualified as councillors, and, following procedures, their places on the Council were filled by the co-option of others.

In the report of the Housing Committee dated 30 September 1916, the joint secretaries, Edmund W. Eyre, and Patrick Tobin, gave a résumé of the recent work of the Committee. Reference was made to the findings of the Local Government Board Departmental Committee report about the immediate need for the erection of 14,000 cottages at a total estimated cost of £3,570,000 (€300 million at 2005 prices). In these circumstances, the Committee felt that, at a minimum, the municipality was entitled to expect the release of surplus funds, insofar as they had been accumulated from Irish sources for the national purpose to which they should be devoted, namely the housing of the working classes.

> We are instructed to state that the Housing Committee expected that the Members of the City and County of Dublin would have taken united action to secure advances from the Treasury to enable the Dublin housing schemes to be carried out, and that the Parliamentary Representatives would have communicated to the Corporation the result of their efforts. The Committee are, therefore, surprised to find that no active steps appear to have been taken to attain this object.[41]

This report was widely circulated.

By October 1916, Kelly, having recovered from his prison experience, had resumed his work on the Housing Committee where consideration was being given to various proposals for getting money to commence building on the sites already acquired. The report for the quarter ending 31 October 1916 gives an up-to-date account of the progress for the various sanctioned housing schemes, such as the purchase of the

---

41 *Dublin Corporation Reports*, 1916, Vol. 3, p. 411, DCA

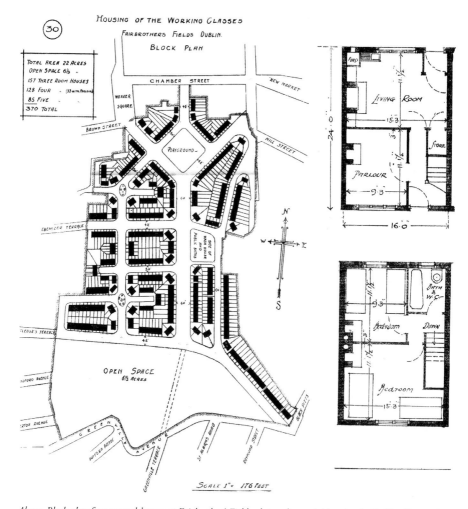

Above: Block plan four-roomed houses at Fairbrothers' Fields, designed as social housing by Dublin Corporation which features extensive open space, a wash-house and public baths, and a playground.
Above right: Section of ground plans for four-roomed houses at Fairbrothers' Fields, designed as social housing by Dublin Corporation.

McCaffrey Estate, Fairbrothers' Fields and Spitalfields. The Local Government Board had applied itself to the most urgent of these, in a direct appeal to E.S. Montague, Financial Secretary of the Treasury in Whitehall. It was made clear that the sums sanctioned were for purchase alone, as there was no money for demolition and rebuilding. All ongoing Housing Committee work was complicated by a shortage of funds due to the war. Another possibility which was considered was to borrow from American banks as the only means of getting funds to commence construction with all possible speed. Because of recent clearances of the worst sites, many unfortunate people had been dispossessed and had nowhere to live. The new Chief Secretary, Henry Duke, (who had replaced Birrell who had had to resign owing to his perceived failure to anticipate the Rising), had admitted the urgency of solving the question. Kelly recommended that an American loan be taken up in such instalments as would enable them to implement the schemes for Fairbrothers' Fields, McCaffrey Estate, St. James's Walk and Spitalfields, these sites being in possession of the Corporation. He proposed also that provision be made for the completion of the Ormond Market scheme. Local Government orders had been obtained for the acquisition of the Crabbe Lane and Boyne Street areas, and the Corporation had approved schemes for Mary's Lane, Newfoundland Street and North Lotts, which would be dealt with insofar as funds would permit. All of the schemes listed amounted to about 2,000 dwellings, and would depend on the Local Government Board giving sanction for the entire loan.[42] A special meeting of the Council was called for 3 November to consider the proposed American borrowing.

In tandem with this work, Raymond Unwin had written a report on how best to deal with the reconstruction of the city of Dublin after the Rising, work which had to be carried out urgently. One can only imagine the difficulty of getting money out of the Treasury, in the middle of the war, for this purpose.

A letter was received from the Board of Works intimating that the Lords' Commissioners of HM's Treasury had agreed to a sum of £3,341 from the Local Loans fund for the acquisition of the McCaffrey estate, the loan to be for 80 years at a rate of 4.5%. The purchase of Fairbrothers' Fields was not approved by the Treasury, and it was recommended that the loan should be raised from private sources for the purchase.[43]

In a further report from the Housing Committee, in October 1916, various proposals to borrow money from American banks were being considered to build on sites already acquired, as the only possible alternative to postponing the improvement of the existing wretched conditions. The report of the Local Government Board of 1914 was again mentioned. Two years previously, when that report was issued, Birrell had described the situation as horrible and intolerable. The present Chief Secretary, Duke, had also freely admitted the urgency of solving the question. Other public men in Parliament had described the Dublin housing conditions as the very worst in the three kingdoms. It was then recommended that the loan be taken up in such instalments as would enable the Corporation to have the schemes for Fairbrothers' Fields, McCaffrey Estate, St. James's Walk and Spitalfields carried out, and for the completion of the Ormond Market site. Local Government orders had been obtained for the acquisition of the Crabbe Lane and Boyne Street areas, and the Corporation had approved schemes for the Mary's Lane, Newfoundland Street and North Lotts areas. Work would be processed on all these, insofar as funds obtainable on foot of the proposed loan would permit. Kelly recommended on 20 October that the offer of the American loan should be taken up, and this proposal was also agreed to by Eyre, the City Treasurer.[44]

---

[42] *Dublin Corporation Reports,* 1916, Vol. 3, pp. 433-441, DCA
[43] Ibid. 1916, Vol. 2, p. 65
[44] Ibid. 1916, Vol. 3, pp. 433-441

The glamour and luxury of a charity subscription ball at the Gresham Hotel is contrasted with the poverty and deprivation of homeless people outside in Sackville Street. Cartoon by Fitzpatrick from The Lepracaun, *January 1908 Courtesy National Library of Ireland.*

In December 1916, the urgency of providing dwellings for the poor was so acute that the City Treasurer, Mr. Eyre, advised the Housing Committee that the loan offered to the Council by Messrs. Lee, Higginson and Co. should be accepted even though the rate had been raised to 6.5%. In December 1916, a letter was sent to the Lord Mayor by Archbishop William Walsh stating that the housing of the working classes was of vital importance, and requesting the Corporation to convene a representative conference to consider putting a plan in place to deal with the issue once the war was over. In addition to the Archbishop, this letter was also signed by Edward Carson, MP (for the University of Dublin), William Cotton, William Field and Alfred Byrne, all prominent men. The inclusion of Carson's name in this letter is interesting. Subsequently, the Lord Mayor proposed that six members of the Corporation be appointed to this conference, together with six members of the Housing Committee.[45]

In February 1917, Laurence O'Neill was elected Lord Mayor, while Kelly continued as chairman of the Housing Committee. Another tribute was paid to his work by the Committee. They thanked him for the very earnest, capable and impartial manner in which he had conducted the Committee business and the keen and unselfish interest he consistently took in finding a solution for the housing problem in Dublin. He was also elected chairman of the newly formed Administration Committee of the Corporation Electricity undertaking.

---

[45] *Minutes of Dublin City Council,* 1917, pp. 108-109, DCA

In March 1917, a major report was prepared by the Housing Committee to formulate a policy for the development of the north side of the city. This referred to industrial and commercial concerns, the number of private and tenement houses, population and density of the slum areas, and developed and waste lands. It also evaluated the various grades of the working classes, i.e., skilled and unskilled workers, casual labour earnings and family conditions. The City Engineer instructed that a survey of the lands be prepared, and that the collaboration of the Borough Surveyor and City Architect be sought to provide new streets to meet the need for future development.

In a further report from the Committee, it was stated that Fairbrothers' Fields, McCaffrey Estate, St. James's Walk and Spitalfields sites were now in the hands of the Corporation, and recorded the good news that the necessary loans for their development were about to be made available from the Treasury. The difficulties they encountered in their dealings with the Local Government Board were described in detail, but the money now became available as a result of the action taken by the Chief Secretary, Henry Duke. A copy of his letter, dated 19 April 1917, was included in the report which informed the Lord Mayor that the sum of £10,000 would be available at once, followed by successive amounts during the subsequent year, and totalling £100,000 by the end of the following March, for the above developments. This was a very courteous letter in which the Chief Secretary conveyed his good wishes to the Lord Mayor. The plan to obtain the loan from the American bank was abandoned in view of the prohibitive rates of interest required. Great difficulties had been experienced in the acquisition of Fairbrothers' Fields, 22 acres in all, the compensation claims for which came to £15,750. The development work on this site was to be divided into three phases. The proposals were to follow the general layout suggested by Geddes and Unwin, and included a reduction from 800 houses to 568, or 26 houses to the acre. They had described the site as excellent.[46]

A big increase in work was being experienced by the housing department due to the many applications for tenancies of the new houses now coming on stream. These were the developments at Beresford Street, Ormond Market, Trinity Ward, Inchicore and Cook Street – about 3,000 dwellings in all. All applicants had to be registered by the Assistant Superintendent, Mr. P.J. Dillon, with dispossessed tenants being placed in order of priority. This work could not be done by day, as applicants were often available only between eight and ten o'clock at night, and Mr. Dillon was seeking an allowance for his staff for the amount of extra work involved. The City Treasurer, E.W. Eyre, strongly recommended the application, saying that he knew of no case more deserving of consideration, and that without the driving force of sympathy with the class to be decently housed, the same loyal service could not have been received.[47]

Kelly (1917) summed up his own views regarding Corporation housing policy and the work of the Committee in the course of a testy interview between the Committee and

---

[46] *Dublin Corporation Reports,* 1917, Vol. 2, pp. 285-295, DCA
[47] Ibid. 1917, Vol. 4, p. 204

P.C. Cowan, Chief Engineering Inspector of the Local Government Board, which took place on 19 October, 1917. It is worth quoting in full:

> The position of affairs is this. The Housing Committee was constituted at the beginning of 1913, and it has continued its work ever since. All the officers are honorary officers; not one of them gets a penny piece for his services, except one or two of the assistants, who get an allowance for any overtime they may give. This is a very important point, and I want to get it into your head. This Committee is really doing the work for absolutely nothing. It doesn't cost the citizens £100 a year. The policy of the Housing Committee is to build inside and outside (the city). I am personally in favour of building entirely inside – that is, inside the old City before its boundaries were extended. Do not take that as the policy of the Housing Committee, but if I were the Housing Authority, I would allow no building outside until the slums were gone. I do believe that if suitable sites in the suburbs were acquired convenient to the City, and where tramway accommodation could be got near them, you might build there, but I object, as a Dublin man, to the centre of the City being allowed to go into a complete ruin. There has never been any definite or practical definition as to what is to be done with the slum areas. I asked Sir John Griffiths at the Spitalfields Inquiry what would he do with these slum areas, and he said that they should be reserved for business purposes. Where is the business going to come from? We would like to see factories erected, but we see no sign of them. If they do come there will always be sufficient space for them.

Kelly then confronted Cowan. 'You must make up your mind to support the policy of the Housing Committee in building within and without. The Housing Committee agrees to work with you, and you agree with the Housing Committee.'[48]

The major survey, compiled by the Housing Committee, of the north side of the city referred to above, became available early in 1918, and gave a most interesting and comprehensive account of the development of that part of Dublin dating from the beginning of the seventeenth century.[49] It described the decay of the large old mansions and residential quarters built by the gentry, from private ownership to acquisition by the 'house jobber', whose only concern was to extract the best return for his investment by letting out the rooms in tenements. This regrettable state of affairs had been brought about since the Act of Union, when numbers of the successors of the original occupants had ceased to retain their town houses and more rapid means of transport enticed the wealthy classes to move from the city to the suburbs. On the other hand, large numbers of the labouring classes had migrated from the provinces to the city, attracted by the many works in progress and the comparatively high wages prevailing there. The tenement population was thus created. Up to the sixteenth century, Dublin had been largely confined to the southern bank of the Liffey. A description then followed of the development of the north side, referring to various streets, churches and bridges. The development of the North Lotts area, east of what was the Strand (Amiens Street area), appears to have commenced about 1756. An account of the reclamation of the strand and foreshore showed the reclamation line drawn from the extreme end of the North

---

48 *Dublin Corporation Reports,* 1918, Vol. 2, pp. 485-488
49 Ibid. 1918, Vol. 1, pp. 81-123

Wall to Clontarf, leaving a course for the river Tolka. The construction of this work had been undertaken since the extension of the city boundaries under the Act of 1900, with the filling in of that portion of the Lotts between the railway embankment and the old sea wall at Fairview.

The survey included a list of North Wall streets, alphabetically arranged from Abbey Street to Wellington Street, with details concerning private houses, business establishments, lodging houses, hotels, public institutions and tenements, and with appropriate dates listed in each case to show how the nineteenth century changes evolved. Blackhall Place, Street and Parade, for instance, has a description taken from *Irwin's Guide to Dublin* by Rev. Dillon Cosgrave in the eighteenth century, which reads as follows: 'This is the part of Dublin enjoying the most mild and genial climate and the gardens have the grape and fig ripen in the open air'.

This comprehensive and interesting report ended with an analysis of the various dwellings, their current state of repair, and recommendations for each category. It concludes that it would be unjustifiable to demolish structurally sound houses, and therefore the solution should be to repair and improve them, a view that was shared also by Geddes and Unwin. First-class tenement houses should be renovated and adapted to letting in flats, each flat to be provided with separate sanitary and scullery accommodation, allotting one family to each floor. This new accommodation should be allotted to families consisting of three or more persons, as the cubic content of the rooms in these old houses was greatly in excess of that in the more modern type of artisans' dwellings. Councillor W.T. Cosgrave wrote a special memorandum disagreeing with these proposals for flats as outlined for first-class tenements. He felt it was an unsatisfactory solution to the problem, and would not justify the money spent on them in the long run.[50]

In 1918, during which Kelly was unanimously re-elected chairman of the Housing Committee for the fourth year in succession, the City Treasurer, E.W. Eyre, drew the attention of the Council to the fact that the English Local Government Board had actively interested itself in the question of providing state assistance to enable English, Scots and Welsh local authorities to grapple effectively with their housing needs after the war. Eyre, seeing that no action was being taken to bring Ireland within the scope of this Government recognition, issued a report himself in which he emphasized the pressing needs of Dublin, and its claims to any state aid which might be given to cities in Great Britain, claims already fully debated and admitted in Parliament, and urged by all sections of public opinion. He quoted from the official circular in which the Government recognised that it would be necessary to afford substantial financial assistance from public funds to those local authorities who were prepared to carry through without delay, at the conclusion of the war, a programme of housing for the working classes approved by the Local Government Board. Eyre stated that, as far as he was aware, no corresponding official undertaking had been given regarding Ireland. Mr. Brady, MP had written to the Chief Secretary who replied in his capacity as president

---

50 *Dublin Corporation Reports,* 1918, Vol. 1, pp. 122-123, DCA

of the Irish Local Government Board, with indifference, saying that it was not clear to what extent and in what manner the Government would subsidise the housing schemes. Eyre recommended that the Housing Committee and the Council insist on an assurance in definite terms that what had been given to English, Scots and Welsh local authorities in substantial financial assistance from public funds be made available also to Ireland.[51]

The Lord Mayor, Laurence O'Neill, wrote to the Prime Minister on 20 November 1918. The letter reminded the Prime Minister in the strongest terms that, notwithstanding the assurances given in Parliament by Mr. Birrell, Mr. Duke and the present Chief Secretary, Mr. Short, Ireland would participate in Government housing grants after the war. The Irish Local Government Board had not, so far, taken any action by way of intimating to the Irish local authorities the extent of the financial assistance to be given to Ireland. He added that Dublin's deplorable conditions were well-known to Government, and had been fully debated at the beginning of 1914 on the consideration of the Department inquiry report. The consensus of opinion as expressed on that occasion by both English and Irish members, as well as the minister responsible for Irish administration, showed that the work in Dublin was beyond the resources of the municipality and that state aid was essential. 'It is one which, on humanitarian grounds alone, demands immediate action on the part of the State, and the people of this city are entitled to know now what measure of assistance the Government proposes to enable the very grave conditions in Dublin to be grappled with.'[52]

This very well-argued letter from O'Neill elicited only a brief reply from Lloyd George, to the effect that he was taking steps to ascertain personally what the actual position was with regard to the progress of schemes for rehousing in Dublin and other parts of Ireland. During 1919, efforts continued to obtain money from various sources to advance the housing programme, but this work was going on against a background of tremendous pressure on many members of Dublin Corporation because of the very grave political situation at that period. A letter written by W.T. Cosgrave to Arthur Griffith, dated 28 August 1919, outlined the mishandling by the British of the housing crux in Dublin. He wrote that the Corporation had made its own reports about the housing conditions, and that in 1916 £300,000 (€25 million at 2005 prices) had been needed immediately for the erection of dwellings for the working classes. Within a month, the Rebellion broke out and Cowan, the chief engineering expert appointed by the British, was quoted in a letter written by Cosgrave to Griffith, dated 28 August 1919, regarding the housing situation:

> The Rebellion of 1916, with its terrible results in loss of life, vast material waste, the re-birth of dying antagonisms, the creation of new enmities and the setting back of the clock in many most vital movements, might possibly have been prevented if the people of Dublin had been better housed. After the declaration of War, the English Government

---

[51] *Dublin Corporation Reports,* 1918, Vol. 2, pp. 465-472, DCA
[52] Ibid. 1918, Vol. 1, pp. 126-128, DCA

passed into law an Act granting £4,000,000 [€450 million at 2005 prices] for Housing in Ireland, but not a single penny of this grant was ever spent in Ireland, and it is now clear that this Act was passed to popularise the War in Ireland… In 1914, £3,500,000 would have sufficed to solve the problem; now the cost would be £12,000,000 which is about the sum collected in Imperial Revenue from the citizens each year.[53]

Kelly, amongst other councillors, had been elected a member of Parliament in the general election of December 1918. During 1919, many nationalists were arrested, deported and imprisoned in British jails for their political activities. W.T. Cosgrave had been arrested for the second time in May of 1918, and was imprisoned in Reading Gaol. In January 1919, his seat on the Corporation was declared vacant. Seán T. O'Kelly suffered a similar fate. Many nationalists were being held in Mountjoy prison in Dublin, where their health deteriorated due to the bad conditions there. A serious influenza epidemic spreading throughout Europe at this time also affected Ireland. In January 1919, the newly formed Irish parliament, Dáil Éireann, was convened for the first time. All these events delayed the needed housing schemes.

In August 1919, J.J. Kelly, a well-known alderman of the Council and prominent business man with a tobacconist shop at the top of Camden Street, informed the Housing Committee that he had managed to negotiate a loan for housing purposes of £150,000 from an American/Scots company at a rate of 5% over fifty years. This company had large trust funds available for investment, some of it available only for improving conditions of the working-class population. J.J. Kelly wished to include houses for the middle classes also, a class, which in his opinion, had been sadly and grossly neglected. He wrote to the Town Clerk informing him that the loan had been secured through his own firm, the National Development Company of Ireland Ltd., and mentioned that money might also be available for the development of shipping in Ireland. He was most anxious to see the establishment of a large shipbuilding yard in Dublin, adjacent to Dublin port, as he wished that 'my own native city can get the full benefit of this great industry. I would, therefore, ask you not to give any options on any property controlled or owned by the Corporation at or adjacent to the Port until I can put a proposition before you in concrete form'.[54] This proposal was addressed to the Town Clerk, Henry Campbell.

At the monthly Council meeting of 1 September, a motion proposed by Kelly and seconded by Councillor P. Doyle was carried, to the effect that the Town Clerk was to write to Alderman J.J. Kelly, informing him that the Corporation was prepared to accept the loan to be applied to the provision of housing schemes and that the City Treasurer and Law Agent be instructed to proceed accordingly.

A report from the Housing Committee outlined in great detail the frustrations being suffered by the Committee due to the lack of any clear action by the Local Government

---

[53] Quoted in Cosgrave to Griffith, 28 August 1919, de Valera Mss. Vol. 2, P150, Item 1404, UCDA
[54] *Minutes of Dublin City Council,* 1919, pp. 451-452, DCA

Board, and stating that their inaction was not consistent with the clear-cut instructions for housing schemes being sanctioned for local authorities in England.[55] No definite pledge of a similar nature had been given to Ireland, despite promises by the new Prime Minister, Lloyd George, twelve months previously to the Irish convention that the Government would be prepared to consider the inclusion in the scheme of settlement of a substantial provision to deal immediately with this vital problem. There was still no information as to the nature and extent of such assistance or indeed if any financial aid at all would be received from state sources.[56]

The Housing Committee, meanwhile, decided to go ahead with their plans for the various schemes, the selection of sites, and the types of houses to be built. The Chief Architect, C.S. MacCarthy, laid out all the issues – nine developments in hand, staff required, possible costs and schedules. Of particular note were the plans for the Marino Estate, which had been in abeyance for a number of years, and the land for which was now owned by the Corporation. Mr. MacCarthy suggested a better type of housing for this scheme, and stated that 600 dwellings could be built on the land at a cost of approximately £395 each (€20,000 at 2005 prices). Kelly commented also on the various issues involved, and stressed the urgency of making decisions, so as to have everything ready should permission come through to proceed with the work.

> Within recent years, the Corporation has increased to a large extent housing accommodation for the workers in the city. In 1911 the number of dwellings was 1,344. On the completion of the McCaffrey estate and St. James's Walk contracts, now in progress, the number of dwellings will have reached 2,232, and these figures will shortly be increased by the addition of 370 houses on the Fairbrothers' Fields site.[57]

The above information was set out by Kelly in relation to the appointment of Patrick J. Dillon to the position of Superintendent of Dwellings for the Municipal Council. Kelly highly recommended this man, stressing his qualities for the position, and his enthusiastic interest in his work. He said that it had to be recognised that there were many people whose conditions of existence varied, and who suffered from unemployment and other genuine causes of disability. By sympathetic and judicious treatment, Mr. Dillon had succeeded in maintaining these tenancies without inflicting unnecessary hardship on the unfortunate people involved.

This was Kelly's last recorded contribution to municipal affairs for many years, because on 11 December 1919, he was taken from his bed by the military, deported and imprisoned in Wormwood Scrubs, where he was kept until 16 February 1920, when he was released on condition that he did not return to Ireland. Thus he was removed as chairman of the Housing Committee, as well as from his many other public and private responsibilities. In common with so many others, imprisonment, with all its long-term uncertainties and anxieties, effectively ruined his health.

---

[55] *Dublin Corporation Reports,* 1919, Vol. 1, pp. 121-147, DCA
[56] Ibid. pp. 121-147
[57] Ibid. pp. 234-236

Chapter Eleven: Conventions and Elections

In the early part of 1917, the business of Dublin Corporation was focused on the financial shortages resulting from the aftermath of the Rising. Kelly, apart from his work for the Housing Committee, was also a member of the General Improvements Committee, and continued to represent the Corporation on the committee of the Royal Hospital. But at this point housing issues were being rendered more acute because, as mentioned earlier, whatever money might have been available was required for rebuilding the ruins in O'Connell Street and the adjoining areas. The matter of the reconstruction work was raised early on in the year within the Council, when, by agreement with the Lord Lieutenant and the Lords Commissioners, the Treasury advances to effect repairs could be made to the contractors on the certificate of architects or buildings supported by a recommendation from the Commissioners of Public Works.

The majority of the Irish political prisoners, i.e. those who had never been charged, had been released from jail just before Christmas 1916, while those who had been charged and sentenced were still in custody. Of major concern to the Council was the absence of four of its councillors: Seán T. O'Kelly, William Partridge, P.T. Daly and W.T. Cosgrave. A motion in the Council was moved by Kelly and seconded by Councillor O'Beirne, demanding the release of these prisoners, as their continued imprisonment was a cause of great irritation to the Irish people. This motion was carried.[1]

Partridge was a very sad case. He had been a trade union activist and a member of the Citizen Army, and had fought with Countess Markiewicz and Michael Mallin in St. Stephen's Green during the Rising. He was subsequently captured, tried, and sentenced to fifteen years in jail for his activities. He was co-opted by the Council to the vacant councillorship in the New Kilmainham Ward in February 1917, and he wrote to the Town Clerk from Lewes prison to express his gratitude to his fellow councillors. He made the point that he was neither a prisoner of war nor a political prisoner, and was not being treated as such. 'I am merely a common convict, allowed certain privileges that are neither comprehensive or numerous.' He wrote that he did not wish to complain about his imprisonment, for 'when I agreed to surrender, in order to protect innocent bloodshed, and the unnecessary destruction of public property in Dublin, I, in common with my comrades, cheerfully accepted any and all possible results of such an act'. He stressed that he did not wish to accept any pardon which might retard or reduce the old original demand of the people of Ireland, and would prefer to finish his full sentence, or die a convict and be buried within prison walls, rather than consent to have

---

[1] *Minutes of Dublin City Council*, 1917, p. 11, DCA

his freedom purchased by the smallest portion of such a price.[2] Kelly proposed a motion that this letter from Partridge be inserted in the minutes of the Corporation, which was put and carried. Time and again, it is noticeable that, through Kelly's intervention, such letters were incorporated in the records, as if he felt that these documents would convey a sense of the history of events more tellingly than in the necessarily formal reports of the Corporation's proceedings.

Partridge also wrote separately to Kelly, with whom he was on friendly terms, after his release from jail in the middle of April 1917. He described himself as 'medically scrap after they had made several unsuccessful attempts to induce me to petition for my release'. On medical advice, he was not allowed to travel home, and was forced to remain in England while he was receiving medical treatment. He described the conditions in Lewes prison where he had been detained.

> My comrades in Lewes prison are no way despondent – talking, singing, laughing and whistling in their old cheerful way. But the pale cheek, the sunken eyes and the skull showing plainly and painfully through their skin tell their own horrible tale silently. Confinement and insufficient food is killing them. These men are going to their death cheerfully but as surely as did our own gallant comrades who fearlessly faced the guns in Kilmainham twelve months ago. The South African Rebellion was suppressed without the carnage or brutality displayed in Dublin… Must my comrades in Lewes wait in confinement until they too become wrecks? It is to prevent this I write to you. I am so helpless myself to do more.[3]

The unfortunate Partridge returned to his brother's home in Ballaghaderreen only to die in August 1917. Countess Markiewicz gave the oration at his graveside. Kelly continued to pester the authorities for permission to visit the Lewes prisoners on his own behalf and on behalf of Dr. Russell, the Assistant City Medical Officer for Health, but to no avail.

Coinciding with the release of the Irish political prisoners in December 1916 was the declaration of a by-election in North Roscommon, due to the death of an Irish Parliamentary Party MP, James O'Kelly. This was a chance for Sinn Féin to make its mark. A representative group of members of Sinn Féin, the Irish Volunteers, the IRB, and the Irish Nation League decided to grasp the opportunity. They were all united in their opposition to allowing the Parliamentary Party a clear run. The Irish Nation League consisted of a group of lawyers, which included George Gavan Duffy, Laurence Ginnell, J.J. O'Kelly and others opposed to any form of Home Rule which would include partition. A suitable candidate had to be found. A key figure in this drive was the dynamic priest, Fr. Michael O'Flanagan, from Crossna, Co. Roscommon, a member of Sinn Féin, and well known to his superiors for being a troublemaker who did not support the Parliamentary Party as did most of the clergy. As Fr. O'Flanagan saw it, winning this seat could rekindle the spirit of the Rising among the people who were

2 *Minutes of Dublin City Council*, 1917, 1917, p. 209
3 Private collection

distressed and angered by the loss of their executed leaders. Dr. Michael Davitt, son of the founder of the Land League, was approached to go forward, but he declined. Then the name of George Noble, Count Plunkett was suggested. His credentials, on one level, were impeccable, as he was the father of Joseph Mary Plunkett, a signatory of the 1916 Proclamation. Joseph had been imprisoned after the Rebellion and then executed, and Count Plunkett had been dismissed subsequently from his post as director of the National Museum even though he had had nothing to do with it. Griffith was dubious about him, but nonetheless, once Plunkett had been selected, threw himself vigorously into the campaign to elect him. T.J. Devine was the Parliamentary Party's choice of candidate, and a third aspirant, Jasper Tully, ran as an independent. He was the editor of the *Roscommon Herald,* and was regarded as an eccentric.

This campaign came to be known as the 'Election of the Snows', because of the heavy snowstorms which swept the country in January 1917. Fr. O'Flanagan was a powerful orator who knew the people and the terrain very well, and addressed the hustings several times each night, despite the weather. There were snowdrifts of up to ten feet throughout the county, and he had to organise manpower to clear the blocked roads between Elphin and Strokestown. It was reported that several people had gone missing and were found frozen to death in the snow. Fr. O'Flanagan repudiated the recruitment propaganda of the Parliamentary Party, and emphasised to small farmers the importance of land reform. He masterminded Plunkett's itinerary throughout the constituency and organised church meetings after Mass on Sundays. Fr. O'Flanagan was ably backed by J.J. O'Kelly, whose journalistic skills contributed hugely to the publicity. Polling took place on 3 February, and all the hard work paid off handsomely. The ballot boxes were transported to Boyle courthouse, where they were kept under lock and key and guarded by the police and volunteers. On 5 February the result was declared, with Plunkett sweeping the board with 3,022 votes to Devine's 1,708, while Tully polled 687. Plunkett, in his victory speech, claimed that the results reflected the feelings of the people who had kept alight the torch of freedom handed down from Tone and Emmet, and not those of the Parliamentary Party leaders, who had expressed horror and detestation of the 1916 Rising. He said that the time had come to reject the present policy of corruption and job-seeking. An engraved memorial plaque, commemorating Plunkett's election, on the courthouse in Boyle is worded: 'In this Courthouse on February 3 1917, George Noble Count Plunkett was elected Sinn Féin MP for North Roscommon. His election was the first step in breaking the Parliamentary link with England.' Fr. O'Flanagan's own account of the 'Election of the Snows' was published in *The Catholic Bulletin*, March 1917.

The Parliamentary Party took its defeat very badly, but, significant as Plunkett's election was, it left Sinn Féin somewhat in disarray with no agreed plan for advancement. Much work had to be done to consolidate the various views into a cohesive whole. The main groupings consisted of those who espoused republican principles and the use of force as expressed in the spirit of the Rising, against the more conservative principles of Griffith and Sinn Féin. It was desirable that the momentum and the experience gained in the campaign to elect Count Plunkett should not be wasted, as there was another by-election pending in South Longford and Sinn Féin was determined to capitalise on its success. Plunkett called a meeting at his house in Fitzwilliam Street in early February 1917 to discuss strategy. Those invited included Griffith, Fr. O'Flanagan, Michael Collins, Laurence Ginnell, Kelly, and William O'Brien of the Labour Party. The aim was to consolidate the diverse views of the various strands of nationalists into a more coherent whole, and thus present a united front to the public. It was not clear whether Plunkett's recent success could be attributed to a wish on the part of the people for what could be called extreme republicanism represented by, for instance, Cathal Brugha, or the more restrained and moderate principles of old-style Sinn Féin. And the label of Sinn Féin also embraced the Volunteer movement and Cumann na mBan, the members of which, while having misgivings, decided pragmatically to avoid a split, and go along under its banner.

Arising from this meeting, and after much discussion, Plunkett decided to summon a conference in the Mansion House on 19 April, to which he invited delegates from all the principal political groups, together with representatives of the local authorities and members of the clergy. Some seventy public bodies were represented at this gathering. A lively discussion took place at a meeting in the Corporation when it was discovered that the Lord Mayor (Laurence O'Neill) had not seen fit to include Plunkett's invitation to take part in the conference on the agenda for discussion. The Lord Mayor said he had taken the decision not to bring it before the Council as he feared it would result in a split. He was taken severely to task by Kelly who said that, in his opinion, it should have been brought before the house, as 'Count Plunkett, because of his opposition twenty years ago to intolerance in Irish national life by British statesmen, was entitled to the courtesy of having his letter put before the Council'.[4]

Count Plunkett's convention was described enthusiastically by Andrew E. Malone in *New Ireland*[5] 'as a definite turning point in Irish political movements':

> First, because it is the largest and most representative meeting of Irishmen in Ireland
> which has stated its claim for full independence, and secondly, because Ireland, through
> this meeting appeals to the nations of the world and no longer to Westminster.

The outstanding features of the meeting were the passing of a vote of honour to the men who had sacrificed their lives, which was passed in silence; a declaration proclaiming Ireland a separate nation, and then the Count's declaration: 'That we, the Assembly of Irish Independence, desire to establish an organisation to unite Irish advanced opinion and provide for action as a result of its conclusions.'

From this conference an arrangement emerged, brokered by Griffith and Fr. O'Flanagan, that a representative group, nine in all, acceptable to all, would work together to achieve their common goal. This supposedly inclusive group, now called the

---

4 *Dublin Saturday Evening Post,* 7 April 1917
5 *New Ireland,* 28 April 1917

Mansion House Committee, of which Kelly was a member, elected William O'Brien as chairman. This was a somewhat surprising development as it was assumed by Plunkett himself, as well as others, that he would take the chair. The work done by this committee resulted in the establishment of Sinn Féin clubs all over the country, set up in many cases by those prisoners who had been released home to Ireland some four months previously.

The expected by-election now occurred in South Longford. Despite some opposition, a jailed nationalist held in Lewes prison, Joseph McGuinness, was selected as the Sinn Féin candidate. It was expected that the fight for this seat would be bitter, which proved to be the case. Longford was a garrison town, traditionally very supportive of the Parliamentary Party, and had responded in huge numbers to Redmond's recruitment drive when the war began. The big guns of the Parliamentary Party came out to support their chosen candidate, but the Sinn Féin election machine won the day again. Sinn Féin had received an unexpected fillip just before polling day on 9 May 1917, when three archbishops, including the Archbishop of Dublin, Dr. Walsh, fifteen Catholic and three Protestant bishops, issued a manifesto proclaiming that 'to Irishmen of every creed and class and party, the very thought of our country partitioned and torn as a new Poland, must be one of heart-rending sorrow'.[6] Archbishop Walsh added his own personal contribution to the manifesto when he wrote in the *Evening Herald* on 8 May stating that, in his opinion, the damage was already done, and the country was practically sold. This statement was widely circulated in Longford on polling day, and undoubtedly further damaged the Parliamentary Party's cause. There was widespread publicity in the newspapers in the days following the election about the significance of the Archbishop's intervention. On 11 May, the *Pall Mall Gazette* commented that his wholehearted support of the Sinn Féin candidate was not a surprise to anyone who knew His Grace's past record, and remarked on how deeply he took to heart the stern suppression of the Irish Rising of the previous year.[7] Polling day was 9 May, and McGuinness won the seat, after a recount, by a margin of only 37 votes. However, a win was a win, and the Parliamentary Party was left to lick its wounds once again. The Dublin correspondent of the *Times* wrote: 'I think the word unique in its strictest sense, may be applied to the fact that eighteen Catholic and three Protestant bishops have united publicly in allegiance to the principle of an Ireland, one and undivided. It is a signpost of a revolution in the social position in Ireland'.[8]

Since early in the year, very conscious of American criticism of his stance on Ireland, Lloyd George had been floating ideas regarding possible solutions for the political impasse. He made an offer, on 7 March 1917 in the House of Commons, to the effect that he was prepared to grant Home Rule to the part of Ireland which had been demanding it, while stressing that no action could be taken to force Home Rule on those to whom it was unacceptable. He proposed that the details of this possible deal could be worked out by a convention representative of all shades of Irish opinion.

---

[6] *Irish Independent*, 8 May 1917
[7] Quoted in Morrissey, *William J. Walsh, Archbishop of Dublin, 1841-1921* p. 301
[8] Quoted in *Curran Papers*, Ms. 17,728, Vol. 2, Mss. Room NLI

Horace Plunkett's Convention

On 16 May, Lloyd George put forward additional proposals. The first was that Home Rule should be applied immediately in the twenty-six counties, and the remaining six should be excluded until they or the British Parliament thought otherwise. His alternative plan was to call a convention with a mandate to submit proposals to the Cabinet for the future form of government for Ireland within the empire. The Unionist Council was apprehensive about taking part in the proposed convention, and Sinn Féin refused to. It was the opinion of nationalists that the composition of the convention, having being handpicked by Lloyd George, precluded the possibility of any settlement being arrived at through this medium. Labour, under the leadership of William O'Brien, felt that it was 90% composed of men who had already consented to partition, and twenty at least of the members were Ulster Unionists of the covenanter type, pledged to agree to nothing Sir Edward Carson and the Ulster Unionist Council did not approve.[9] Archbishop Walsh supported it with serious reservations, as it was his opinion that it was a Government device to save the faces of the British before the world.

The convention went ahead under the chairmanship of Sir Horace Plunkett (founder of the agricultural co-operative movement and no relation of Count Plunkett). It had the support of the Parliamentary Party. Redmond, who was far from well, had told Lloyd George that the only possible hope for the success of the convention lay in the participation of Irishmen of all creeds, interests and parties. Sir Horace Plunkett, well known and much respected for his work in social and agrarian issues, had felt that the continued retention of the remaining 1916 prisoners was a major handicap to meaningful negotiations. On 15 June, it was announced that in order to help the work of the convention, the prisoners were to be released on the following day. The first meeting of the convention took place in Trinity College in July 1917.

Apart from Horace Plunkett, there were significant figures who genuinely believed that in the convention there was the possibility of a way forward. Decent men such as A.E. (George Russell), Fr. Tom Finlay, Stephen Gwynn and Edward MacLysaght were determined to give it their all. There were nine southern Unionists, led by Lord Midleton, who were anxious about their own future in whatever compromise might be brokered for Ireland. Several of them had contributed to a document entitled 'Thoughts for a Convention' which they had submitted for the consideration of the Imperial Conference in London in advance. A.E. wrote that he had accepted Lloyd George's nomination because he could not have it on his conscience that he had refused to help to bring about an Irish settlement if there was a ghost of a chance of success.[10] However, in view of such diverse and tenaciously held views, the enterprise was doomed from the start. Having tried to induce Dillon to become chairman and failed, Horace Plunkett himself was elected chairman, and was well aware of the potential pitfalls. He fully understood the Ulster unionist fears about how they would be treated under Home Rule. But he rightly concluded that their fears about Home Rule were a front to what in fact was their real

9   Macardle, Dorothy. *The Irish Republic*, p. 205
10   Quoted in West, T. *Horace Plunkett: Cooperation and Politics,* Colin Smythe, 1986, p. 160

reservation – the economic one – that a Home Rule government in Dublin, dominated by agricultural interests, would be inimical to industrial and commercial Ulster. The convention's report was issued in the spring of 1918, signed by fewer than half the members. It recommended a form of Home Rule under which the Irish parliament would have no power over the army, navy, police, postal or certain other services. Less than half of the members had signed it. A.E. had resigned from it long since, declaring that the Sinn Féiners were right in their intuition from the first. 'If I had followed my own intuitions, I would have remained away also. A man must either be Irishman or an Englishman in this matter. I am Irish'.[11] A subcommittee of five reported separately against conscription.

Horace Plunkett travelled to London on 8 April 1918 to present the convention's report to Lloyd George, and found himself, to his horror, in the House of Commons the following day in time to hear Lloyd George introduce the Military Service Bill – conscription – which he proposed to extend to Ireland.

The East Clare Election

Redmond had been shattered by the death of his brother, Captain William Redmond, killed in the War on 7 June, but the fallout of this tragedy, apart from his own personal grief, was that it caused a by-election in East Clare. Dillon's instinct was not to fight the election. The party had a good candidate who, in normal circumstances, could have been expected to retain the seat, but Sinn Féin had put forward the recently released prisoner from Lewes, Éamon de Valera. The mood of the country was in his favour and supporters flocked into Clare in huge numbers to help him to victory. The location of this by-election was very significant because of its resonances. It had elected Daniel O'Connell to the House of Commons in 1828. It now was putting forward a candidate of impeccable credentials in Éamon de Valera. The nationalist election machinery again swung into action, with Volunteers in uniform playing a prominent role coming up to polling day. The Parliamentary Party had few resources, and their fight to elect their candidate, Patrick Lynch, was a puny effort. It crumbled under the onslaught of Sinn Féin's well-organised and disciplined workers, and on 10 July, de Valera won the seat with a large majority of 5,010 votes to Lynch's 2,035.

The last in this quartet of by-elections occurred in Kilkenny (the vacancy was in the city of Kilkenny) one month later, occasioned by the death of Patrick O'Brien, a Parliamentary Party member. W.T. Cosgrave, of Dublin Corporation, who had taken part in the Rising and had been sentenced to life imprisonment, was, on de Valera's suggestion, proposed as the Sinn Féin candidate. He received 772 votes, nearly double the number polled by the party candidate.

Sinn Féin called its own convention in October 1917, at the time of year when traditionally its conventions were held. Griffith was still president of the movement. He was

---

[11] Quoted in West, T. *Horace Plunkett: Cooperation and Politics,* Colin Smythe, 1986, p. 173

not an ambitious man, and when it became clear that de Valera was going to challenge him for the leadership, he willingly stepped aside. He felt that this procedure would be best for the continuing success of the Sinn Féin Party, instead of a possible unseemly contest. Thus, at the convention, de Valera was elected unanimously to the position of president, with Griffith and Fr. O'Flanagan agreeing to act as vice-presidents. De Valera's selection as chairman endorsed the convention's acceptance of the actions of those who had participated in the Rising of Easter Week. De Valera now had the job of trying to reconcile the two wings of the movement – that of traditional Sinn Féin, as propounded by Griffith, and the newer republican element personified by Cathal Brugha. De Valera defined the objectives of the movement at this point:

> Sinn Féin aims at securing the international recognition of Ireland as an independent Irish Republic. Having achieved that status, the Irish people may by Referendum freely choose their own form of Government.[12]

Griffith's address stressed that Ireland had achieved its goal, as she had renounced the British Parliament, and when Cathal Brugha proposed that all stood united for an Irish republic, his proposal was accepted unanimously by the assembly, the numbers attending being something in the order of 1,700. It was decided to continue to use the name of Sinn Féin. It was made clear that every possible means would be used to fight the imposition of conscription.

From October 1917, Lloyd George had begun to worry at the bellicose tone of de Valera's speeches:

> They are not excited and so far as language is concerned, they are not violent. They are plain, deliberate, and I might also say cold-blooded incitements to rebellion … There is a great deal of talk among the Sinn Féiners which does not mean Home Rule. It does not mean self-government. It means complete separation – it means secession … This country could not possibly accept that under any conditions.[13]

Apart from the disquieting rumours from Ireland, Lloyd George had to deal with the shortage of manpower for fighting the war. Some of his colleagues felt that it could solve a lot of difficulties if conscription were introduced to Ireland, as they could scoop up all the men who had been drilling with the Sinn Féin clubs over the previous few months, and at the same time put them to good use in fighting the war. Redmond wrote to Lloyd George on 13 November 1917, warning him that if the convention failed, it would mean governing Ireland at the point of a bayonet. Dillon wrote in similar terms, but the British government, ignoring the warnings, reorganised the constituencies in Ireland, thus giving Unionists additional seats, and by 9 April 1918, as noted above, Lloyd George had announced the new Bill permitting the extension of conscription to Ireland.

---

[12] Macardle, Dorothy. *The Irish Republic*, p. 217
[13] Ibid. p.220

This Bill was passed in the House of Commons on 16 April, and for the last time, led by Dillon, the Parliamentary Party left the House. The members returned to Dublin and joined in a conference of representatives of all parties united in the national cause, to fight the common enemy.

Horace Plunkett's convention held the previous year in Trinity College, had been John Redmond's last attempt to salvage Home Rule, the campaign to which he had devoted his life. He died on 6 March 1918. In contrast to the elaborate funeral arrangements made by Archbishop Walsh for his popular brother, Major William Redmond, on the occasion of his death in the War, John Redmond was not given a requiem mass in Dublin's Pro-Cathedral. His body was brought directly to Wexford for burial, where Dillon delivered the encomium. The Archbishop did not even send a message of condolence. A requiem mass was held in St. Francis Xavier's Church, Gardiner Street, by Clongowes Wood College, where Redmond had gone to school. John's son, also William Redmond, contested his father's Waterford seat in March 1918, and retained it, due, no doubt, to a sympathy vote and also the family's popularity in the constituency.

A further by-election which took place in South Armagh in early 1918 was a difficult one for Sinn Féin to contest. It quickly resolved itself into a struggle between Sinn Féin and the Parliamentary Party, the latter having chosen a local man, Patrick Donnelly, a Newry solicitor, who was well known, whereas Patrick Mc Carton, the Sinn Féin candidate, was a native of Tyrone, and, at that time, was working in America. The outcome was a victory for the Parliamentary Party which won the seat handsomely with a result of 2,324 votes to 1,305 for Sinn Féin.

From the beginning of 1918, Sinn Féin was in election mode in anticipation of a general election. There was a sense that the results of this election were going to presage a most important political development in the evolution of the nationalist movement. It took a great deal of manoeuvring to consolidate the various elements. Since the Rising, No. 6 Harcourt Street had become the headquarters not alone of the traditional Sinn Féin members, but also of the Volunteers, and figures such as Cathal Brugha and Michael Collins, representing the extremist point of view, who could not see any way of progressing without the use of force. They were uneasy bedfellows, and there was many a fracas while the strategy of planning for the election was in progress.

As a pacifist, Kelly's misgivings, which he had expressed earlier about the taking over of the Sinn Féin movement as he knew it, were not unfounded. An ongoing account of the evolution of the movement, now with many Volunteer elements, appears in the minutes of what were called the Sinn Féin Standing Committee meetings, dating from 17 January 1918, immediately subsequent to the South Armagh election. They continue until 31 March 1922. These weekly reports are contained in two handwritten notebooks, together with minutes of meetings of the Ard-Chomhairle of Sinn Féin, and an occasional Ard-Fheis throughout the same period.[14] The meetings were long and there

---

[14] Sinn Féin Standing Committee Minute Book, NLI, Microfilm Mss N. 3651 P 3269, p. 167

was always a demanding agenda. They were remarkable for the faithful attendance of those involved. Each minute lists the names of those present, and gives a detailed account of the main subjects dealt with, including conscription, strategies for the forthcoming general election, particularly in the North, the release of prisoners and finally plans for the transition from the Standing Committee to a national government when Dáil Éireann came into being. Various leading figures were arrested throughout this period, and contingency plans had to be prepared for substitutions to the major positions, such as the president, vice-president, the honorary secretaries and treasurers, as any one of these people was liable to be taken up at any time, and indeed were. In fact, de Valera and Griffith were arrested simultaneously on the night of 17 May 1918. Those who acted as proxies in their absence were Fr. O'Flanagan, Mrs. Wyse Power and others, depending on availability. Kelly was one of the honorary secretaries and he frequently took the chair at the meetings. He also handwrote the minutes and frequently signed them. The first notebook contains over forty sets of minutes in his handwriting, until he himself was finally arrested in December 1919, and he is not mentioned after that date.

The meeting held on 17 January 1918 was chaired by de Valera. The attendance included Griffith, Count Plunkett, Laurence Ginnell (called Labhrás Mac Fionghail), Seán Milroy, Mrs. Wyse Power and Kelly. A meeting held on the 6 February recorded Griffith in the chair, and noted that Cathal Brugha would be unable to attend for the following five or six weeks due to illness. Ginnell was appointed secretary of the election fund, with the power to spend £200 (€11,000 at 2005 prices)[15] at his discretion. It was decided to authorise a chapel collection for the Sinn Féin fund on 24 March. At this time, the question of those who had access to funds, and the vulnerability of funds during the period when the Sinn Féin Bank was being raided, was a source of great worry. On 21 February a resolution was passed that no money from funds be issued except on the requisition of the president, and that the heads of all departments should furnish detailed accounts of all proposed expenditure of their departments to the executive committee. It was decided to authorise a chapel collection for the Sinn Féin fund on 24 March.

The Bill to enforce conscription in Ireland had been passed in the House of Commons on 16 April, and had been a continuous subject for discussion during all the standing committee meetings held at this period. It was agreed on 10 April that de Valera and Griffith should accept the invitation of Lord Mayor O'Neill to meet with delegates of the Irish Party and of the Trades' Council, to encourage co-operation and to formulate a national policy to defeat this menace. The first meeting was called by O'Neill on 18 April, and the group came to be known as the Mansion House Conference. William O'Brien, who was one of the delegates, wrote an interesting account of its initial meeting.[16] A decision was made to send a delegation from the meeting to Maynooth to brief

---

[15] See footnote 4, Chapter1, for calculation methodology
[16] O'Brien, W. *Forth the Banners Go*, Three Candles Ltd. 1969, pp. 163-169

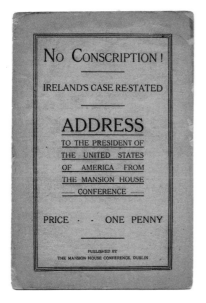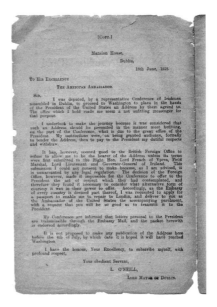

Anti-conscription address from Mansion House Conference to President of the United States, June 1918; with covering letter from Laurence O'Neill, Lord Mayor of Dublin. Dublin City Archives.

the bishops who had convened there to formulate their own stance on conscription. At the meeting between the politicians and the bishops, it was decided that an anti-conscription pledge would be drawn up for countrywide circulation at masses on the following Sunday. O'Brien credits de Valera with the wording of the anti-conscription pledge

> Denying the right of the British Government to enforce compulsory service in this country, we pledge ourselves solemnly to one another to resist Conscription by the most effective means at our disposal.[17]

The bishops also authorised a national church-gate collection to finance the anti-conscription campaign at all the Masses. There is no doubt that the strong and united attitude against conscription adopted by the all those at the Maynooth meeting on that occasion had a profound influence on public opinion.

At a special meeting of the standing committee held on 10 May, it was decided that on the day the order for conscription would be issued, everyone throughout the country should refuse to purchase any commodities on which the British government levied tax, with the exception of necessary foods, and also refuse to pay instalments due in respect of land purchase and every other direct or indirect tax. The Mansion House conference funds were to be used by parishes on a limited basis, and any general arrests were to be treated as attempts at conscription.

---

17 Morrissey, T.J. *William J. Walsh, Archbishop of Dublin, 1841-1921,* pp. 310-311

The standing committee issued a poster against conscription and asserted that: 'For the first time for generations England's will in Ireland is opposed by a practically unanimous Ireland, and England's will shall be broken and Ireland's honour upheld.'[18]

On May 17, Lord French (Commander-in-Chief of the military) authorised a series of arrests across the country on the grounds that Sinn Féin was collaborating with the Germans. Griffith and de Valera were among those arrested, deported and imprisoned in England without charge. The full list of those arrested and deported included W.T. Cosgrave, Count Plunkett, Darrell Figgis, Countess Markiewicz, Walter Cole, Maud Gonne and Michael Lennon.

The standing committee meeting held on 19 May was chaired by Kelly. Temporary appointments to replace the detainees were made, and included MacNeill (replacing de Valera, and representing the Volunteers) and Kelly (substituting for Griffith, and representing Sinn Féin) at the Mansion House Conference. After these arrests, Sinn Féin issued a statement giving the names of the substitute officers and instructed that all were to carry on with their work. 'The country might rest assured that no matter how many of the Leaders might be arrested; there would be men and women to take their places.' This was signed on behalf of the first substitute committee: M. O'Flanagan CC, vice-president, George Nesbitt and J. Wyse Power, honorary treasurers, and Alderman Tom Kelly and P. Sheehan, temporary honorary secretaries.

With regard to the disbursement of funds, William O'Brien remembered that, at this time, Kelly was effectively in charge as 'John Dillon was very nervous about the disbursement of funds, and said that he would leave the payments to Kelly and myself'.[19] As O'Brien, by his own admission, did not want to get involved in money matters, Kelly continued to control the Sinn Féin funds until he was arrested and deported to England in December 1919. He used the money from the fund to alleviate the distress, not only for dependants of internees, but also for those on the run. He colluded with Michael Collins to give grants to Sinn Féin supporters whose business establishments had been destroyed by the crown forces, and also for the benefit of IRA volunteers who were ill. With the ending of the threat of conscription and the campaign against it in November 1918, the conference decided to return the anti-conscription fund to the subscribers. By May 1919, £164,000 was returned or resubscribed to church charities, £21,000 was ceded to the conference, and £15,000 resubscribed to Sinn Féin, leaving £50,000 with Laurence O'Neill, honorary treasurer of the fund. During the next few months another £46,000 was returned to subscribers.

The meeting of the standing committee held on 27 May was chaired by Kelly, who also signed the minutes. Seán T. O'Kelly reported that he had requested Michael Corrigan, solicitor, to go to England to try to get in touch with the interned prisoners, whose relatives at the time were unaware of their whereabouts. It was decided that a protest had

---

18 Sinn Féin Standing Committee Minutes, 10 May 1918
19 Gaughan, J. A. *Thomas Johnson*, Kingdom Books, Dublin 1980, pp. 103-4

to be made against the arrests and subsequent maltreatment of the prisoners, an issue that would be dealt with by the Mansion House conference. The custody of the funds was again discussed, and it was decided that all monies should be lodged in the Sinn Féin Bank in the first instance.

An Ard-Comhairle (senior council) meeting of Sinn Féin was held on 4 June. The agenda included the recent arrests and treatment of the prisoners, together with a discussion on the constitution of the standing committee, the attitude of Sinn Féin towards the Mansion House conference, and a discussion of the victory of Sinn Féin in the East Cavan election, which resulted in the election of Arthur Griffith. He was returned with a vote of 3,785, as against his Parliamentary Party rival's 2,581 votes. A further meeting on 13 June discussed whether the Mansion House conference should make provision from their funds for the dependants of the deported men. Three members of the standing committee, Messrs. Boland, Beaslaoi and MacMahon, were chosen to co-operate with three delegates from each of the Volunteers and Cumann na mBan organisations, to look after the interests of the Sinn Féin prisoners' dependants. It was also decided to apply to the British authorities for the return of property taken away from the office at Harcourt Street, by agents of the English military government in Ireland. The meeting held on 21 June noted, with satisfaction, that the freedom of Sligo was to be conferred on Fr. O'Flanagan, and the committee was instructed to write to the Mayor of Sligo expressing its gratitude for the honour to be conferred on its acting president. The 27 June meeting invited Lord Mayor O'Neill to convene a public meeting to demand the release of the prisoners, the emphasis of which was to be put on the fact that Ireland was a separate nation. It was felt that conscription was imminent.

At another special meeting held on 29 June, with Kelly again in the chair, it was stated that information had been received indicating that the British Government was likely to suppress the Republican movement, and it was decided that the monies in the Munster and Leinster Bank should be drawn out in the Treasurers' names, and dispersed safely by them in whatever way they deemed advisable. Contingency arrangements were again made should the current officers be arrested, and for their substitution should it occur.

An order issued from the Metropolitan Police Court, Inns Quay, Dublin, dated 2 July 1918, signed by T.C. Drury, Divisional Justice, informed the secretary of the Dublin Workmen's Club, John J. Mooney, that the house and premises of the club at 41 York Street were to be closed, as there was evidence that they were being used for purposes prejudicial to public safety by persons attempting to cause sedition. The order mentioned that Alderman Thomas Kelly had been honorary secretary for the previous twenty-five years. At this time, it had thousands of members, and its loan fund had a capital of over £20,000 (€1,100,000 at 2005 prices).[20]

---

20 Private collection

On 8 July, a special meeting of the standing committee of Sinn Féin was held, with Fr. O'Flanagan in the chair. The level of harassment from the military authorities was so great at this time that it was decided that, in the event of the Sinn Féin organisation being suppressed, the title Self-Determination League should be used instead. It was also reported that two representatives of the French Ministry of Agriculture had visited Ireland with the object of offering Irish agricultural workers opportunities to settle in France, together with their families. It was felt at this meeting that if there was to be emigration, it should be to France rather than to England.

At a subsequent meeting on 16 July, Piaras Béaslaí spoke of how difficult it was for him and certain others to attend at the usual Harcourt Street venue, due to the possibility of raids. Kelly gave an account of the work of the Mansion House conference, and the director of elections, Robert Brennan, outlined his plans for the forthcoming general election. He had ensured that every voter in every constituency would be personally canvassed, and from the detailed returns, he was able to forecast the results with a great degree of accuracy. Sinn Féin had developed strong local organised committees, banishing forever the idea that the party was Dublin-oriented only. David Hogan, who had worked with Brennan, wrote a full account of these preparations in his book *The Four Glorious Years*. He outlined the detailed structures for covering the country with publicity and information from Dublin.

> Since O'Connell's day there was no movement so closely knit yet so flexible. It had begun
> in the street or the townland, came up through the parish, the constituency, the county,
> the province, all joining like the rays to a star at the National Headquarters. An order
> from Dublin would be in operation within a week in 2,000 cumann (constituency)
> areas.[21]

At a meeting held on 25 July, Peadar Ó hAnnracháin reported that he had visited the East Cavan area, and had been told that several of the local priests who had assisted in the election of Griffith had been transferred from their parishes, as a punishment, by the bishop of the diocese.

Early in August, the selection of candidates for the forthcoming general election was discussed. Harry Boland was instructed to arrange a conference between the Sinn Féin and Labour representatives with a view to reaching agreement with them on election strategies. Kelly's credibility, because of his socialist leanings, appears to have been vital in brokering the deal with Labour.[22] Initially, Labour had decided to contest four of the seven Dublin seats, but subsequently withdrew, thus leaving Sinn Féin with a clear field. Thomas Johnson, secretary of the Irish Labour Party, explained that Labour was withdrawing lest the nationalist vote be split. Kelly was nominated for St. Patrick's and St. Stephen's Green wards, both of which had urged their claims on him as a candidate. He finally agreed to run for St. Stephen's Green.

---

[21] Hogan, *The Four Glorious Years,* Irish Press Ltd., Dublin 1953, p. 46
[22] Fitzpatrick, D. *Harry Boland's Irish Revolution*, Cork University Press, 2003, pp. 103-109

The date fixed for the opening of Parliament was 15 October, and it was on this day it was thought that the dreaded order for conscription would be issued in Council. It did not materialise, and the threat disappeared with the armistice declared on 11 November. It now seemed that the general election was imminent, as Lloyd George was anxious that a coalition government would be returned in Great Britain. A statement issued by Sinn Féin on 19 October 1918, warned that the party had to be prepared to face a general election at any moment.

> An opportunity has come to Ireland such as never before appeared in the long centuries of her struggle. Ireland's fight has always been for self-determination. Sinn Féin invites the Irish people to make a bold appeal to the Court of Nations ... At the General Election the polling will take place on one day. Every constituency must be prepared to stand upon its own feet. Now is the time to prepare; there is not a day to be lost.[23]

This general statement from Sinn Féin was signed by Fr. M. O'Flanagan, acting president, G. Nesbitt and J. Wyse Power, honorary treasurers, R. Ó Breandáin (Robert Brennan) director of elections, and H. Boland and T. Kelly, honorary secretaries.

On 25 October, a most important Sinn Féin Ard-Fheis (annual convention) took place in the Mansion House, with approximately 1,700 delegates present. The purpose of this convention was to elect a president and other senior party officials and to make preparations for the forthcoming general election. Monsignor Curran (Archbishop Walsh's secretary) was present and has left an account of the day. The delegates included:

> ...priests by the score mostly the younger clergy with the dust of Maynooth still on their boots. There were professional men, town clerks and others representing county councils from every part of Ireland. It was remarkable in its organisation and marked the passing away of the old Mansion House conventions of the heyday of the Land League and later the Parliamentary Party. The Round Room was full, as full as it had ever been in the halcyon days of Parliamentarianism.[24]

At this convention a lot of consideration was given to achieving the optimum results from the Northern constituencies, and the Lord Mayor had informed Sinn Féin that he had been approached by the Northern Catholic bishops to know if anything could be done to avoid three-cornered contests, which would give Unionists a chance to capitalise on a split nationalist vote.

This matter was further discussed at a special meeting chaired by Kelly on 19 November, when it was decided that a letter be written to the press to the effect that a plebiscite of nationalist voters would be taken at an early date to decide whether Republican or Irish Parliamentary Party candidates should contest the constituencies against the representatives of the British garrison. But Dillon, leader of the Parliamentary Party, would not agree. Another issue that had created difficulties was the

---

23 *New Ireland,* 19 October 1918, p. 379
24 *Curran papers,* Ms. 27,728, Vol. 1, Mss Room NLI, p. 226

possibility of more than one candidate contesting a particular seat. De Valera, for instance, while still in jail, was nominated for East Clare, East Mayo, and the Falls division of Belfast. He went on to win East Clare and Mayo, but in the Falls he ran against Joe Devlin, who won the seat.

The bitterness between Sinn Féin and the Irish Parliamentary Party endured until the end. Dillon continued to denounce Sinn Féin policies, and despite many attempts by the latter party to broker deals with him in relation to specific seats, Dillon refused to co-operate. As late as 22 November, Dillon reiterated his intention to contest the election. 'The Irish Party', he said, 'will not be absorbed and will not give a clear field, but will fight Sinn Féin with all the resources at its disposal.'[25] With less than a fortnight left before the election date, the Parliamentary Party could only put forward some fifty-five candidates against Sinn Féin.[26]

The attitude of Dillon had alienated many of his supporters throughout the country, none more so than the Catholic clergy, many of whom had been traditionally the party's staunchest supporters. On 29 November, the Archbishop of Dublin, Dr. Walsh, wrote to the papers to make his own position clear. He had not intended to make any public statement he said, but as in 1904 he had been one of the most prominent supporters of the policies of the party. He stated that he had ceased to give it support of any kind, in view of what he considered to be a disastrous change in their policies. Dr. Fogarty, Bishop of Killaloe, summed up the new Irish view on the political situation by sending his best wishes and a subscription to Sinn Féin, handicapped though it was by the unjust imprisonment of its leaders.

On 11 November, the date on which the war had ended, Sinn Féin Headquarters were attacked by a mob flying Union Jacks, who set fire to the building. Hogan describes the attack vividly, stating that the following morning the building looked as if it had been hit by a hurricane. To add to their problems, Robert Brennan, director of elections, was captured by the military, and imprisoned without charge in Gloucester prison. His post as director of elections was filled by James O'Mara. Many of the contestants were in prison, some of them taken up just before polling day on 14 December. The final rally was held in O'Connell Street, into which gathered representatives from every constituency. Brennan's long-planned election strategy swung into action and delivered the hoped-for results. After the polling booths closed, the boxes were kept in sealed rooms, and were supervised by volunteers, who stayed on duty during the fourteen long days it took to count the votes. As the results started to come in, it was clear that Brennan's meticulous plans had borne fruit. Sinn Féin won 73 seats, and swept away the Irish Parliamentary Party forever. A noticeboard had been fixed on the second-floor window of No. 6 Harcourt Street to record the results, and as the extent of the victory became clear, the delirium of the crowds knew no bounds. 'For those whose names the people knew well, Harry Boland would come to the window, and in the silence that immedi-

25 Quoted in 'The General Election 1918', Thomas P. O'Neill, *Capuchin Annual*, 1968, p. 398
26 Walker, B.M. (ed.) *New History of Ireland*, Royal Irish Academy, 1978 (Ancillary Publication)

ately fell, would call out: 'Countess Markievicz is in', or 'Seán T. O'Kelly has been elect-ed', or 'Alderman Tom Kelly beats them both in Stephen's Green.'[27] De Valera defeat-ed John Dillon in East Mayo by 8,843 votes to 4,451. Monsignor Curran recorded that Archbishop Walsh voted twice: once in Drumcondra for Richard Mulcahy, and once for Lawless, the candidate in Finglas.[28] The Parliamentary Party won 6 seats, and Unionists 26. The nation had turned its back on the Parliamentary Party in what Dillon described afterwards as a landslide. He blamed the inept policies of Lloyd George and felt that the only course the party could now take was to stand aside and give Sinn Féin its head.

It was a tragic end to the once-powerful Parliamentary Party, which had enjoyed such a huge amount of loyalty and respect for so long. History had conspired in its down-fall, as the postponement of Home Rule at the commencement of the war could not have been anticipated. Dillon, but not Redmond, had seen clearly the disastrous effects for the party; both men had lived out their lives in its service, and had inspired most of Ireland to accept the policy and the dream of Home Rule. The thousands who had turned out to greet Asquith on his visit to Ireland in 1912 bore eloquent evidence to the party's success. Redmond badly erred in urging enlistment in 1914, and did not dis-play wisdom in his later despairing years when he clung to the promises of a cunning Westminster government. The end for both men was tragic. Redmond was dead, and for Dillon, now the leader of his party, the future belonged to Sinn Féin.

---

27 Hogan, *The Four Glorious Years,* Irish Press Ltd., p. 50
28 Quoted in Morrissey, *William J. Walsh, Archbishop of Dublin, 1841-1921,* p. 317

Chapter Twelve: The First Dáil

On 19 December 1918, a few days after polling day, the standing committee of Sinn Féin met at No. 6 Harcourt Street. The matters discussed were the state of the party's finances after the election. George Nesbit, acting financial director, stated that having made a grant of £200 to the Irish Republic Prisoners' Committee, a substantial sum of approximately £3,900 (€217,000 at 2005 prices)[1] still remained. The results of the general election were announced on 28 December and Sinn Féin, having gained the day, did not procrastinate. The plight of the political prisoners was an immediate issue, and the national executive organised one hundred meetings of protest to be held throughout the country on 5 January 1919. 'Release the Prisoners' became a national slogan. A special Foreign Affairs committee was appointed to present Ireland's cause at the peace conference which was taking place in Paris, and Messrs. O'Kelly, Barton, Collins and Gavan Duffy were instructed to proceed immediately to London.

At a meeting of the standing committee on 1 January 1919 with Kelly in the chair, it was decided that certain items would be referred to the new Irish parliament, to be called An Dáil, which was being summoned to meet. Firstly, the relationship between the Sinn Féin organisation and the new Dáil had to be clarified. Then a declaration of independence was to be drawn up, and lastly a message to the free nations of the world was to be composed. It was felt that it was essential to retain intact the political organisation and its newly acquired election skills. It was also decided that a new premises for the organisation should be purchased, and Kelly was one of three members entrusted with the task of finding a suitable building. A decision was then taken that the financial director should instruct the constituency directors of finance that the anti-conscription fund be handed over to the Dáil and that this directive be issued immediately.

The attitude of the British to the results of the general election in Ireland was one of complete bewilderment. The authorities were at an immediate loss as to what should be done, but it was not long before they decided on intensified repression. But that did not interfere with the plans of Sinn Féin, which had called a conference of the newly elected TDs in the Oak Room of the Mansion House on 7 January to plan the first public meeting of the new assembly, Dáil Éireann.

At this preliminary event, over which Count Plunkett presided, all elected Sinn Féin members who were not in prison, attended. Count Plunkett himself had just been released after seven months' imprisonment in England, and it was he who signed the

---

[1] See footnote 4, Chapter 1, for calculation methodology

Christmas Card to Tom Kelly from Micheál Ó Foghludha, 5 Cabra Road, Dublin. This card was printed and issued by Sinn Féin and the cover includes a list of prisons where Irish nationalists were held. [1918]. Private Collection.

letter of invitation to every representative elected, in whatever interest, to attend on 21 January for the inaugural meeting of the Dáil. There are 29 names, including Kelly, on the attendance list, all members of the Sinn Féin Party. De Valera and Griffith were conspicuous by their absence through imprisonment.

A copy of the Orders of the Day survives.[2] Count Plunkett called the assembly to order. The pledge was then signed by all those in attendance, declaring that each committed himself to work for the establishment of an independent Irish republic; that nothing less than complete separation from England was acceptable, and finally that each newly elected representative would abstain from attending the British Parliament. The chairman, secretary and staff were then appointed. A series of motions was proposed, the first of which was by Boland, Collins and Eamonn Duggan, concerning the imprisonment without charge of the 37 Dáil members being held in British jails and thus debarred from exercising their duties as elected representatives of the Irish people. Thirty had been imprisoned for eight months, and four others were sentenced to be detained in Ireland by courts martial. The remaining three were exiled for their activities in the 'Cause of Irish Freedom'. A motion was proposed on behalf of the Irish people demanding their release. A resolution was then adopted, with Alderman Kelly dis-

---

2 Private collection

Postcard from Seán T. O'Kelly, Paris, to Alderman Tom Kelly. Seán T. represented the First Dáil at the Peace Conference in Paris in 1919, an appointment which was consistently defended by Tom Kelly. Here O'Kelly express-es his appreciation of this support. 3 March [1919]. Private Collection.

senting: 'That we, the Republican Members of the Irish Constituencies in accordance with the National Will are empowered to call together the Dáil Éireann and proceed to act accordingly'. The motives for Kelly's objection are not clear.

The task of drawing up the Declaration of Independence and the Message to the Free Nations of the World was delegated to 15 members who were also members of the executive committee of Sinn Féin, who were to prepare and submit draft statements regarding same. This drafting committee included MacNeill, O'Mara, Collins, Brugha and Kelly. It was decided that a further private meeting be called for 14 January at which the question of representation at the peace conference would be raised. Funding was also discussed, and it was agreed that a statement be issued to the press giving the names of the members present, and their resolution regarding the imprisonment of elected representatives. At this second meeting, it was decided that 21 January at 3.30 p.m. would see the first national assembly to convene on Irish soil since the disbandment of Grattan's parliament under the Act of Union of 1800.

On 21 January 1919, the Sinn Féin members of the Dáil trooped into the crowded Round Room of the Mansion House. Admission was by ticket only, and the Round Room was full to capacity, leaving many outside to share in the excitement and cheers of the Dawson Street crowds. All seats were occupied, save those in the front row, which had been left empty in deference to the elected prisoners who could not be there. The non-Republican elected deputies did not attend. Count Plunkett presided and pro-

Members of the First Dáil, photographed in the Mansion House garden on 21 January 1919.
Front row (left to right): Joseph O'Doherty; Seán Hayes; John Joseph O'Kelly; Count George Noble Plunkett; Cathal
Brugha; Seán T. O'Kelly; Pádraic Ó Máille; James J. Walsh; Tom Kelly
Centre row (left to right): Joseph Sweeney; Kevin O'Higgins; Domhnall Ó Buachalla; Eamonn Duggan; Piaras
Béaslaí; Dr. James Ryan; Dr. John Crowley; Peter Ward; Patrick J. Moloney; Roger Sweetman
Back row (left to right): Robert Barton; Richard Mulcahy; Conor Collins; Philip Shanahan; Seamus A. Burke
Photograph by Layfayette; courtesy National Museum of Ireland.

posed that Cathal Brugha be elected speaker. A prayer in Irish was read by Fr. O'Flanagan, and then the business of the day commenced. The order paper was completed. The speaker, now to be called the Ceann Comhairle (Cathal Brugha) and clerks of the day were appointed. The roll was called, and in so many cases the reply had to be 'faoi ghlas ag Gallaibh', (imprisoned by foreigners) as each imprisoned absentee's name was left unanswered. A ripple of laughter ran through the assembly when the name of Edward Carson was called, but needless to remark he did not confirm his presence. The Constitution, the Declaration of Independence and the Message to the Free Nations of the World were all approved. Cathal Brugha delivered the Declaration of Independence in Irish, and it was repeated in English by Eamonn Duggan, and then in French by George Gavan Duffy. The Message to the Free Nations of the World was read by J.J. O'Kelly (Sceilg) in Irish, Count Plunkett in French, and Robert Barton in English. This proclaimed to the world that the nation of Ireland had achieved her national independence, and called upon every free country to support Ireland's national status and her right to its vindication at the peace conference which had convened in Paris under the presidency of Woodrow Wilson three days previously. Then followed the reading of the democratic programme.

Piaras Béaslaí read the Democratic Programme in soft Kerry Irish and Alderman Tom Kelly read it in English in the voice of a Dublin worker. It laid down the foundations on which the new Ireland would be built in accordance with the principles of Liberty, Equality and Justice for all … The children would be the Republic's special care and no child would suffer hunger or cold, and to all there would be open means to education and training as citizens of a free and Gaelic Ireland.[3]

Included were provisions for the welfare of the poor and the aged, and for the utilisation of the country's resources for the benefit of all, and promises that the conditions in which the working classes lived and worked would be changed through social legislation. The preparation of the democratic programme is generally attributed to Seán T. O'Kelly, representing Sinn Féin views, and to Tom Johnson of the Labour Party, but it is not hard to discern the hand of Kelly also in those promises. Brian Farrell has described the proceedings of this meeting as 'the constitutional cornerstone of the new Irish state; the origin of a cabinet system of government that has persisted to the present day'.[4]

On the same significant day for the whole of Ireland, while the achievement of her own parliament was being celebrated, there occurred an event in far away Tipperary which presaged tragedy. At Soloheadbeg, nine armed men from the Third Tipperary Brigade of the Volunteers led by Dan Breen and Seán Treacy, attacked two policemen in charge of a load of gelignite and shot them dead.

Thus began the sequence of violent events remembered today as the War of Independence or, more colloquially, the Troubles. The Irish Volunteers, now called the Irish Republican Army (the IRA), and the crown forces engaged in escalating confrontation. Raids, ambushes, and mutual atrocities took place, especially after the arrival of the ill-disciplined auxiliary police (the Auxiliaries and the Black and Tans). There were arrests and deportation to Britain of many nationalists, hunger-strike protests by prisoners, and retaliatory destruction of property in towns and villages. De Valera escaped from Lincoln jail, resumed his presidency of Sinn Féin and the Dáil, and went to America to promote the nationalist cause. Terence MacSwiney, Lord Mayor of Cork, died on hunger strike. The Truce (July 1921), the Treaty (December 1921) and the tragic Civil War (1922-1923) followed. Griffith and Collins died and the seemingly precarious Irish Free State came into being, soon to establish itself as a politically, if not financially, self-confident entity.

Throughout this turbulent period, the Dáil continued to assert its authority as parliament, appointing government ministers, sanctioning the issue of a loan and setting up courts with civil and criminal jurisdiction which proved surprisingly successful for tribunals functioning in opposition to the established legal system. While nationalist commentators then and later would exaggerate the degree to which the Dáil controlled the country, there was no doubting that it severely undermined the authority of the British

---

[3] Farrell, Brian. *The Four Glorious Years,* David Hogan, p. 61
[4] *The Founding of Dáil Éireann,* Brian Farrell, Dublin 1971, p. 51

administration, attracted massive popular support outside the entrenched unionist areas in Ulster and increasingly won sympathy abroad – not least in the United States, which was a major factor in persuading Lloyd George to seek a settlement.

Tom Kelly could take little part in this evolving situation once he was himself arrested in December 1919 and deported to England, where he was interned without charge in Wormwood Scrubs prison. However, prior to that he had been an active member of the Dáil. As early as 22 January 1919 he had introduced the vote permitting the Minister for Finance (Collins) to raise £2,000 for necessary expenses. On 10 April he addressed the assembly on the issue of political prisoners:

> At this very moment in British jails there are about forty of our countrymen. They have for over twelve weeks been in solitary confinement, and they are not allowed the necessities for human cleanliness. These men have had to lie on their cell floors and their food has to be taken off the floor of the cell. This is the class of treatment meted out by the power that boasts of her Christianity and civilisation, and still, with the resources that that power can command, she is unable to conquer these Irishmen.[5]

He again seems to indicate that he held certain doubts, when he says that:

> … some of us have our faults, but it is our right to put our individual point of view and live up to the promises of the people who gave us their votes … We must regard these men as brothers in suffering, and since I do not like that suffering should be inflicted on myself, I do not like to see it inflicted on my fellow countrymen. We stated on the opening day that we wished this country ruled by the principles of justice and equality for all, and in doing so I must mention that I am one who believes that Christ's Sermon on the Mount was the greatest deliverance ever made. Liberty, equality, and justice for all – that is the motto that was declared here at the first opening day of the Dáil. It is, I believe, the spirit that eventually will crown the President's deliberations and his Executive with complete success.[6]

It is interesting that he made a point of saying that it must not be assumed that he was 'at the back' of the Government, while nonetheless, wishing it well.

The next day, 11 April, Kelly, still pursuing his own agenda, asked for a statement from de Valera regarding the social policy of the Ministry. He drew attention to the fact that in the democratic programme outlined at the first meeting of the Dáil it was stated that 'it would be the first duty of the Government of the Republic to make provision for the physical, mental and spiritual well-being of the children, to abolish the present poor law system, and to take such measures as would safeguard the health of the people'. Kelly felt it would be wrong to adjourn without making some reference to their duty in connection with the welfare of the people. 'Let them take the city of Dublin and see how its condition has been impoverished and demoralised from the time that the rapacity of British Imperialism became the creed immediately after what was known in history as

---

5 *Proceedings of Dáil Éireann 1919-21-22* (henceforth *DE*), January 1919, pp. 26-27, Stationery Office, Dublin 1994
6 Ibid. 10 April 1919, pp. 64- 65

Nelson's victories.' He believed that in asking de Valera to outline the work of the Dáil in connection with the democratic programme he was only asking him to do what would be a pleasing duty.

De Valera, replying, said that it was quite clear that the democratic programme, as adopted by the Dáil, contemplated a situation somewhat different from that in which they actually found themselves. They had the occupation of the foreigner in their country, and while that state of affairs existed, they could not put fully into force their desires and their wishes for their social programme. He offered to consult organised Labour to examine more closely the conditions under which the people lived, but he had never made any promise to Labour, because, while the enemy was within their gates, the immediate question was to get possession of their country.[7]

On 9 May, a further public session of the Dáil was held, specifically to greet a commission from America, to whom the President of the Executive extended a warm welcome. A private session was convened on 17 June, at which it emerged that de Valera had left the country without reference to the members of the Dáil. Griffith became deputy president in his absence. Seán MacEntee asked for an explanation of the absence of the president. He claimed that no member of the Dáil had been consulted, and that it was neither right nor fair to them that they were unable to say whether the president had gone away, and where he was. It subsequently transpired that de Valera had gone to America. Kelly's contribution at this session was that he felt that it was not proper that the monies of the Dáil should be in the hands of a bank which flew the Union Jack. This view was generally supported. It was explained that £2,000 had been lodged with the Munster and Leinster Bank for convenience, and that it would be withdrawn without delay. With reference to the salary paid to Gavan Duffy, it was stated that it was never sanctioned by the Dáil, and was in excess of that paid to members of the ministry. Kelly said that it was not a sound principle that members of the Dáil should be appointed to salaried positions without the approval of the Dáil.[8]

At the session on 19 August, which was held in private, Griffith reported on satisfactory progress achieved on various issues. The success of President de Valera's visit to America was noted. This session resumed on the following day, when Kelly was appointed substitute Minister for Labour, to replace Countess Markievicz who had been arrested and imprisoned. Kelly immediately drew attention to the necessity of establishing and strengthening the conciliation boards, and pointed out that their success depended to a great extent on the attitude of Labour to the Dáil. After some discussion, it was agreed that to enable the conciliation boards to deal effectively with local Labour disputes; it was the duty of each deputy to furnish to the Ministry of Labour immediate information regarding the outbreak of local disputes and strikes as they occurred.[9]

---

7 *DE 1919-21*-22, April 1919, pp. 78, Stationery Office, Dublin 1994
8 Ibid. 17 June 1919, pp. 115-116
9 Ibid. 19 August 1919, pp. 142-143

On 20 August, the executive discussed the matter of setting up an agricultural land bank, a suggestion received with approval. Kelly thought well of the scheme, but reminded the assembly of the existence of the Sinn Féin Bank. He also asked certain pertinent questions regarding the proposed method of doing business, and whether the contingency of the seizure of money by the English government had been provided for.[10] Funds were needed to proclaim Ireland's case to the world, to finance the setting up of a civil service, together with a court system, and to develop Irish national assets such as fisheries, forestry and other industries.

The Dáil then discussed the matter of an oath of allegiance, the Secretary for Defence (Brugha) proposing that all deputies, Irish Volunteers, officers and clerks to the Dáil should be required to swear allegiance to the Irish Republic and to the Dáil. Kelly had serious reservations about its necessity. He believed that any man who would not keep his word would not keep his oath. It had been said that the one object of the suggested oath was to make the Irish Volunteers subject to the Dáil. In his opinion the two bodies should remain separate. He reminded them of the fate of the Volunteers in 1782. A time might come when a military demonstration might be necessary. It was a species of coercion to force this issue. Griffith and others, however, spoke in favour of the oath and it was decided that it should be required.

The session of the Dáil held on 27 October was in private, and in accordance with the decision previously taken, the deputies and officials advanced to the speaker's table and signed the oath. The acting president then pointed out that, since its last meeting, the Dáil had been proclaimed a dangerous association by the enemy. Certain members had been asked not to attend that session, because of the possibility of being arrested. He referred to the activity of the British government which, since 13 September, had been trying to suppress Sinn Féin, the Irish Volunteers, the Gaelic League, Cumann na mBan and the Sinn Féin clubs. They had also tried to suppress the nationalist press. Griffith regarded all the British actions as tremendous publicity value to the campaign being conducted by de Valera in America.

However, all during the autumn of 1919, the British authorities were deploying additional troops in attempts to suppress nationalist activities, such as meetings and gatherings of all kinds, including economic as well as political and sporting activities. All nationalist papers were affected, and publicity for the cause was achieved only through the publication of a bulletin, a mimeographed type of propaganda sheet, which was circulated every few days. The raids and the imprisonment of prominent nationalists continued.

In early December 1919, Kelly was arrested in the middle of the night and transported to England, where he was imprisoned in Wormwood Scrubs. Kelly was one of many. Sinn Féin Headquarters had been raided by the military and many members of the

---

[10] *DE 1919-21-22*, 20 August 1919, p. 147

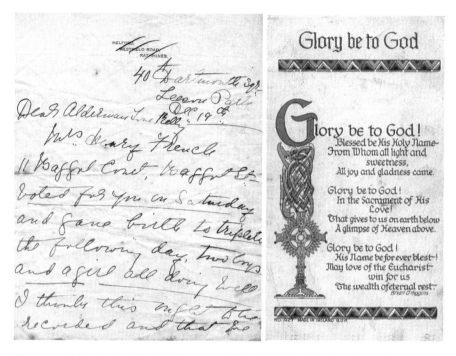

Christmas card (not dated) to Tom Kelly 'from your old friend Mrs. Pearse' (mother of executed 1916 leaders, Patrick and Willie). The cover features a Celtic design with a poem by Brian O'Higgins.

organisation had been similarly treated. At this time Kelly was in his early fifties, and the long-term effects of this experience was to be the destruction of his health. Initially, he was full of resolve, and a letter to his wife written from prison and dated 15 December 1919 expresses his belief that things would come right again, even though it was hard to be away from home at Christmas. He told her that he was not able to write anything regarding the treatment he was receiving but, to ease her mind, he informed her that the prison officials he had encountered were courteous and obliging. He told her not to worry overmuch, and wrote out a list of instructions regarding all the work which was being left undone because of his absence. Characteristically, he was concerned about the plight of Dublin's poor and mentioned certain individuals. He asked his wife to see Mr. Cosgrave and others about these unfortunate people. He instructed her not to send any food, as none would be allowed into the prison. He asked for clothing and some of the tobacco he normally smoked, and told her that one letter per fortnight was all that was permitted.[11]

The British repression continued. On 17 December 1919, the Lord Mayor, Larry O'Neill, felt compelled to write to the newspapers to explain why the Aonach, sched-

---

[11] Private collection

uled as usual to take place in the Mansion House coming up to Christmas, had to be closed down.

> A few days ago Aonach na Nodlag, which has been held every year since 1907 for the sale and exhibition of Irish Industries and Irish works of Art, was prevented from being held by the Authorities at the last moment, at the point of the bayonet, 150 police and over 500 soldiers fully equipped taking part in the operation … Therefore in view of what has taken place, and what may happen at any moment, I feel compelled to close it down, as I do not desire to have any conflict between the citizens and the soldiers and the police which might end in bloodshed.[12]

Kelly's family received another letter from him early in the new year, saying that he and his three comrades had got through Christmas well enough. He requested them to send word to all his old '41' friends (York Street Club) that he wished them a happy new year. He complained that he had missed Mass on New Year's Day through an error. After that date Kelly's health began to deteriorate badly. He became mentally unstable and from his file which survives in the Public Record Office at Kew, the progress of his illness can be followed from medical records and other documents.[13] A note on the file cover indicates that Lord Parmour (Charles Alfred Cripps) called attention to the reported ill-health of the prisoner on 30 December, in a letter to the Home Secretary. He wrote:

> A doctor who is to be trusted, writes about the health of Alderman Kelly, who is said to be mad in Wormwood Scrubs prison. I know nothing of the conditions, but think it best to let you know, seeing that the health is said to be precarious and quite unfit for prison.[14]

On 7 January, W.R.K. Watson, the medical officer, examined Kelly, and noted that he was a man of rather poor physique, but showed no sign of serious disease. He was offered a special diet, but refused to have anything different from the others. Mentally, he was beginning to fret over his imprisonment, being worried about 'the indefiniteness of it'. Watson wrote that Kelly was not as well as he had been, and that if the deterioration continued, the question of his fitness for further imprisonment would have to be considered.

A medical report on Kelly's condition was received at the Home Office on 8 January 1920. A memo (handwritten, and initialled HBS), was attached to the file, and instructed that a copy of the medical officer's report be sent to the Irish government, because, should the prisoner's condition deteriorate to such a degree as to endanger his reason, the Secretary of State might feel it impossible to refuse his release. The writer presumed that, as the question might present itself in a very urgent form, the Lord Lieutenant should be willing to leave the decision in his (the writer's) hands, but if His Excellency felt so disposed, the prisoner should be at once moved back to Ireland. The following was written to the Secretary of State on 10 January 1920:

---

12 NLI Mss. Room 10, 723
13 *Public Record Office London* HO, 144/1615/395988. File embargoed until 2020.
13 Ibid.

I enclose copy of correspondence about Alderman Kelly, one of the Irish internees. As this man's condition might become serious at any moment, I should be glad to have your instructions on two points: If the Chief Secretary asks you to decide on the question of release, shall we take the responsibility and release if he is certified unfit? And secondly, if the Chief Secretary or the Irish Government insists on his being detained at all risks, will you accept this at all risks? I do not know how dangerous he is, but if we keep him, will he become insane? It would, I think, do more harm than could possibly come of his release.[15]

This note was initialled, but illegibly. A note in another hand follows:

His illness is not due to hunger striking. He should be carefully watched and if the MO so advises should be released. (Initialled 12 January.)

A letter written from the Irish government (meaning the British administration), dated 15 January reads:

I presume Kelly's state of health is being carefully watched as directed by the Secretary of State.

A further note was recorded on 19 January. This note is initialled, but the initials are illegible, as is the co-initial:

I am afraid his probable election as Lord Mayor is not likely to improve his health in prison. He is said to be first favourite but has he yet been elected? Secretary of State to see, and a copy to be sent to the Irish Office.

On 16 January, a report was drawn up headed 'Irish Internee 3658 Thomas Kelly' which stated:

The general deterioration of the above-named internee's health, to which I referred in my report of 7th inst. still continues. I have consequently found it necessary today to admit him to Hospital. It is to be hoped that with nursing, rest and suitable diet, his condition will improve, but I am not over-sanguine. I propose to report further in a few days.
Signed: WRK Watson, Medical Officer.

This report was forwarded to the Home Office for the information of the Secretary of State, on 17 January 1920.

Kelly's unanimous election as Lord Mayor occurred on 30 January 1920. The event was marked by the running up of the Republican flag on the City Hall amidst great cheering from the crowd outside. Laurence O'Neill, the retiring Lord Mayor, presided at the Council meeting. He described the arrest of Kelly by the soldiers of the King, who broke his windows, hammered on his hall door with trench tools, and openly and gross-

---

15 *Public Record Office London* HO, 144/1615/395988
   All quotations following, which relate to Kelly's condition, are from the same source.

'His Majesty's Pleasure'. *The British Prime Minister, David Lloyd George, has invited all Sinn Féin MPs to attend the formal opening of the Westminster Parliament by King George V. As Tom Kelly is a political prisoner in Wormwood Scrubs it is not possible for him to attend. Cartoon from* Freeman's Journal, *5 February 1920.*

ly insulted his family and himself at the whim of some 'under-strapper who pulled the wires in Dublin Castle'. O'Neill referred to Kelly's work on the anti-conscription committee and in the Corporation for over twenty years, and said that on such a man the British government had placed their claws. Alderman Cosgrave then read a message just received from Wormwood Scrubs which stated that Kelly's health had improved, and that he had been moved to the hospital for two days to receive special treatment.[16]

At this meeting, it was decided not to forward any names to the Lord Lieutenant for the appointment of High Sheriff, as the Council declined to recognise the Lord Lieutenant's right of appointment. A motion to remove the sword and mace from the chair and place them in the muniments room as they were 'emblems of feudal authority, and their exhibition at the meetings of the Corporation was a perpetual symbol of servitude', was deemed out of order.[17]

Meanwhile, as his condition continued to worsen, a letter dated 4 February 1920 addressed to Thomas Kelly MP arrived at his address in Dublin, containing an invitation headed 10 Downing Street, Whitehall, from Lloyd George, stating:

16 *Irish Independent*, 31 January 1920
17 *Morning Post*, 31 January 1920

Sir, On Tuesday February 10 1920 His Majesty will open Parliament in person. An
address will be moved and seconded in answer to the Gracious Speech from the Throne.
I hope you may find it convenient to be in your place, Yours faithfully, D. Lloyd George.

The newspapers had great fun with this. The *Freeman's Journal* published a cartoon
showing Kelly in a prison cell, and regretting that a previous engagement with His
Majesty would prevent him from accepting the Prime Minister's kind invitation. The
Evening Telegraph reproduced the envelope and commented: 'Similar invitations have
been sent to other Irish representatives who are held in jails in similar circumstances. Is
the incident an ill-conceived and unmannerly practical joke, or is to be deemed merely an outstanding example of the crass ignorance – not to say stupidity – of those who
assume the right to rule in Ireland. The English language knows no words to suit the
situation.[18]

On 9 February, despite the two days in hospital for special treatment, Watson reported
Kelly's health showed definite signs of deterioration. 'The strain of imprisonment and
uncertainty as to his fate are more than his mind can stand with safety. He complains
of constant nightmares, of visions of executions and similar horrors ... I therefore feel
bound to record my opinion that further imprisonment and suspense are not without
danger to his bodily and mental health'.[19]

King George V, in his speech at the opening of Parliament on 10 February, stated that
the condition of Ireland was causing him grave concern and promised that a bill would
be laid before Parliament to give effect to proposals for the better government of that
country. He specifically mentioned the lack of educational facilities for children. He also
announced that the partition bill promised by Lloyd George would be introduced immediately. At the parliamentary session on 12 February 1920, Lieutenant Commander
Kenworthy asked the Chief Secretary if he would state on what grounds the Hon.
Member for St. Stephen's Green had been imprisoned and if he was aware that the Hon.
Member had been unanimously elected Lord Mayor of Dublin. He asked if it was proposed to bring him to trial and if so, when. A reply was given stating that Kelly had been
arrested under a rule made in pursuance of the Defence of the Realm regulations, as a
person having acted or being about to act in a manner prejudicial to the public safety.
As to whether he would be brought to trial, the order was for deportation.[20]

On 12 February, 10,000 sympathisers gathered in the Albert Hall in London to protest
against the imprisonment of the Lord Mayor of Dublin and other Irish prisoners. No
serious interference by the police was reported. This meeting, held under the auspices
of the Irish Self-Determination League of Great Britain, was addressed by Arthur
Griffith and Eoin MacNeill. The president of the league, P.J. Kelly, moved resolutions
demanding the recognition of the Irish Republic, and the immediate release of

---

[18] *Evening Telegraph,* 4 February 1920
[19] PRO, London, 144/1615/395988
[20] *Evening Telegraph,* 12 February 1920

Alderman Tom Kelly, Lord Mayor of Dublin, who was seized many weeks before by the British army of occupation in Ireland, deported and held in Wormwood Scrubs prison in London. He also demanded the release of 64 other Irishmen, who, in similar circumstances, had been deported and imprisoned in recent weeks. This evoked an outburst of cheering, and a message of greetings to the Irish prisoners in Wormwood Scrubs was enthusiastically endorsed. In his speech, Griffith said that Ireland had voted by a majority of five to one for an Irish Republic and that the British army was using every instrument of tyranny and sabotage against the declared will of the Irish people.

On 13 February, the *Manchester Guardian* published a leading article on Kelly's imprisonment. It stated that the Chief Secretary for Ireland was asked on the previous day how the Lord Mayor had come to be shut up in an English gaol. The reply was that he was a

> person suspected of acting, or being about to act, in a manner prejudicial to public safety … The British Government chose to seize, deport, and intern Alderman Kelly of Dublin, while he was still only an alderman, under this doubtful sanction. Dublin, in that inconvenient way she has, has made him Lord Mayor. In consequence, his arbitrary imprisonment becomes a matter of public notice, and Sinn Féin secures a first-rate advertisement … Any adequate intelligence work in Ireland would have warned the Government that Alderman Kelly, if arrested under the discredited Defence of the Realm Act, would become a world-figure that would further stultify British rule in Ireland. And such he has become. If there be evidence against him that British law can substantiate, the law should be invoked. But to arrest him under rules tolerable only in a state of war is to play surely, but not we hope deliberately, into the hands of the forces of disorder in Ireland and to make them a gratuitous offering of a *cause célèbre*.[21]

Kelly was released from Wormwood Scrubs on Monday 16 February at approximately 10 p.m., on health grounds. A statement issued by the authorities read:

> Alderman Thomas Kelly, Lord Mayor of Dublin who has been interned in Wormwood Scrubs has been conditionally released by the Government owing to the state of his health. The order of internment has not been revoked: its enforcement has been merely suspended. He has been informed that if he attempts to return to Ireland he will be immediately re-arrested. He has been in failing health for some time past and his release was an act of imperative necessity if his health is to recover from the effects of his imprisonment.[22]

Kelly was suffering from a severe mental breakdown – a not unexpected result of prison treatment upon a man of his age and constitution. In a recent letter to his sister, he had written that he did not know how or when he would be out. He said that he was in fairly good health but took no interest in anything and had no energy. He also commented that the prison was filling up rapidly and was much livelier. He also said that if he had been asked, he would not have accepted the position of Lord Mayor![23]

---

21 *Manchester Guardian*, 13 February 1920
22 *Daily News*, 18 February 1920
23 Private collection

On 19 February, the Irish government (meaning the British government in Ireland) asked if this man had signed the declaration of acceptance of the Lord Mayoralty of Dublin. This resulted in a request from J. J. Taylor to Mr. Brickland:

> Will you kindly enquire from the Governor of Wormwood Scrubs prison, and let me know whether Alderman T. Kelly has signed the declaration of acceptance of the Lord Mayor.

On 21 February Mr. Wall said that the Government was sure that Kelly never signed any formal acceptance while he was in Wormwood Scrubs, but that he may have intimated his acceptance or readiness to accept in a letter.[24]

The papers commented on his release and stated that it had taken place only just in time to prevent another tragedy of the Thomas Ashe type being laid at the doors of the Government.

> Among Dublin citizens of all classes, a feeling of deep sympathy will be extended to their Chief Magistrate, whose speedy recovery and resumption of his civic duties will be welcomed by people of all shades of politics. The patient is receiving all possible care, medical and otherwise, and his friends are hopeful that a few weeks' rest in congenial surroundings will be the means of putting him on the road to recovery. It is felt that a considerable amount of time will elapse before he can take up the duties of Lord Mayor.[25]

On his release, Alderman Kelly was met by Arthur Griffith, Desmond Fitzgerald, William Sears MP and J.H. MacDonnell, his solicitor. He was put into the care of Dr Mark Ryan, a well-known Irish nationalist sympathiser, and taken to a nursing home, where he remained for some time. His wife and eldest son, Isaac, immediately travelled to London to be with him. On seeing her husband, Mrs Kelly found him suffering from great physical and mental strain, though they were able to converse a little on family matters. Dr Ryan said he was in a delicate condition, and would require constant medical attention and very careful nursing as he was in a state of nervous and general debility and suffering from insomnia. He was much thinner in appearance. His wife was very indignant that a statement had been put out which seemed to imply that he had agreed to any condition as the price of his release. He had refused to give any undertaking whatsoever. It was recalled that following his arrest and imprisonment after the Rising in 1916, he had suffered from a nervous breakdown, similar in all respects to the present one, and he did not recover his health afterwards for fully two months.[26]

The allegation that the Lord Mayor was released conditionally was denied by J. H. MacDonnell, Kelly's solicitor and also by Arthur Griffith and others in a position to know.

---

24 PRO, London, 144/1615/395988
25 *Evening Telegraph,* 17 February 1920
26 Ibid. 18 February 1920

Neither the Lord Mayor nor anybody acting for him gave any undertaking whatsoever as a condition precedent to the Alderman's release. His friends make no disguise of their conviction that the British Government has really released their victim because they wished to avoid having to hold another inquest.[27]

The editorial in the *Evening Telegraph* on 17 February paid a very warm tribute to Kelly on all levels. It referred to his love and knowledge of Dublin, and singled out for special mention the contribution he made to the art section of the Aonach exhibition held in 1916. It claimed that the treatment meted out to him was illegal, even according to English law, and there was no legal redress for arrest and deportation. The authorities could arrest any man, woman or child and confine them in prison without charge, and without any rights or privileges.

On 21 February, there was a report to the effect that Kelly had shown some improvement, and had slept naturally for four or five hours. By 5 March, he had been removed from the nursing home to the south coast of England. Dr Ryan felt that this change to a more bracing atmosphere might help with his recovery. His wife accompanied him, and they were staying where he had the advantage of meeting some Irish friends. From Ireland, his colleagues in the Dáil were keeping him in mind and had deputed Séamus de Staic to remain in close contact with him, and keep them informed. De Staic, giving an address in Boscombe, near Bournemouth, wrote to Oifig an Rúnaidhe (Secretary's Office) at the Dáil on 4 March that Mr. and Mrs Kelly were staying at the Boscombe Spa Hotel. De Staic said he was taking him for long walks every morning, and that physically he was improved. His opinion was that if the ban were lifted and Kelly could return home to Dublin and be amongst his friends, he would soon recover.[28] He wrote again to the Dáil on 5 March to the effect that Mr. Dixon of Dublin (presumably Kelly's old friend Henry Dixon) was travelling over to visit him. De Staic reiterated his opinion that Kelly would not recover until he could return to Dublin. It is now known, from a separate source, that Kelly subsequently left Boscombe, and went to stay near the convent of the Sisters of St Joseph of Peace, at Grimsby, in the north of England, where his sister was a member of the congregation and had offered to look after him. He did not actually stay in the convent, but in a house nearby, where, according to Sister Evangelista (a member of the congregation) 'the nuns would give him their best attention and care. He suffers terribly from imaginations … I suppose the man was losing his mind in that awful prison'. [29] At this time, Kelly was still poorly and, according to newspaper reports on 29 March, Dr Ryan felt that there was no improvement, that his health left much to be desired, and it had been decided to call in a specialist. So far as is known, Kelly remained with the nuns at Grimsby until he was given permission to return to Dublin.

---

27 *Evening Telegraph,* 17 February 1920
28 NAI DE. 2/86
29 Letter from Sister M. Evangelista, dated 24 February 1920, Archives of Sisters of St Joseph of Peace, Grimsby

On 23 April, the order of internment was revoked by the Government. J.H. MacDonnell, Kelly's solicitor, was informed of this decision and was, in turn, requested to inform Kelly. Sir Basil Thomson, British Director of Intelligence, was requested to stop the surveillance on Kelly, if he had not already done so.

Kelly finally arrived home on the morning of 28 April 1920. He was accompanied on the journey by Councillor Joseph Clarke, an old friend and colleague from No. 6 Harcourt Street, who had also been released. His wife and a number of friends met him at Westland Row station and brought him home. The newspapers reported that he was still in very poor health and would remain under medical care for the time being. Sometime in the late 1960s, the present writer spoke to Joe Clarke, who described that journey. It seems that Kelly was sleeping in the corner of a crowded railway carriage on the way to Holyhead, when the train stopped without warning in the middle of the countryside. Kelly immediately got up and, before anyone could stop him, managed to open the door of the carriage, jumped out and ran away across the tracks. He was closely followed by one of his companions who succeeded in catching him and getting him back on the train before it started moving again. Joe Clarke identified this man as Michael Collins. Kelly and Collins were always on good terms with each other, as is evidenced from surviving correspondence regarding the provision of financial help to prisoners, during 1918 and 1919.[30]

The Corporation met on 30 April 1920, and Larry O'Neill, still acting Lord Mayor, warmly welcomed the news that Kelly had returned to Dublin. He said:

> I am sure you will all join with me in extending a welcome to Alderman Tom Kelly on his returning once more amongst us. I am also sure that you join with me in expressing the hope that he shall soon be restored to his usual health, and his usual vigour, and take his place once more amongst us, and above all take his place in the position to which you have elected him, that of Lord Mayor of this city.[31]

---

[30] NLI 10723 Manuscript Room
[31] *Evening Telegraph*, 30 April 1920

Chapter Thirteen: The Tragic Year of 1920

The absence of Tom Kelly had consequences within the Corporation. Apart from being chairman of the Housing Committee, where his absence was most keenly felt, he had been a member of the School Meals & Scholarships Committee, the Electricity Supply Committee, the Estates and Finance Committee, and the Improvements Committee. He also represented the Corporation on the board of the Royal Hospital for Incurables in Donnybrook, as he had done for many years.

On 2 January 1920, the Local Government Board had convened an inquiry concerning the major housing scheme for Marino, the first under the new Housing Act which became law in August 1919. Under this legislation, each local authority was required to submit to the Local Government Board a survey of the housing needs of their districts within three months of the passing of the Act, specifying the number and nature of the houses to be erected, the approximate quantity of land to be acquired, and the average number of houses proposed per acre, together with an estimate of the time required to carry out the developments. The Lord Mayor, Laurence O'Neill, was reluctant to proceed with the Marino inquiry without Kelly. He had sent a telegram to the Chief Secretary asking for Kelly's release in view of his importance as a witness and an advisor. The Chief Secretary regretted that the request could not be granted. Then the Lord Mayor, after consultation with the Corporation, decided to go ahead with the inquiry. The inspector, P.C. Cowan, stated that no one could regret more sincerely Alderman Kelly's absence than he did, as very many important issues needed to be worked out, in particular the great and dominating difficulty of finance, and the nature of the houses to be built. He said that Kelly was one of the pioneers who projected schemes like these in Dublin, and that his heart and soul had been centred in this particular scheme. The inspector added that he would have been a principal witness here today if he were free. The scheme was described as ideal, and had been prepared with up-to-date planning principles: apart from standard accommodation, each house was to be provided with a scullery, larder, bath and WC. Mr. W.J. Larkin, president of the Dublin Tenants' Association, was also present at the inquiry, and expressed regret at the absence of Kelly, describing him as 'an honourable and upright citizen, and as clear a gentleman as there was in public life'.[1] In spite of many reservations, the inquiry went ahead on the grounds that the City Architect and his staff had done much preparation and, furthermore, it was generally felt that Kelly would have been the last to wish the work to be postponed by even a day.[2]

---

[1] *Evening Telegraph,* 2 January 1920
[2] *Dublin Corporation Reports,* 1921, Vol. 11, pp. 386-7, DCA

At the meeting of the Housing Committee held on 13 January, the Lord Mayor deplored that a man of Tom Kelly's worth should be deprived of his liberty without charge or trial. The climax was reached, he added, when application was made to the authorities to allow the alderman to attend the Local Government Board of Inquiry into the Marino housing scheme, in connection with which his valuable aid was so badly required. He had taken a great interest in the scheme, but was denied the pleasure of attending the inquiry and the Corporation were denied the pleasure of his assistance. The Lord Mayor moved a resolution, which was carried unanimously, recording their confidence in their chairman, Alderman T. Kelly, MP.

> We regret exceedingly that his confinement in a British gaol, without accusation or trial, has deprived us of his able counsel, and the citizens of the services of a man whose chief object has always been to improve the conditions of his native city. W.T. Cosgrave acknowledged the vote of thanks on behalf of the Alderman.[3]

The municipal and urban council elections, which were held every three years, took place on 15 January 1920. For the first time, they were conducted by the method of the single transferable vote. This change applied only to Ireland. The British government felt, wrongly as it turned out, that proportional representation would be of advantage to the pro-British minority of the population, and would reduce the Sinn Féin majority at the polls. The councils managed certain local services, and were directly responsible to the Local Government Board which controlled the purse strings. For some weeks before the election, both sides had engaged in hostile activity. The military authorities went around tearing down Republican posters, and placed the counties of Waterford, Wexford and Kilkenny under martial law. But these methods only succeeded in stimulating resistance and resulted in another victory for Sinn Féin.

In the elections, Kelly topped the poll in Area 3 of Dublin with 3,438 votes. This comprised Fitzwilliam Square, Mansion House, Royal Exchange and South City wards. The Catholic archbishop, Dr. Walsh, who had been ill for some time, sent a telegram of congratulations to Kelly, and had telephoned the acting Lord Mayor to ask him to communicate to Kelly's wife and family how delighted he was at his success.

On 7 January 1920, the military and police had raided the headquarters of Dáil Éireann and Sinn Féin, both situated in Harcourt Street, together with the offices of the New Ireland Assurance Society, in O'Connell Street. A large force of military and police appeared at No. 6 Harcourt Street and were in possession of the premises when David Kelly, younger brother of Tom and manager of the Sinn Féin Bank, arrived at work. They said they had orders to close the bank. All the rooms and the hall door were walled up, and the books and effects were shifted into the hall until alternative premises could be procured. David Kelly asked whether the order was a police or military one, but received no reply. He was told that he could apply to have the bank reopened, but he said he would make no application to do so as the bank was established by an act of the

---

[3] *Dublin Corporation Reports,* 1921, Vol. 1, p. 102, DCA

British Parliament under the Industrial and Provident Societies' Act. Furthermore, he pointed out that the Inland Revenue was willing to take two pence on each of the bank's cheques, as were the income tax authorities to accept tax. Arrangements were subsequently made to transfer the business of the bank to No. 3 Harcourt Street.

There was continuing anxiety in Dublin regarding the state of Kelly's health. Alderman Cosgrave MP (who topped the poll in Area No. 7 – New Kilmainham and Usher's Quay Ward, with 2,033 votes) said he had been informed that Kelly's health was dangerously impaired in Wormwood Scrubs, and that his continued detention might have tragic results. He recalled that Dr. McWalter stated on 15 December, that after Kelly's arrest in 1916 he had examined him in Richmond Barracks, and had given a certificate showing that his heart was not strong, and that imprisonment would have a serious effect on him, and possibly terminate his life. He said that this document still existed at that time in the military archives in Dublin.[4]

As already recorded, Kelly was unanimously elected Lord Mayor at a packed meeting of the Council on 30 January 1920, during which ceremony the Republican flag was hoisted over the City Hall, for which the Corporation officials disclaimed responsibility. Kelly was proposed for office by Laurence O'Neill who stated that for over twenty years Kelly had given the very best that was in him to uplift his native city and to better the poorer class of citizen amongst whom he had lived. Kelly's election as Lord Mayor was seconded by W.T. Cosgrave who recalled how, on his previous arrest after the Rising in 1916, his house was rifled by the military who had removed priceless old documents and memoirs, one of which was a protest from Napper Tandy over the grant of the freedom of the city to Lord Chatham. However, Kelly was not now being proposed as Lord Mayor because he was in an English jail, but because he had given good and honest work in the Corporation. Even those councillors who traditionally held different views to Kelly's now voted for him. Alderman O'Brien (Labour) said that Alderman Kelly would give a square deal, and he believed his election would throw open his prison doors. McWalter, who described the Sinn Féin movement as the most infamous tyranny Ireland ever suffered, worse even than Orangeism and Carsonism, said that he could not vote against Tom Kelly because of his record as a corporator. Alderman Beattie expressed similar opinions. Alderman Joseph MacDonagh and Councillor Mrs. Sheehy-Skeffington stated that one of the reasons they were in favour of Kelly as Lord Mayor was because of his record on conscription.[5]

It was reported in the newspapers on 6 February 1920 that Kelly's presence as chairman of the Housing Committee was required at an investigation in connection with twenty-nine people living in Upper Mercer Street and Little Digges Street. On his evidence would depend approximately thirty evictions, and the Lord Chief Justice gave liberty to serve notices on the Chief Crown Solicitor to have Kelly in attendance, to no effect.[6]

---

4 *Irish Independent,* 31 January 1920
5 Ibid. 31 January 1920
6 *Evening Telegraph,* 6 February 1920

On 18 February according to the reports, it seemed that Kelly's installation as Lord Mayor would have to be deferred. The Town Clerk, Henry Campbell, and the city Law Agent, Ignatius Rice, stated that the present Lord Mayor would continue automatically in office until his successor was installed. The possibility of sending a deputation of officials to England to invest Kelly with the insignia of office was also discussed. A letter to the newspapers from Serjeant A.M. Sullivan[7] stated that he had used every means at his disposal to secure the release, not alone of Tom Kelly, but of another member of his party, who also seemed to be a victim of oppressive injustice.

> I have devoted my time and my skills to bring home to the mind of the Executive, in the most effective means at my disposal, the resentment of every lover of liberty to the claim of the Government to imprison men, not alone without trial, but without charge.

Sullivan wrote to Kelly on 17 February telling him that he welcomed his liberation, and that he had interviewed the Lord Lieutenant to protest against his detention, and pointed out that 'tribute to your character came from every section of the community, and to its voice I ventured to add my own. It has taken nearly a month of hammering to make this good but I am glad to have lent my aid'.[8]

At a Council meeting held on 23 February, a long discussion took place regarding the problems associated with the absence of Kelly, and what should be done. O'Neill said he would visit Kelly at the earliest possible moment, but that there was no option but to postpone the installation for the present: 'Whatever action I take is not to please anyone, is not for my own piece of mind, is not for the sake of popularity, but solely for the sake of Tom Kelly for whom I have more than a passing affection'.[9]

There was speculation in Dublin as to whether or not Dublin Corporation would send over the Lord Mayor's chain by deputation to Kelly for the installation date of 17 March. It was felt that there could not be any reason why the authorities would refuse to let him have it, as he had been merely an internee and was not accused of any crime. However, it was considered possible that the Catholic Alderman Kelly would refuse to accept it, as the chain had been presented by William of Orange. Daniel O'Connell was the first Catholic to wear it when the old Orange corporation was broken up in 1841.[10]

The Sinn Féin Bank was raided again on 27 February, when sums of £1,166 in notes and cash, gold, and deposit receipts for £7,204 were taken by the police. This resulted in an action by the Sinn Féin Co-operative Peoples' Bank against Colonel Edgeworth Johnstone, Chief Commissioner of the Dublin Metropolitan police. A writ for the return of the money and documents had been signed by T.M. Healy QC and James Murnaghan. The solicitors Corrigan and Corrigan acted for the bank. The case was

---

[7] Serjeant to the King, one of the last holders of this old legal title, a well-known barrister and Roger Casement's barrister during Casement's trial for treason

[8] Private collection

[9] *Evening Telegraph*, 24 February 1920

[10] Ibid. 18 February 1920

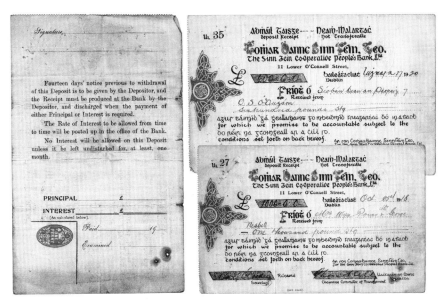

Sinn Féin Co-operative People's Bank receipts, written in Irish. Names on receipt no. 35 are those of Mrs. Jennie Wyse Power and Eamonn Duggan: signature on receipt no. 27 is Daithí Ó Ceallaigh, i.e., David Kelly, Manger of the Sinn Féin Bank. Mrs. Wyse Power and George Nesbitt lodged money receipted in no. 27, and were acting treasurers at the time, substituting for Austin Stack and Harry Boland (October 1918). The sums are £100 (no. 35) and £1,000 (no. 27). Private Collection.

heard in court on 20 March, but was adjourned for a month.[10] The sequel was reported in the newspapers on 15 June 1920. The authorities kept the gold, but returned the money, notes and documents to the manager through E.J. Duggan, MP, solicitor.[11]

Meanwhile, the harassment of nationalists by the military and police authorities (now including the ill-disciplined Black and Tans) continued. On 20 March 1920, Tomás MacCurtain, Lord Mayor of Cork, was shot dead in front of his wife and children. The Council was adjourned for one week as a mark of respect, and an official delegation consisting of Mrs. Jennie Wyse Power and the Lord Mayor was appointed to attend the funeral. On 24 March, Alderman William O'Brien was reported to be seriously ill in Wormwood Scrubs prison where he had been on hunger strike for the previous seven days. The Chief Secretary was asked if there was any intention of bringing him to trial, but the reply was in the negative. On 25 March, Cosgrave was detained in the Bridewell, and on 26 March Joseph MacDonagh was deported to Wormwood Scrubs. In retaliation, Alan Bell, a magistrate, was pulled off a tram in Ballsbridge and shot dead. Accommodation was offered in Dublin Castle to officers of the military for their own protection.[12] William O'Brien was released on 27 March, on the same conditions as Kelly had been, and warned that he would be rearrested if he returned to Ireland.

---

10 *Evening Telegraph*, 20 March 1920
11 Ibid. 15 June 1920
12 Ibid. 26 March 1920

Driven to desperation by the arrests of so many significant members of the Council, the Lord Mayor wrote to the Prime Minister, Lloyd George, on 26 March 1920, outlining the dilemma in which he found himself. He addressed his letter from the Mansion House in Dublin.

> Dear Sir,
>
> When one is in a dilemma as to the proper authority to approach, it is a very safe procedure to approach those who are in authority over all.
>
> For three years I have been Lord Mayor of Dublin. When my term of office expired on the 23rd of February last, my successor, Alderman Thomas Kelly, was unable to take my place, owing to being in a very precarious state of health as a result of having been interned in an English Prison. The duty still rests upon my shoulders to carry out the duties of Lord Mayor.

The Lord Mayor went on to recall how the Sinn Féin Party had won a majority in the Corporation at the recent municipal elections but the arrest 'one by one' of the Sinn Féin councillors was making it impossible to carry on the Council's work for the people who had elected them. He concluded his letter with a plea:

> Although I am in a very, very minor position compared to you, Sir, I put it to you this way. If the members of your Government were picked off one by one and say deported to Ireland, or America, detained in Prison, away from friends, relatives and admirers, without any charge, and without any trial, how would they and you feel? And how would you carry on the Government of your Kingdom? That is the position I find myself in at the moment. In my endeavour to carry out the work of my little kingdom (and after all every man, woman and child in this world has a kingdom of their own), I find I cannot do so, if my colleagues are taken from me.
>
> Will you please give this whole matter your serious consideration, and oblige one whom you invited to act as a member of the ill-fated Convention you set up, and who accepted in good faith that invitation.
>
> Yours respectfully, L. O'Neill.

Lloyd George replied from Downing Street on 31st March 1920.

> My dear Lord Mayor,
>
> I deeply sympathise with you in the dilemma in which you are placed, but I appreciate also the difficulty from the other side. Ireland to-day is menaced by a formidable organisation which seeks to promote its ends by terrorising public officials and the Irish people by the weapons of murder and assassination. This campaign has attained such proportions that it is impossible to obtain evidence in the ordinary way which will lead either to the arrest or conviction of murderers and assassins. In these circumstances the Executive which is responsible for the maintenance of government and the protection of the life, liberty and property of the individual citizens is placed under great difficulties. They certainly do not wish to arrest the guiltless. On the other hand, their first and imperative duty is to leave no stone unturned to enable them to lay their hands upon those who are terrorising society, and they may at times have no option, if they are to grapple with the problem of organised murder, but to dislocate in some degree the normal life of the community.

The Prime Minister then denounced the policy of Sinn Féin which he said depended upon 'violence in opinion and violence in action'. It was a policy which could never lead to the union of Ireland. Like the Lord Mayor, he ended with a plea:

> The Government, however, is most anxious to make as easy as possible the task of those who are endeavouring to carry on the administration of the country on reasonable lines. And if there are any means by which moderate men can be helped and encouraged to withstand and oppose the present campaign of intimidation and so bring nearer a settlement of the Irish question, I will gladly co-operate in bringing them into effect.
>
> Ever sincerely, D. Lloyd George.[14]

On 10 April, the newspapers carried stories of a crisis in Mountjoy prison where one hundred and four prisoners were on hunger strike, with many at the point of death. The prison hospital was full, and the men were determined to die rather than abandon their protest against their imprisonment. The Municipal Council met on 12 April and decided to adjourn for one week, commencing on 19 April, as a protest against the ill-treatment of the prisoners, contrary to the agreement previously negotiated between Mr. Duke, the Chief Secretary, and the Lord Mayor, and an agreement later arrived at between Dr. McRory, Bishop of Down and Connor, the Lord Mayor, and Mr. Shortt, the new Chief Secretary. It endorsed the action of the national executive of the Irish Labour Party and the Trade Union congress in calling a general strike on 13 April.[15] The Lord Mayor was asked to intervene, and on 13 April a telegram was sent to Sir Hamar Greenwood (Undersecretary for Home Affairs and soon to become Chief Secretary for Ireland) signed by both O'Neill and Alderman McWalter, saying:

> Dublin in fever of excitement owing to dangerous condition of political prisoners at present on hunger strike in Mountjoy Prison. We fear a dreadful tragedy pending. In the interests of peace and humanity we expect you to interfere.[16]

That same day, 13 April, brought a general cessation of work throughout Ireland: business came to a standstill in Dublin, Cork, Limerick, Waterford and Galway.

In the course of a report on the activities of the British during the month of April 1920, the *Catholic Bulletin* described the conditions of the political prisoners on hunger strike in Mountjoy prison without charge or trial. It complimented the tireless work of the Lord Mayor in working for their release, and also referred to Kelly, still in exile in England. 'In the midst of it all, it is not to be forgotten that Labour's oldest friend in Dublin, Ald. Tom Kelly and Lord Mayor elect, is still held untried and uncharged in England, admittedly broken in mind and body through the tyranny of the Government of Lloyd George, self-styled champion of human freedom'.[17]

---

14 NLI Ms. 35294/10
15 *Minutes of Dublin City Council,* 1920, p. 210
16 *Evening Telegraph,* 10 April 1920
17 *Catholic Bulletin,* May 1920, p. 257

On 14 April, the Lord Lieutenant sent for the Lord Mayor to inform him that the prisoners would be released unconditionally. The national strike was called off. A resolution of gratitude to the Lord Mayor was passed for his work in mediating in their release. Many of the released prisoners were in a weak and dying condition and Fr. Albert OFM ministered to them at Mountjoy prison. The Lord Mayor announced on 24 April that he would be setting up a fund for them and invited contributions from the public. He recommended the establishment of a committee to collect funds throughout the country.

On 3 May, the Council had moved a resolution acknowledging the authority Dáil Éireann as the duly elected government of the Irish people, and undertook to give effect to all decrees promulgated by the Dáil insofar as they affected the Council. It instructed that copies of this resolution be forwarded to the Minister for Foreign Affairs for transmission to the governments of Europe and to the President and Chairman of the Senate and House of Representatives of the United States of America. Councillor Michael Dowling said that in his opinion the motion was out of order as it would be illegal for the Council to pass a resolution which proposed disregarding the parliament and executive government as constituted under existing laws. This motion resulted in 38 votes in favour and 5 against, and thus was carried.[18]

On 30 April 1920, at a special meeting of the Corporation at which the Lord Mayor presided, he asked that all would join with him in extending a welcome to Alderman Kelly on his return. 'I am certain that you will join me in expressing the hope that he shall soon be restored to his usual health and vigour, and take his place once more amongst us, and above all, take his place in the position to which he has been elected, namely that of Lord Mayor of this City.' A similar resolution was passed at a meeting of the Housing Committee on the same day.

It appears that a more constructive atmosphere grew between the Corporation and the Local Government Board as the year advanced. Apart from the progress achieved with the earlier housing schemes such as Fairbrothers' Fields and Marino, others were being developed, for example those at Crabbe Lane, Spitalfields, Mary's Lane, Boyne Street, North Lotts and Newfoundland Street. Guidelines were issued by the City Architect and the Housing Committee for the design of the new houses. They specified room sizes, and recommended that living rooms and parlours should have a southerly aspect if possible. Bathrooms and larders, and a space for prams and bicycles were to be included. The position of beds was to be shown on bedroom plans. Native materials were to be used if available. Plans for all of these were submitted for approval, and all had been accepted by the Local Government Board by 31 July 1920. The board's architects provided professional and constructive comments on each of the proposals, and suggested various modifications in a positive way. Having considered the board's proposals, the Housing Committee wrote thanking them for their prompt reaction, and suggested a conference between the Local Government Board and the Housing Committee and its

---

[18] *Minutes of Dublin City Council,* 1920, p. 307, DCA

officials. This took place on 13 August. Each site was carefully considered in great detail and mutually acceptable courses of action were planned. The dedicated work of the City Architect, Charles J. MacCarthy, greatly contributed to the successful outcome of these negotiations.

The final session of the Dáil during 1920 was held on 17 September, when once again reports from the various departments were recorded. The plight of the political prisoners was brought to the attention of the meeting by J.J. Walsh of Cork, who wished to tender the sympathy of the Dáil to their relatives. The Minister for Finance, Michael Collins, stated that he wished to propose that a payment of £250 (€11,000 at 2005 prices)[19] be made immediately to Alderman Thomas Kelly, to help with the heavy expenses incurred by his recent breakdown and illness. Michael Staines seconded the motion, which was carried.[20] A reference to this payment to Kelly also occurs in Dáil correspondence dated 14 September 1920, in a memo written by Collins, on paper headed Dáil Éireann, Department of Finance, Mansion House, Dublin, where he recorded that the only matter he wished to refer to, apart from matters raised in his department report, was that of Alderman Kelly.[21] This initiative resulted in the order by the Dáil that a payment of £250 be made immediately to him.

In the Council, Alderman Cosgrave, seconded by Alderman McWalter proposed a motion that Laurence O'Neill, acting Lord Mayor, be asked to convey to Alderman T. Kelly MP (Lord Mayor elect) and to Mrs. Kelly and family, their sincere sympathy in the trouble they had experienced, and the hope that Kelly would soon be able to attend the Council again. This motion was carried.[22]

The friction between Dublin Corporation and the Local Government Board seems to have been resurrected when a letter from Cyril Browne, Local Government Auditor, announced his intention of coming to Municipal Buildings to audit the accounts of the Dublin County Borough and Council, and requested that all books and accounts be produced. It was moved, by Alderman Cosgrave and seconded by Councillor Lyons, that no books or accounts of Dublin Corporation be furnished to the British Local Government auditor. A letter was sent by C. Ó hUiginn (Kevin O'Higgins), assistant to the Minister for Local Government, to the Town Clerk (Henry Campbell) directing that no books or accounts were to be submitted to any local government official of a department of the British government and no facilities were to be extended to him. The letter further stated that in due course the accounts of Dublin Corporation, in common with those of the other public bodies of Ireland, would be audited under the auspices of Ó hUiginn's department. The original motion, and subsequent amendments and counter-amendments not to co-operate with the British Local Government auditor, were proposed and carried, with 27 for and 13 against.[23]

---

19 See footnote 4, Chapter 1, for calculation methodology
20 *DE*, 1919-1920, p. 232
21 NAI DE. 238A
22 *Minutes of Dublin City Council*, 1920, p. 518, DCA
23 Ibid. 1920, pp. 512-513, DCA

The dispute regarding the auditing of the Corporation accounts by the Local Government Board official rumbled on, when on 4 November Alderman O'Brien asked the Town Clerk, through the Lord Mayor, why the order of the Council regarding the non-submission of the books was not acted upon by the Town Clerk and his assistant. The Town Clerk replied that as the order was illegal, and they had been advised to that effect by the law agent, he had been unable to comply with the Council's resolution. It was then moved by Alderman O'Brien, and seconded by Councillor Raul, that, as the Town Clerk had refused to carry out the decision adopted by the Council, he and his assistant be suspended from duty. The Town Clerk, and his assistant Mr. Flood, withdrew. This motion was then put and carried.[24]

A special meeting on 15 November 1920 considered a notice of motion, proposed by Alderman W.T. Cosgrave, that the services of Campbell and Flood be dispensed with and that the Estates and Finance Committee report as to the retiring allowances to be paid to these gentlemen, and that Michael J. Walsh, BA, LLB be appointed Town Clerk, pro tem.[25]

David Kelly, the manager of the Sinn Féin Bank, was arrested on 24 November at his residence at 132 Great Brunswick Street, in a raid by the auxiliary police. However, he was released and was back at work on 27 November, having been detained at Portobello Barracks and Arbour Hill. He declared that the watchword was 'business as usual'. But by 29 November, the Sinn Féin Bank was raided again. Auxiliaries blew open the safe and took about £500 in coins and notes. They also took account books. Kelly and the caretaker's family emerged safely. Subsequently, the building was exhaustively searched and considerable damage was done. On 30 November, the premises of the Sinn Féin Bank and the *Freeman's Journal* offices at 27 Westmoreland Street were set on fire, but were saved by the prompt arrival of the fire brigade.[26]

On 26 November, Griffith and Eamonn Duggan were arrested, and attempts were made to arrest Cosgrave and Alderman Joseph MacDonagh. Early in December 1920, Eoin MacNeill was arrested together with his two sons. Countess Markiewicz was court-martialled on conspiracy charges of organising and promoting Fianna Éireann 'for the purposes of committing murders of His Majesty's police'. She refused to recognise the court.

The Lord Mayor received the resignations of Henry Campbell and John J. Flood from their positions in Dublin Corporation as Town Clerk and assistant Town Clerk, on 14 December. Campbell wrote a bitter letter to the Lord Mayor, stating that the Lord Mayor's attitude had ensured that he could not possibly remain in office. He referred to 'the illegalities, irregularities and indecencies perpetrated or attempted to be perpetrated by the Council in reference to his position as Town Clerk and the duties and obli-

---

24 *Minutes of Dublin City Council,* 1920 pp. 518-519, DCA
25 *Dublin Corporation Reports,* Vol. 3, p. 455-456, DCA
26 *Evening Telegraph* 27, 29, 30 November 1920

gations therewith, which had forced him to conclude that he would best serve the citizens of Dublin and his own honour and dignity by severing his connection with the Municipal Council'. He concluded that he had always performed his duties in accordance with the law, the statutes and the standing orders, under which alone the municipal council and its officers could act. He was thus forced to resign. Flood, in a shorter letter to the Lord Mayor, cited similar difficulties with reference to his own resignation.[27]

A further letter from Campbell called attention to the fact that Alderman T. Kelly MP and Alderman John T. O'Kelly (Seán T. O'Kelly) MP, having failed to make and subscribe the statutory declaration of acceptance of office, and having also been absent from meetings of the Council for a period of over six months, were, consequently, no longer members of the municipal council. The Law Agent stated that if the members could show just cause for their absence, they would not be disqualified. Alderman McGurk and Councillor J. Murphy moved that no action be taken in the matter. This was carried.[28]

The Lord Mayor and Council were served with a mandamus (a judicial writ) from the Local Government Board, ordering the Corporation to produce all books, accounts and documents relevant for the audit, thus resulting in a major confrontation with the British authorities. Alderman McWalter and Councillor Beattie attempted to have this order complied with; their motion resulted in a division which was lost by 11 votes to 14.

A Council meeting of 6 December was broken up by the entrance of armed forces of the Crown, who arrested several members of the Council.[29]

Under the Defence of the Realm Act, an order from Captain Herbert Quare was issued to the Council, requiring the premises at Municipal Buildings, Cork Hill, and also the offices of the Veterinary Department at Castle Street, to be delivered up to the military by 8 a.m. on 7 December. A subsequent order, in a similar vein, was issued by Major General G.F. Boyd, dated 10 December, in respect of the City Hall. In view of these developments, the Lord Mayor called a special meeting of the Council for 20 December, the earliest date on which a legal meeting could be held. He wrote to Quare on 9 December explaining why it would be impossible to vacate all these premises due to their constant use. The City Treasurer's office, for instance, handled sums of about £50,000 per week (€2.2 million at 2005 prices) involving such payments as rates and employees' salaries, and the public health offices were particularly busy at that time due to a serious outbreak of typhus in the city. The Council could not agree to co-operate in surrendering these offices, as no alternative accommodation existed, and to vacate them would be to jeopardise the public health of the city and dislocate its financial

---

27 *Minutes of Dublin City Council*, 1920, pp. 579-582, DCA
28 Ibid. 1920, p. 584, DCA
29 Ibid. 1920, p. 575, DCA

arrangements. Boyd replied that his decision was to appropriate the City Hall and adjacent Municipal Buildings and must be treated as final, and that they were to be vacated by 22 December. Alderman McWalter proposed that the order be complied with, but that the military authorities be requested to permit the Council to retain the lower portion of the building on Cork Hill and Castle Street. Alderman Mrs. Kathleen Clarke moved that no action be taken regarding the notices from the military authorities. This latter proposal was put and carried by a large majority.[30]

The Lord Mayor proposed that the municipal offices be closed on Friday 24 December and Tuesday 28 December. This was carried, thus ensuring that all buildings were closed for four days. This was intended to buy the Council a little time, but to no avail, as the British army occupied City Hall from 22 December 1920 until 21 January 1922, when the building was ceded to the newly established Irish Free State. The City Council was obliged to move to the Mansion House, where it remained for nearly four years, holding its meetings in the Round Room.[31]

[30] *Minutes of Dublin City Council,* 1920, pp. 606-613, DCA
[31] *Dublin Corporation Reports,* 1923, vol. 2, pp. 683-686

Chapter Fourteen: The Fall of the Corporation

From the beginning of 1921, there was great concern about the numbers of unemployed in Ireland. An organisation called the White Cross was established in America to assist republicans and their families who were suffering hardship through their involvement in the Anglo-Irish war. The money collected amounted to £1,374,795 (€66 million at 2005 prices). This fund was administered under the aegis of Sinn Féin, and Griffith helped in its organisation. Money was distributed to all victims on a non-sectarian basis, and was also used to aid Catholics who had to flee Northern Ireland. Cardinal Logue was one of its patrons, and contributors included Count John McCormack and Pope Benedict XV.

By the new year, there were many issues causing concern to the Corporation, stripped as it was by the absence of many of its most competent and experienced members. The Local Government Board had refused to distribute normal resources to hospitals and other public institutions, on the grounds that they were withholding funding from all organisations which supported Dáil Éireann. The Dáil urged all local government bodies to apply for grants while they still could, particularly for housing, before the source dried up.[1]

In the matter of housing, the acting Town Clerk endeavoured to restart the construction works on the Fairbrothers' Fields development, work on which had been suspended due to lack of funds, but was now at an advanced stage. By this time, the land was completely owned by the Council, and a considerable portion of the roads and sewers had been completed. The British treasury had agreed to advance the necessary sums to complete the scheme, and every possible avenue was being explored to obtain loans to proceed with this and the other housing projects which had been held up because of the financial situation.[2]

The row over the resignations of the Town Clerk and his assistant had dragged on into the new year, with a letter from Campbell disputing the right of the Corporation to dismiss him without superannuation, and stating that he was applying to the Local Government Board to have the amount of his allowance determined. The Corporation responded was that it was his duty to comply with their request, but he had both neglected and refused to produce the accounts to the officials of the Corporation for the annual audit. Campbell now threatened legal action, and declared that he was not in a position to hand over various matters in his custody until his successor had been 'duly,

---

1 Collins, Stephen. *The Cosgrave Legacy*, Blackwater Press, Dublin 1996, p. 19
2 *Dublin Corporation Reports*, 1921, Vol. 1, pp. 84-85

validly and legally' appointed to the position of Town Clerk.[3] An order to compel him to do so was issued by the Clerk of the Crown, James O'Brien. Meanwhile, John J. Murphy was appointed Town Clerk on 14 February 1921.[4]

As referred to above, the Corporation and its officials were going through a difficult phase of disengagement from the British system of the Local Government Board, while developing a working relationship with the new Dáil administration and the provisional government. The curious situation was that, while disengaging, the Corporation was still trying to get as much money as possible from the Board before finally severing the link. O'Neill was re-elected, once again, to the position of Lord Mayor, as Kelly had still not returned to public life. O'Neill had offered to vacate the post, and only reluctantly agreed to take it on for another year. He indicated that his family felt that after four years of strenuous work, he had done his part and also had taken his share of the risks that were going. He had been looking forward to handing over to Kelly. Seán Mac Caoilte paid an appreciative tribute to O'Neill, and also to Kelly. He expressed the hope that they would soon welcome Kelly back to the Council which he had long honoured with his presence and guided in its decisions by his wonderful knowledge of Dublin and its problems. Mrs. Sheehy-Skeffington said she hoped that Kelly would be again elected as Lord Mayor, when it would not be, as it was previously, a post of difficulty and danger. Dr. McWalter also spoke in his favour.[5] McWalter died suddenly a few days later, at the age of fifty-three. He had been a schoolfellow of Kelly's. They were often politically at variance but shared a mutual concern for the welfare of Dublin's poor, and relations between them had always been cordial. McWalter had qualified as a medical doctor. He was also an engineer, and had served in the Great War in Palestine before taking up his municipal duties once again on his discharge from the British army in 1918.[6] Tributes were paid to him in the newspapers, universally regretting his passing. A Council meeting on 7 February 1921 was deferred as a mark of respect. A letter from W.T. Cosgrave voiced a personal tribute:

> I should like to point out that there had always been a very close friendship between the Doctor and myself, and the fact that we were on opposite sides never warped our personal relations. There were many occasions on which he showed remarkable character the most notable of which, to my mind, was his strenuous opposition to the removal of the name of Dr. Kuno Meyer from the Roll of Honorary Freemen of the City. The circumstances leading up to, and perhaps responsible for, his tragic demise call for no emphasis from me. The city has lost a brilliant son, the Corporation a gifted colleague, the medical profession an able and generous practitioner, and we have lost a friend. Go ndéanaidh Dia trócaire ar a anam.
>
> L.T. Mac Cosgair (W.T. Cosgrave)[7]

[3] *Dublin Corporation Reports*, 1921, Vol.1, p.151, DCA
[4] *Minutes of Dublin City Council*, 1921, pp. 124-126, DCA
[5] *Evening Telegraph*, 31 January 1921
[6] Ibid. 5 February 1921
[7] *Minutes of Dublin City Council*, 1921, p. 101, DCA

The resolutions being passed in the Council during the first half of 1921 indicate the many atrocities inflicted on the people not only in Dublin but throughout the country during that terrifying year. Six men who were executed in Cork prison occasioned another motion of sympathy by the Corporation. Letters were received from three councillors, Joseph Clarke, J.V. Lawless and James O'Brennan, stating that they were all imprisoned in Ballykinlar Internment Camp, Co. Down, and therefore unable to attend meetings, and requesting that copies of all Council reports be forwarded to them there.

Then the Kelly family suffered another blow. On the evening of 14 March 1921, David Kelly, manager of the Sinn Féin Bank, was shot dead beside his home at 132 Great Brunswick Street, (now Pearse Street). A serious street battle had taken place up and down the street that evening. A bomb had exploded directly opposite the police station and crossfire took place between auxiliaries and armed men. Three of the latter were killed, and five auxiliaries were wounded. The conflict continued further down the street, near the public library, and it was in this skirmish that David Kelly was killed. He was a well-known and much-esteemed figure in Dublin, and at the time was about fifty years of age. He had not been involved in the military action. He had suffered from an infirmity of the leg and had been in delicate health, facts which probably contributed to his death as he was unable to seek cover quickly enough in the crossfire. His body was brought to the George V Hospital (later St. Bricin's).[8] His death notice read:

> **Kelly** (Dublin): Shot in Great Brunswick Street on 14 March 1921. David Kelly,
> Manager Sinn Féin Bank, youngest son of the late Isaac Kelly of Wicklow, and of the late
> Mrs. Sarah Kelly, of 132 Gt. Brunswick, Street. To the great grief of his sisters, brother
> and friends. His life for Ireland.

A photograph of his coffin being carried out through the crowds at St. Andrew's Church, Westland Row, appeared in the *Evening Telegraph,* together with a description of the funeral and a list of those attending who included Sister Aidan of Grimsby, Miss Kathleen Kelly and Mrs. Coyne (sisters), Mrs. (Thomas) Kelly (sister-in-law) together with many prominent persons in the national movement, corporation councillors and officials. Thomas Kelly's name is not included in the list of mourners, probably because he had returned to Grimsby to continue his convalescence in the care of the nuns. The Corporation met on 16 March and the Lord Mayor proposed a message of sympathy to the Kelly family, which was seconded by Councillor George Lyons.[9] Councillor Lyons said that David Kelly was a mild-mannered and peaceful man, of no importance as a fighting man, as he was a cripple. Nevertheless, Lyons went on to say that it appeared that those who had custody of his body in the George V Hospital had mistakenly identified him as a man of importance and significance in the Irish Republican Army. His death could not be regarded as a victory for anyone.[10]

---

8   *Evening Telegraph,* 16 March 1921
9   *Minutes of Dublin City Council,* 1921, p. 143, DCA
10 *Evening Telegraph,* 16 March 1921

Máire Comerford has left us a vivid picture of David Kelly in his office at the Sinn Féin Bank:

> No. 6 Harcourt Street was the property and headquarters of the Sinn Féin Bank. Entering the house, the first thing you met was the polished mahogany counter surmounted by a brass grill and David Kelly, manager of the Bank, looking as if money and savings were the only things that mattered. He was a lame man but that was not to save him from being shot by Crown Forces in the days ahead.[11]

Lloyd George resolved to call elections in southern and northern Ireland with the object of electing two separate parliaments in an effort to solve the impasse. The general election was held in May of 1921. Sinn Féin met no opposition in the south, and its members were returned with 124 seats. In the six counties comprising Northern Ireland, 52 seats were on offer, of which the unionists won 40 and nationalists the remaining 12, and this in spite of sabotage and intimidation prior to polling day, a state of affairs which continued after the election. In opening the Belfast parliament on 22 June, King George V pleaded for peace in the whole of Ireland. Lloyd George made contact with de Valera, from which evolved the truce announced on 11 July.

As mentioned above, it would appear that at this time Kelly had returned to stay, once again, under the care of his sister (known as Sister Aidan) and the nuns, at the Convent of St. Joseph of Peace in Grimsby. It seems reasonable to conclude that he could not endure, from the point of view of his health, the constant threatening environment in Ireland. The daily accounts of murders and executions must have been impossible for someone in such a frail condition to deal with, and he knew that at least he could expect peace and quiet with the nuns. Obviously, the sad death of his one surviving brother would have adversely affected his health.

Some letters corroborate this assumption. One written by his daughter Eileen, dated 14 July 1921, points to much concern and affection on the part of his family in Dublin, who were obviously missing him. This letter also contains a reference to the peace move, and expresses a hope that he would be coming home soon to take his rightful position in Ireland's government. Eileen wrote that the town had nearly gone mad on the previous Monday as a result of the peace initiative (presumably she was referring to the King's speech, and its aftermath). She described the rejoicing in the St. Stephen's Green area, and the arches of Republican flags which were flying in Mercer Street and Cuffe Street. She recounted how a band came up the South Circular Road at about one in the morning and played outside the Kellys' house for about twenty minutes, before calling for a cheer for Alderman Tom. She mentioned that there were also cheers for him outside the Mansion House in the same week, and that 'all of us in 23 (Longwood Avenue) couldn't possibly express how proud we are of you'.[12] Another letter, this time from de Valera to Kelly, addressed from the Mansion House and dated 9 September 1921, expressed a desire to see him back in Dublin amongst his colleagues:

---

11 Comerford, M. UCDA, LA18
12 Private collection

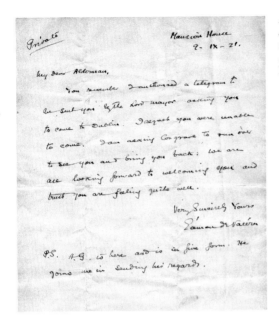

Letter dated 9 September 1921 from Éamon de Valera to Alderman Tom Kelly, written at the Mansion House, expressing a desire to see him back in Dublin amongst his colleagues. Private Collection

I am asking Cosgrave to run over to see you and bring you back. We are all looking forward to welcoming you and trust you are feeling quite well.

De Valera added a P.S:

A.G. (Arthur Griffith) is here and is in fine form. He joins me in sending his regards.

The date confirms that Kelly had not as yet returned to Ireland at that time.[13]

The activities of the Corporation in the early 1920s continued despite all the difficulties. The work of the Housing Committee, now under the chairmanship of Councillor J. Murphy, progressed. Sanction was sought for the construction of 60 houses on the Fairbrothers' Fields site, specifying that Irish materials and labour be employed in the construction of these houses.[14]

At this point, with Dr. McWalter dead, C.J. McCarthy and Edmund W. Eyre (City Architect and City Treasurer respectively) both retired, the absence of Kelly, and of Sir Henry Campbell, Town Clerk – a familiar figure for so long and now no longer acceptable – the dynamics within the Council must have been greatly changed. In fairness to Campbell and his assistant, Flood, they were both carrying out their duties as they always had done, within the legal framework to which they were accustomed, and to which they owed their allegiance.

---

13 Letter from de Valera. Private collection
14 *Minutes of Dublin City Council,* 1921, pp. 308-310, DCA

Two other deaths of note took place at this time. The first was that of Sir Charles Cameron, who had been connected with the Corporation since 1862, when he was appointed Public Analyst. He had served in many other capacities over the years, and became Medical Officer of Health in addition to being City Analyst and Executive Sanitary Officer. His salary for holding these three positions was £1,000 per annum. He died on 27 February 1921, and was replaced by Dr. Matthew Russell, who had been assistant Medical Officer for Health since 1911. Then on 13 April 1921, Dr. William Walsh, the Catholic archbishop of Dublin, also passed away. Archbishop Walsh had been appointed in 1885. He had been a strong supporter of the nationalist movement, and of the efforts of the Corporation to achieve social justice over a period of thirty-six years.

Peace negotiations with the British continued during the truce throughout the summer months of 1921. The North remained the main sticking point, with Sir James Craig, now leader of the northern Unionists, declaring that the designated counties of Ulster must remain a separate political entity. A number of position papers were issued by both Lloyd George and de Valera. De Valera was urged to accept the peace terms on offer, which were dominion status for the south and the acceptance of a separate status for the northern counties, effectively partition, at least for the time being. It was envisaged that the northern issue could be addressed separately at a later stage, and that the frontier between the north and south would be decided by a boundary commission. Craig continued to insist that he would not meet de Valera, unless the separate status of the six counties was recognised. After protracted negotiations, the Treaty was finally signed on 6 December 1921 and resulted in the well-known tragic outcome: widespread dissension followed by civil war.

Kelly wrote to the speaker, in a letter dated 22 December 1921, indicating that he would support the agreement with the British government. The Treaty had been negotiated by the delegation led by his great friend and colleague, Arthur Griffith, and, while Kelly had serious reservations about it, he obviously considered that it was the best that could be achieved at the time and so indicated his support. Kelly wrote to the speaker of the Dáil, Eoin MacNeill, as follows:

> I am unable to attend the meeting and I wish my vote to be recorded for the ratification of the Treaty. Mise do chara, Thomas Kelly.

His eventual support probably was due to his conclusion that Griffith and the rest of the delegates had achieved the maximum that could be obtained from the wily Lloyd George, and perhaps felt that not to do so would result in greater evils. As he was not present, his vote was not included in the reckoning.

Kelly's reservations about the Treaty were referred to in a tribute, written in Irish, and published in the *Irish Times* on the occasion of his death in 1942. The writer, identified only by the initial C, included the following comment:

Is cuimhin liom an t-am sin an bhróin a's an dóláis, an bhliadhain 1922, nuair nár aontuigh Ó Ceallaigh leis an gConnradh a chuir Ó Gríobhtha a ainm leis i London Shasan, ní raibh Ó Gríobhtha in annamh a thuigbheáil caidé mar a thuit sé amach nach raibh Ó Ceallaigh ag cuidiú leis.[15]

The Dáil voted on the Treaty on 7 January 1922, resulting in a margin for acceptance of 64 votes to 57. As a result of this vote, de Valera was succeeded by Griffith, who became president of the executive. The standing committee of Sinn Féin continued to meet until 31 March 1922, and the last recorded minutes of that date were signed by de Valera. The proceedings in the Dáil during 1922 are written about extensively elsewhere, from the time of the Treaty and the ensuing civil war. As already noted, at this period, Kelly was staying with the nuns at Grimsby.

The Oireachtas Library

This second stay with the nuns led to an interesting outcome. The congregation of St. Joseph of Peace, where Sister Aidan, Kelly's sister, was a member of the community, had been founded in 1884 by Margaret Cusack, popularly known as the Nun of Kenmare. She was born in Dublin in 1829 into an Episcopalian family. Her father was a medical doctor who had rooms in Digges Street, at the rear of the Royal College of Surgeons, St. Stephen's Green. She entered an order of Anglican nuns in London, but subsequently became a Catholic, and joined the Poor Clares in Newry in 1859. She worked in the deprived communities of Kenmare, and subsequently Knock, before deciding that she wished to establish her own congregation, and travelled to Rome where she obtained permission from Pope Leo XIII to do so. This new order became known as the Congregation of St. Joseph of Peace. The first convent of the new congregation was at Grimsby. Then a larger building was erected in Nottingham, which became the motherhouse. Eventually it spread to different parts of the world, but especially to America. Over the years, the Nun of Kenmare had written several books on aspects of Irish history herself, and succeeded in making quite a lot of money by her pen. She had also acquired an extensive library of books of Irish interest. When Kelly started to regain his health under the care of the nuns at Grimsby, he must have become aware of the existence of the Nun's collection which, through him, was to become part of the Dáil Éireann library.

Kelly's involvement with this library came about when, towards the end of 1921, a decision was taken to establish an official library for Dáil Éireann. A memo survives referring to provisional decisions taken at a meeting of the Dáil held on 26 November 1921 which indicates that his colleagues in the Dáil were continuing to take an active interest in his welfare. At this meeting, it was decided to offer Kelly the appointment of librarian to Dáil Éireann. This decision was recorded in a government file together with

---

[15] I remember the time of sorrow and distress in the year 1922, when Kelly did not agree with the Treaty to which Griffith had put his name in London, England, Griffith was unable to understand how it came about that Kelly was not supporting him. *Irish Times,* 21 April 1942

a comment to the effect that, in view of the fact that Alderman Kelly would almost certainly refuse to accept the subsistence allowance of £250 per annum to which he was entitled as a TD, it was decided that he be appointed librarian to Dáil Éireann at a yearly salary of £250; his first duty to be to prepare a catalogue of books suitable for an official library.[16] The librarian would act as a central buying agent for all departments. This document is signed by Diarmuid Ó hÉigeartaigh, Rúnaidhe na hAireachta. Kelly would have been regarded as a fitting choice to acquire items for this significant enterprise, because of his interest in, and knowledge of, history and antiquarian books. However, it is worth pointing out that a librarian already existed in the person of Henry Egan Kenny, who had been the librarian in the Chief Secretary's department in Dublin Castle, and at some point had transferred to Dáil Éireann. Kenny's position as librarian seems to have been ignored while these arrangements regarding Kelly were being discussed. W.T. Cosgrave undoubtedly felt that the project would be a way of gradually encouraging his former colleague to resume his political career, and had probably made the suggestion as an act of kindness towards an old and respected friend. In any event, Kelly undertook the task.

A sparse file survives in the Oireachtas Library concerning Kelly's work in the capacity of Dáil Librarian.[17] This file includes a booklet entitled *Rough List of Books Procured for Leabharlann na Dála,* printed at Mahon's Printing Works, Yarnhall Street, Dublin in 1924. The proprietor, Patrick Mahon, was also a councillor whose premises had been raided twice and wrecked by the armed forces of the Crown during 1920, thus forcing their closure. He published nationalist journals such as *Young Ireland* and the *Fr. Mathew Record.* The business was obviously up and running again by 1924, in view of the date of the list of books as referred to above. There is a short, unsigned introduction to this list of the library's contents, dated 12 February 1924, and it is reasonable to conclude that it was written by Kelly. The document states that the books were in good condition with few exceptions, and enumerates the sources from whence they came. Those books which came from the convent in Grimsby were described as being the remainder of the library of the Nun of Kenmare, and were considered to be 'a good lot' when they were acquired.

There is mention in the general council notes of the congregation of St. Joseph of Peace, 6 March 1923, of a request from Mr. Thomas Kelly for the books, stating that 'both he and President Cosgrave of the Free State Republic thought they might be useful in the Dublin Library'. Their request was sanctioned by the council of the congregation in 1923, and there was, apparently, no question of payment. A list of 107 titles (many of them comprising several volumes) survives in the above-mentioned file. The books were described as the foundress's personal library of Irish history, and the superior thought it would be a good idea for the books to be presented to the new Free State. The Nun of Kenmare had died in 1899. She had a controversial reputation at the end of her life, and had come to regard herself as an incubus within the congregation she had estab-

---

16 D.238A NAI
17 This file was brought to my attention by Dr. Patrick Melvin, Librarian, Oireachtas Library

lished.[18] She decided that she would best serve it by resigning her position both from the congregation and from her religious life. She died as a layperson, in Leamington Spa, where she is buried in the Anglican plot. The manner in which these books were acquired explains why the stamp of the congregation appears on so many of the books contained in the Oireachtas Library. In Dublin, in 1992, a dignified plaque was erected by the Cusack Society, commemorating this radical, courageous though controversial nun on the approximate site of her father's rooms in Digges Street. This site is now known as Cusack Corner.[19]

Apart from the books from the Nun of Kenmare's collection, the library eventually contained the remains of the Chief Secretary's library, in addition to a collection which had been acquired, over the years, by Kelly for the library of the Workmen's Club in York Street which was no longer functioning. He also acquired some volumes from a sale of books when the contents of Carrigoran House, Newmarket-on-Fergus, Co. Clare, were auctioned after the death of Clara, Lady Fitzgerald in 1922. This Fitzgerald family were descendants of Edward Fitzgerald, MP for Co. Clare. The house still stands, and is now run as a nursing home by the Sisters of the Incarnate Word.[20]

The involvement of Kelly in the affairs of the Oireachtas Library came to an abrupt end sometime during 1924, or perhaps 1925, though exactly when is not clear. He was obviously still working on the project on 12 February 1924, as referred to above. By 26 February 1926, a memo from Colm Ó Murchadha, Clerk of the Dáil, refers to the fact that a joint library committee of the Dáil and the Seanad was being set up to advise and assist the Ceann Comhairle and the Cathaoirleach in the direction and control of the library.[21] The only evidence to explain Kelly's severance from the library is based on family hearsay. It seems that it was imputed that he was using his position in the library to further his own financial interests, and this was a slight which he could not ignore, so he withdrew. To sum up, there is nothing to suggest what policy directive, if any, was given to him and with little or no money to spend, he could not acquire all the material he would have liked. The closing sentence in the 1924 report noted:

> It is a matter for regret that as so many rare, interesting, valuable and curious items were offered for purchase during the past months, the money not being available, they had to be declined.

The Corporation proceedings were recorded until its dissolution in May 1924. O'Neill was re-elected once again as Lord Mayor for the two years February 1921 to February 1923, though there are references to his being seriously ill at this time, and that his

---

18 See Carden, S. 'The Origins of the Oireachtas Library' in *Dublin Historical Record*, Vol. LVII, No. 1, Spring 2004

19 Three biographies exist: Eagar, I. ffrench, *The Nun of Kenmare*, Mercier Press, Cork 1970; Vidulich, D. A. *Peace Pays its Price*, Sisters of St. Joseph of Peace, Washington 1975; O'Neill M. R. *The Life of Mother Clare*, 1990, no publisher listed

20 Weir, H. *Houses of Clare*, Ballinakella Press 1986, p. 62

21 Oireachtas Library file, Leinster House, courtesy Dr. Patrick Melvin

place was frequently taken by Alfie Byrne, acting Lord Mayor.[22] C.J. MacCarthy, the former City Architect, was replaced by Horace O'Rourke who had been working in the post in an acting capacity. MacCarthy wrote to the Council to thank them for the liberal manner in which they dealt with him on his retirement. Progress was reported on various housing schemes such as St. James's Walk, the Marino and Oblate sites, Boyne Street and others.

Under the auspices of the Paving Committee, a special committee was set up to consider street names on 12 April 1921.[23] A survey found that 19 of the existing names derived from kings and queens, 49 from viceroys and their families, and probably upwards of 120 in honour of state officials, lords mayor, noblemen, property owners and their connections. The system of street nomenclature was attributed by the Corporation to a policy pursued in the past to anglicise the outlook and habits of the Irish people. Many of these names represented individuals hostile to the national spirit, and the Corporation felt that few cities in the civilised world had honoured the names of such people to the same extent as our own city of Dublin. A special committee was convened to recommend alternatives, and consisted of Risteard Ó Foghludha (chairman), Charles O'Neill, Peadar Mac Fhionlaoich, and Seán Mac Caoilte. Kelly had also been nominated to act on this committee, but his health, at the time, had not recovered sufficiently to contribute to its work. It recommended that the Irish name of the street should take precedence, and that various other new procedures in relation to numbering, identification, and nameplates be put in place.

Another issue which was preoccupying the Council in 1921 was the ownership of the Dublin squares, and the legal conditions under which they were held. At this time Rutland (now Parnell) Square was declared to be the property of the governors of the Rotunda Hospital. George III had given power to the governors to erect an enclosure and impose a tax on certain of the houses in Rutland Square for a single year to defray the work, and access to the square was by means of a key given to residents of the square and some neighbours, on payment of a certain annual sum. The governors were legally the trustees, and could not abandon the revenue derived by opening them to the public. Merrion, Mountjoy and Fitzwilliam Squares were controlled by commissioners appointed under George III to enclose, upgrade and ornament them. A tax was imposed on the houses, not exceeding three shillings per square foot, to pay the expenses of maintaining the square, payable for 147 years from 1791. In order to now open the squares to the public, provision would have to be made for paying off the debts of the commissioners, for which an Act of Parliament would be necessary.[24]

On 13 February 1922, it was noted by the Council that the Estates and Finance Committee had given temporary possession of the City Hall and Municipal Buildings to the representatives of the provisional government, on the surrender of the premises by the military authorities.[25]

---

[22] *Minutes of Dublin City Council,* 1922, p. 140, DCA
[23] *Dublin Corporation Reports,* 1921, Vol. 1, No. 71, pp. 506-507, DCA
[24] *Minutes of Dublin City Council,* 1921, pp. 468-469, DCA
[25] Ibid. 1922, p. 117, DCA

On 3 May 1922, the Council passed a resolution reaffirming its allegiance to Dáil Éireann as the sovereign government of the country, and declared its readiness to accept all orders emanating from the Government or any of its properly constituted departments. On 4 May at a special meeting of the Council the following motion was addressed to the Rt. Hon. The Lord Mayor of Dublin:

> That inasmuch as the Provisional Government of Ireland has been set up and clothed with authority by virtue of the Treaty made between Ireland and Great Britain, and approved by Dáil Éireann, to whom this Council has pledged its allegiance by resolution of 3 May 1922: Now therefore, this Council acting in pursuance of this pledge, in accord of such approval, hereby declares that it recognises and will conform to the lawful Orders and Decrees of the Provisional Government of Ireland. Signed: L.T. MacCosgair (W.T. Cosgrave), Siobhán Bean an Phaoraigh (Mrs. Wyse Power), Geo. A. Lyons, Thomas Cassidy, T.J. Loughlin, Seán Ó Ceallacháin.

Obviously it was essential for the provisional government to ensure that it had the support of the municipal authority.[26]

Against the deteriorating national situation, the Council struggled to develop its housing policies during 1922. Various issues continued to cause anxiety. Two councillors called for policy guidelines to be instituted in respect of the types of houses to be built, together with the eligibility criteria and selection procedures for the applicants. There was trouble about the newly erected houses on the Fairbrothers' Fields development, and a view that the first 25 completed houses had been allocated unfairly. Two councillors called for policy guidelines to be instituted in respect of the types of houses to be built, together with the eligibility and selection procedures to be used in their allocation.

A motion by Councillor P.T. Daly proposed that the interests of tenants should be properly safeguarded, and that they should be allocated houses according to the order of their application, and number and family size, those with the largest families and the worst housing accommodation to get preference. Applicants for housing on this site numbered 1,775 and no further applications could be accepted. The superintendent was instructed to select a preliminary list of applicants for consideration by the committee, with maximum earnings to be not more than £7 per week, and the number in each family to be not less than five. The possibility of building a further 198 houses on the site was to be examined, using a superior type of design, incorporating an additional room at ground-floor level, and three bedrooms were felt to be essential for the average family. Thus a five-room unit ought to be the minimum standard, each having a cubic content of 6,062 cubic feet.[27]

So many allegations continued to be made about the allocation of the houses on the Fairbrothers' Fields site that a sworn inquiry was initiated by the Local Government

---

26 *Dublin Corporation Reports, 1922,* Vol. 1, Report No. 111, p. 677, DCA
27 Ibid. 1922, Vol. 1, pp. 411-412

Department of Dáil Éireann to investigate the matter. This inquiry in turn alleged that the members of the Housing Committee attempted to give possession to their friends of houses which cost £1,025 (€57,000 at 2005 prices)[28] at prices ranging from £246 to £379 each. The inspector stated that without rigorous selection criteria the most deserving persons could not be sure of securing the support of the committee in every case. He also found that the committee had no housing policy, demanded no definite qualifications from intending tenants, and had not issued guidelines to the councillors regarding the selection of such tenants. Had the order of the Housing Committee made the previous October, specifying a list of suitable applicants, been enforced, much of the present difficulty might have been avoided.[29] Councillor Lawlor proposed a motion to the effect that the Town Clerk be instructed not to proceed with the sale of any houses or other property of this Corporation, until such sales were approved of, and sanctioned by the Council, and that any resolution to the contrary be rescinded.[30] It is tempting to speculate as to what the position might have been had Kelly still been in charge.

A delegation from the Council consisting of the chairman, Mr. P.F. McIntyre, and three other members of the Streets Committee visited Birmingham, Glasgow, London and Paris in July 1922, to inquire into methods of road clearing and construction. They were well received by public officials in all the cities visited, and developed useful contacts with their opposite numbers. They were received formally by the municipal council of Paris, and by the prefect of the Seine, and much was made of the cordial relationship existing between France and Ireland.[31]

Griffith died suddenly on 12 August 1922. It is unlikely that Kelly was at the funeral of one of his oldest and closest friends, as he was probably still out of the country. This sad event undoubtedly further contributed to his health problems. The deaths of Griffith and subsequently of Cathal Brugha and Harry Boland were marked in the Council by votes of sympathy to their families. On 26 August, at a specially assembled meeting, the members recorded their grief over the untimely and tragic death of Michael Collins, and his irreparable loss to the Irish nation. The tragedy and futility of Collins' death, and his loss to the national cause, would have deeply affected Kelly also, in view of the close working relationship that had existed between them.

The last Council meeting attended by W.T. Cosgrave seems to have been on 3 April 1922. He became Minister for Local Government in the provisional government, and subsequently, on the death of Griffith, became president of the Dáil, and on the death of Collins, chairman of the provisional government. He formally wrote to the Town Clerk, J.J. Murphy, tendering his resignation to the Corporation on 14 September 1922 as follows:

---

28 See footnote 4, Chapter 1, for calculation methodology
29 *Dublin Corporation Reports*, 1922, Vol. 2, pp. 87-93, DCA
30 Ibid. 1922, Vol. 2, p. 101, DCA
31 *Minutes of Dublin City Council*, 1922, p. 372, DCA

It is with the greatest regret that I find myself in the position of being obliged to tender, for the acceptance of the Corporation of Dublin, my resignation of the position of Chairman of the Estates and Finance Committee and Alderman representing the New Kilmainham and Usher's Quay Wards, which step is rendered necessary by my election as President of An Dáil and of the government responsible thereto. For many years I have been associated with my fellow members of the Corporation in the work of local government in our City, and during those years we have laboured together to maintain it in its place as the premier City of Ireland. I take away with me most pleasant recollections of that association, and of the cordial relations which have always existed between us, and I shall always follow with keen interest the proceedings of the Corporation of Dublin, of which I am proud to have been a member for so many years. I take this opportunity of recording my appreciation of the courtesy and assistance which at all times I have received from yourself and the officials of the Corporation.[32]

In accepting Cosgrave's letter of resignation, the Council recorded its high appreciation of his services to the city during the many years he had been associated with municipal administration.[33]

The Civil War, by then in progress, and the conditions under which the political prisoners were being detained by the new Irish government, continued to cause concern to the Council. At a meeting of the Council on 17 July, a motion proposed by Mrs. Hanna Sheehy-Skeffington, and seconded by the Lord Mayor, requested that in accordance with the universal practice prevailing in civilised countries, prisoners taken recently in action should be treated as prisoners of war.[34] A letter was received acknowledging the Council's letter of 17 July referring to the treatment of prisoners, and asked what treatment was being complained of, or in what particular the Government had been remiss in the custody of prisoners.[35]

In her response to the Government, Mrs. Sheehy-Skeffington set out the detailed complaints from the prisoners. She stated that prisoner-of-war treatment had been withheld from political prisoners, including the rights of free association with fellow-prisoners, one visit and one letter per day, and the right to receive books, papers and food parcels.

Other councillors protested in similar terms and persons outside the Council, including Maud Gonne MacBride, Mrs. Despard and Dr. Kathleen Lynn, appealed to the Council to exert pressure on the provisional government to remedy the situation. The Council tried to do so, appointing a delegation to visit the prisons and a special committee to receive evidence from prisoners' relatives. In November 1922, it received a letter from Councillor Joe Clarke describing rough treatment to which he had been subjected in Portobello and Wellington Barracks. The Government, however, made little response although it did concede that the number of prisoners inevitably resulted in overcrowding. The Council recorded votes of sympathy on the deaths of those killed on either side in the course of the conflict.

---

[32] *Minutes of Dublin City Council,* 1922, pp. 446-447, DCA
[33] Ibid. 1922, p. 447
[34] Ibid. 1922, p. 335
[35] Ibid. 1922, p. 399

At this time, concern was again being expressed about the health of the Lord Mayor, Laurence O'Neill, and, by 20 November, Alderman A. Byrne was once more listed as Lord Mayor, locum tenans. A further letter, received from the Lord Mayor's secretary, dated 27 November, informed the Council that Mr. O'Neill was seriously ill, and his doctor felt he should remain away for some time longer, as his health was completely broken down.[36]

During 1922, the only indication of Kelly's activities concerns his stay with the nuns at Grimsby, and the subsequent acquisition of the books for the Oireachtas Library, described above. His health remained indifferent, and in 1923 he resigned from the Corporation.[37] However, by 20 December of 1923, Daily Sheet No. 40 from Sinn Féin Headquarters, 23 Suffolk Street, describes a meeting Kelly had had with Messrs. Cosgrave and McGrath to plead for the release of the political prisoners, many of whom had been on hunger strike. There were continuous complaints from the prisons regarding ill-treatment and bad conditions. This meeting took place a few days before a general hunger strike had ceased. During that interview, Kelly was informed that all the interned prisoners would be released, including de Valera, but that those already tried and convicted would be retained. Those who had been convicted of armed robbery were specially mentioned, but Kelly was not quite certain whether there were convicted political prisoners involved also. The question of the date of release was not settled as Cosgrave considered that Christmas was too soon.

It was always claimed within the Kelly family that more men would have been executed at that time were it not for his intervention. These meetings and discussion, to some extent, bear out the view that Kelly acted as a kind of intermediary between Cosgrave and the Republicans during the Civil War.

A major reorganisation and restructuring of Dublin Corporation took place throughout 1923, and there are several references to this work in various reports. A new City Accountant for the Corporation had been appointed in the person of Henry Mangan. The Town Clerk, J.J. Murphy, set out the financial position of the Corporation for the year ended 31 March 1924, and contrasted its then situation with its accounts on 31 March 1920, when the existing Corporation had been elected. At that time there had been a total debit balance of £59,000 (€2.6 million at 2005 prices). The current balance he claimed to be £105,800 better than when they took up office. In the intervening period, the Corporation had restricted loans and had instituted a new method of collecting rates. But sadly the end was nigh for this Corporation, as the report of Nicholas O'Dwyer, BE, Chief Engineering Inspector of the Local Government, who had been instructed by the Minister for Local Government, Séamus de Búrca, to inquire into the performance of the councillors, was about to be made public. The inquiry arose from the alleged misconduct of certain councillors regarding the allocation of the Fairbrothers' Fields houses as outlined above, but it could be supposed that

---

[36] *Minutes of Dublin City Council,* 1922, p. 482, DCA
[37] Ibid. 1923

with the absence of so many of the experienced and competent councillors through imprisonment and illness, and the resignations of Eyre, McCarthy and Campbell, other matters might have gone adrift. The scope of the inquiry was exhaustive and protracted, and the conduct of the different departments was investigated minutely. It was made clear that certain councillors only were involved, and that there were many individuals whose conduct was above reproach. The Corporation was represented by two barristers. The Dublin Citizens' Association was also represented. The Lord Mayor, Laurence O'Neill, while being legally represented, also attended in person. The result was generally regarded as a foregone conclusion, and even the fact that municipal and local elections were scheduled for July of the same year did not allay the apprehension that the Council would be abolished. The blow fell on 20 May 1924, when its functions were handed over to three commissioners, Séamus Ó Murchadha, Dr. D. O'Dwyer, and P.J. Hernon. It was understood that the Lord Mayor, who had held the office for the previous six very difficult years, was invited to accept the chairmanship of the commissioners, and to continue as Lord Mayor for a period of four years, an offer which he had declined. He was interviewed on the following day, 21 May, and said that as it was the people who had elected him Lord Mayor, he would resign his trust only to the people. He claimed that it was a question as to whether the law or the will of the people would prevail. 'The President paid me the compliment of asking me to retain my position. I cannot see anything that would warrant the appointment of Commissioners, and I feel elections should be held. It is a gross insult to the citizens'.[38]

In view of the opinions expressed by the Lord Mayor, and those of certain councillors such as Seán T. O'Kelly and Mrs. Sheehy-Skeffington, whose integrity was beyond question, there must have been something more behind the decision to abolish the Council than the matter of the Fairbrothers' Fields houses. It is possible that the level of criticism emanating from the Council at this time, about the executions and the treatment of prisoners, was not acceptable to the Government, and thus the difficulties which had arisen regarding the allocation of the Fairbrothers' Fields houses provided it with an opportunity to abolish the Corporation.

The commissioners carried out the functions of the elected members of the Council until 14 October 1930, a period of over six years.

---

[38] *Irish Independent*, 20 and 21 May 1924

Chapter Fifteen: The Final Years

Apart from the matter of the Oireachtas Library, how Tom Kelly occupied himself during the year between 1923 and 1924 is not known. At one point, perhaps in 1924, he travelled with his wife to Lourdes, after which visit his health started to recover. Some records state that he terminated his connection with the Oireachtas Library as late as 1927, but it must have been earlier, because by February 1926, as referred to above, a committee consisting of three TDs and two senators had taken over the running of the library. This information appears in a memo held on file in the Oireachtas Library, from Colm Ó Murchadha, Clerk of the Dáil, to Henry Egan Kenny (the writer who used the pseudonym Seán Ghall), dated 4 February 1926. As referred to earlier, Kenny was the Dáil Librarian, and the instruction from Ernest Blythe, then Minister for Finance, was that the books purchased for the library should be of a parliamentary nature, and that duplication with the National Library should as far as possible be avoided.

The Dublin Workmen's Industrial Association in South William Street, of which Kelly had been secretary and manager since its inception in 1901, had disappeared by 1929, according to *Thom's Directory*.[1] The company had been very successful in the earlier years, and was the only known source of income for the Kelly family during the first decades of the century. There is no record of its business being attended to during Kelly's illness. It is listed in *Thom's Directory* up to and including 1928 and the premises are described as vacant in the 1929 edition. By 1929, however, Kelly had recovered sufficiently to open a bookshop at 8 Trinity Street. This was a small shop stocked with books and prints, mostly relating to his beloved city of Dublin. He was selective about his customers – those who were truly book lovers, however impecunious, were always welcomed, but woe betide those who sometimes tried to purchase one of his treasures in order to sell it on at a higher price. These customers he quickly came to recognise and his practice, when he saw them coming, was to lock the door and pull down the blinds. Later on, when he had returned to public life, he used to close the shop and walk to the Dáil or the City Hall whenever his presence was required.

When, in October 1930, the Government decided to reinstate the Corporation, Kelly went forward as an independent councillor, and proceeded to take on some of his previous responsibilities with much of his old vigour. There were many new faces in the Council, but he also found there some of his old friends and familiar colleagues such as Seán T. O'Kelly, Alfred (Alfie) Byrne, Mrs. Kathleen Clarke (Tom Clarke's widow) as well as the two James Larkins, senior and junior. On their first day back, 3 November

---

[1] *Thom's Directory*, 1928, 1929

1930, there was a tussle for the position of Lord Mayor. Alfie Byrne was proposed initially. Kelly and Mrs. Clarke then proposed Seán T. O'Kelly. This latter proposal was defeated by 20 votes to 12, and thus Byrne was elected, going on to become one of the longest-serving and best-known of the Lord Mayors of the twentieth century. Kelly became a member of the Housing Committee, and by autumn of 1931, he was once again its chairman. His tenure as chairman of the Housing Committee had run from 1914 until the end of 1919, and then from 1931 until 1940, after which it would appear from the records that the duties of chairman of the Housing Committee were subsumed into the duties of the City Manager.

The records of the new Corporation show that its activities were completely directed towards municipal matters. Its areas of responsibility were much more limited than in the past, since there was not the same need to raise national political issues because the Dáil was now the national forum. As far as can be gathered from reading the minutes of the Corporation, its business was conducted in a brisk fashion. At a Council meeting on 5 January 1931, Kelly requested the City Manager to furnish returns to the councillors of its financial affairs for the period 31 March 1923 to 31 March 1930 (when the Commissioners had replaced the Corporation) such as the total capital debt for each year, estimates regarding loans and stock, and various other financial matters. In March 1931, he moved an amendment to the street trading by-laws, which had been made in 1926 under the Commissioners, and proposed that the area of Camden Street and South Great George's Street be excluded from the schedule, and that the traders be allowed to continue working in these streets. The name 'street traders' was given to those who had traditionally sold fruit, vegetables and sometimes fish, from stalls erected on the kerb. Seán T. O'Kelly was concerned about the traders who worked in Dorset and Parnell Streets, and proposed that these be allowed to continue as well. A committee was appointed to report on the possibility of providing suitable alternative accommodation for them.[2] The committee's report was presented to a Council meeting on 17 December, which recommended that no street trading be allowed in South Great George's Street, but it was felt traders could be accommodated in Camden Street, which was wider, and also in Parnell Street and Dorset Street, provided that the shopkeepers were agreeable.

The Council received a letter from Maud Gonne MacBride, Honorary Secretary of the Women Prisoners' Defence League, who wished to address them on the matter of re-establishing the ancient right of nominating visiting justices to visit the Dublin prisons. It was agreed that a deputation from the Women's Defence League be received by the Council, which subsequently occurred. At this meeting, Kelly proposed that the Government be asked to allow two members of the Council to visit Mountjoy prison. The two nominated were Kelly himself and Alderman Dr. Myles Keogh.[3]

On a personal note, the Kelly family suffered another tragedy with the unexpected death of their eldest son, Isaac, in October 1932, at the early age of thirty-six. His par-

---

2 *Minutes of Dublin City Council*, 1930, p. 240, DCA
3 Ibid. 1931, pp. 254-255, DCA

ents had relied upon him greatly, particularly during the difficult days of his father's imprisonment and illness, and his loss was always spoken of within the family with great pain. He, also, had been caught up in politics and was imprisoned after 1916 in Knutsford, and subsequently, in 1921, in Ballykinlar Prison Camp. Like his father, he had an aptitude for figures, and was employed as a clerk in the Hibernian bank at the time of his death. His daughter, Kathleen, was the only grandchild to bear the Kelly name.

Kelly went on to offer himself for election on the Fianna Fáil platform when de Valera called a sudden election in 1933. At a certain point during the 1920s, his relationship with W.T. Cosgrave had deteriorated, which must have been sad for both of them. Kelly had been horrified at the decisions taken by the Cumann na nGaedheal government during the Civil War in relation to the executions and ill-treatment of Republican prisoners. By the early 1930s, when times were hard and unemployment was rampant, he found the aims of the newly established Fianna Fáil Party were more compatible and closer to the traditions of old Sinn Féin, than those of Cumann na nGaedheal. He probably thought that he could work more effectively with Fianna Fáil to help the people he cared most about, the poor and the dispossessed. The record of Cumann na nGaedheal on social issues was disappointing. In the international slump following the Wall Street crash, cuts were made to the pensions of the elderly and the blind and little was being done to alleviate the housing problem. The reduction of the old-age pension by one shilling remains vividly in folk memory to this day. In the Cumann na nGaedheal manifesto for the election of 1932, one paragraph only out of fourteen was devoted to social and economic policies while, at that time, the bulk of Fianna Fáil's programme was directed towards welfare issues.[4] This lack of engagement in social issues on the part of Cumann na nGaedheal was probably what prompted Kelly to join the Fianna Fáil Party in 1933, when he was elected once again to the Dáil.

From his entrance into the Dáil as a TD in January 1933, Kelly took on his new responsibilities with enthusiasm, and engaged in a wide range of subjects about which he often knew very little. However, he tackled, head-on, contentious issues relating to the housing record of Dublin Corporation about which, obviously, he knew a lot. He was very contemptuous about the work of the commissioners, and obviously deeply resented the manner in which the Corporation had been disbanded by the Cumann na nGaedheal government in 1924. Frequently, he felt compelled to defend the housing record of the old corporation, and it was his opinion that the restored corporation had nothing like its previous powers. He claimed that three-fourths of the original powers the Corporation possessed were now in the hands of the official known as the City Manager.[5]

Some of Kelly's speeches during this period in the Dáil were somewhat rambling and irrelevant, and tended to a humour which was not always appreciated by his colleagues.

---

[4] Lee, J.J. *Ireland 1912-1985 Politics and Society,* Cambridge University Press 1989, pp. 168-169
[5] *DE,* 1933, p. 1072, 17 May 1933

He threw his weight completely behind de Valera in a very partisan way, comparing him at one point with Parnell and other national heroes. He dismissed Cumann na nGaedheal in an uncalled-for and contemptuous fashion, and was not prepared to see any good in any of its achievements. He also claimed the Cumann na nGaedheal government had been absolutely and completely in control of Dublin Corporation. He engaged in a contentious discussion regarding the setting up of cement factories in Ireland, which, he held, would have the effect of increasing the cost of cement for housing by £1 per ton when it could be imported at a cheaper rate. He admitted that he would prefer to see brick houses being built, but because of the cost he had to accept that cement houses were good enough. Kelly also derided the commissioners for altering the appearance of Dublin by ripping up some of the paved streets of the city and replacing them with cement.[6]

On 17 May 1933, Kelly electrified the Dáil when he admitted that he did not see anything wrong with electoral impersonation, saying that he had probably encouraged a lot of it in his day. He justified this statement by arguing that if one knew the opinions a man held while he was alive, there would be no harm in voting in his place when he was dead. General Mulcahy asked whether these were the instructions given to the Fianna Fáil candidates in the Dublin elections. Kelly said that they were and that the policy had been to vote early and often. Deputy Rice spoke about impersonation, and said that it threw a lurid light on how elections had been won during the previous fifteen months.[7] James Dillon also queried him about his 'early and often' speech and Kelly agreed that he did say it. Dillon said:

> I have no doubt that Deputy Kelly, as he always does in this House, spoke frankly the truth. I only hope that when his colleagues hear the truth spoken and realise how shocking it is, that they will mend their ways not only in local government elections, but in parliamentary elections as well.

Another deputy interjected, and told Dillon to have a sense of humour. Dillon replied that he had, but that he thought it was very necessary that Kelly's words should be put on record.[8] Thinking about it now, it is possible to understand why Kelly would have said this, as he came from a time at the beginning of the century when electioneering in Dublin was conducted in a corrupt manner, and some politicians, particularly publicans, used bribery and other dubious means, including impersonation, to capture votes.

Kelly frequently crossed swords with James Dillon. Dillon, also, was much given to making long and sometimes irrelevant speeches. During a protracted discussion on housing issues, Dillon claimed that the policy being followed in the Corporation appeared to him to indicate that people were being taken out of tenements and put into cheaply constructed blocks of flats, which would be the tenements of the future. He

6 *DE,* 1933, pp. 622-623, 4 May 1933
7 Ibid. 1933, p. 1074, 17 May 1933
8 Ibid. 1933, pp. 2016, 2018, 31 May 1933

said that not one tenement dweller in the city of Dublin had been taken out of a tenement by the Fianna Fáil government, which led to a contentious exchange with Kelly.
The question was finally dealt with by Deputy Belton, who said that it had been agreed
that housing matters should be addressed by the Corporation, and not by two political
parties. Belton was in a position to correct Dillon as he himself was a member of the
Corporation, and knew that many slum dwellers who had been accommodated in the
two previous years had been moved into houses built under schemes in progress before
the current government had come into office, and not into tenement flats as Dillon had
alleged. Belton further regretted the wrong impression given by Dillon concerning the
work of Dublin Corporation, a body which was doing its best to solve the housing
problem. Kelly said he hoped that Dillon would be more careful in the future.[9]

During a discussion on the subject of the *Irish Press* and its funding, Kelly sprang to its
defence and stated that any money put into it by bondholders or others had been well
invested, and that only for it de Valera and his executive council would not now be in
power. The men involved had an honest belief in the future of Ireland and in what
could be accomplished without any further horrible experience of civil war.[10]

In 1933, at a Corporation meeting attended by the press, Kelly announced that plans
were under consideration for the clearance of the slum areas of Summerhill,
Buckingham Street, Talbot Street and Marlborough Street, a site of about 40 acres in
all. He cited the Medical Officer of Health who had been compelled to describe the area
as unsanitary and unfit for human habitation. He stressed that this project would give
much employment for many years ahead in the building trade. He referred to the fact
that the life of the present Housing Committee was nearly over, as within a few months
an election would be held. No matter who came after the present committee, there
would be no going back on this scheme, and that was one of the reasons for inviting
the press to hear the details. Kelly appealed, through the press, for investors to come
forward, and stated that the project would be a very fine investment for those who
could afford to put money into it. He said that the members of the committee had
given earnest attention to providing accommodation in the heart of the city, near places
of employment and in order to save bus and tram fares for the working men. Details
were also given of the number of houses currently under construction, the sites for
which were being cleared and developed, as well as further sites which were acquired by
compulsory purchase. The City Manager was in negotiation for large tracts of vacant
land in the Crumlin and South Circular Road districts. The estimated programme in
hand at the time would provide accommodation for approximately 6,500 families.[11]

Another issue under active consideration at this time was the Electricity Amendment
Bill relating to the provision of electricity for the country. Kelly had been chairman of
the Electricity Committee in the Corporation, when it had been first established. This
committee had performed tremendous work in getting to grips with the many prob-

[9] *DE*, 1933, pp. 430–436, 22 November 1933
[10] Ibid. 1933, p. 1827, 5 July 1933
[11] *Irish Times*, 21 February 1933

lems involved in electricity supply. He had, with great foresight, ensured that the various housing schemes developed during the second decade of the century would be suitably equipped to receive electric power. Various syndicates were tendering for the work, but the Corporation decided that the project should be municipally controlled for the benefit of the citizens. To this end, a deputation had been sent to Switzerland to study the electricity schemes being developed in that country. In 1927, the Shannon Electricity Supply Bill was passed by the Dáil, one of the provisions of which licensed the Electricity Supply Board to take over the operation of the electricity supply from the Corporation scheme, which, after suffering a deficit at the start, had become a financial success. The Corporation was very disappointed when, subsequently, the enterprise was handed over in its entirety to the newly formed ESB. This decision was very controversial at the time. During the discussions on the Electricity (Supply) Amendment Bill, 1934, Kelly vented his annoyance:

> I submit, having regard to the fact that the Shannon scheme started on its career by absorbing the old Corporation supply, assets money and everything else, that I am entitled to have placed on record the position as it affects the Dublin Corporation and the Shannon scheme.[12]

He described the care that the Corporation had taken at the beginning to provide a supply of both light and power for the city:

> The advice of the best engineers was obtained. Vigorous opposition came against the undertaking remaining in the hands of the Corporation. Various syndicates put up brass plates around Dublin, representing themselves as great engineers, and as having any amount of capital behind them. Application was made by the Corporation to the Local Government Board for a first loan of £250,000 with which to start the undertaking, and the Board finally agreed to allow the Corporation to borrow the money and to proceed with the work.[13]

Kelly then gave an account of what he called the immense assets which were handed over by the Corporation to the ESB when the excess of assets over liabilities at that date (1927) amounted to £1,445,670 (€87 million at 2005 prices).[14] The current year's statement (1934) amounted to a surplus of just £5,000. Kelly said that while he wished the enterprise well, he felt that no additional monies should be put into it. He stated that the newly created Electricity Supply Board should be a not-for-profit organisation whose mission was to ensure the availability of an adequate supply of power and light all over Ireland, at a reasonable price. A secondary function of the ESB was to be a good employer. He went on to list complaints he had received about the rates being paid to ESB employees, and went on to compare them to rates of pay in the Corporation to the detriment of the ESB. It was his opinion that the Minister for Industry and Commerce should retain some control over the board, so that Irish citizens would be sure of hav-

---

12 *DE,* 15 February 1934, p.1538
13 Ibid. p. 1540
14 See footnote 4, Chapter 1, for calculation methodology

ing a say in the operation of the board. Deputy D. Bourke, a deputy from Limerick, agreed with what Kelly had said concerning control of the board, as in Limerick, consumers had had a satisfactory electricity supply system of their own until the Government had swooped down and taken control. Now Limerick consumers were paying a higher price for their electricity than consumers elsewhere, while employees had been made redundant with the advent of the ESB and should, in his view, be compensated for having lost their jobs. In response, Deputy McGilligan outlined the financial demands on the board because of the projected investment and because it was liable to repay the State all outstanding monies. He also claimed that he could boast that the system was able to supply Dublin with electricity at a cheaper rate than it had ever got before, a fact which Kelly promptly contested.[15]

By 1935, with Kelly again chairman of the Housing Committee, the Summerhill scheme was ready to go forward. The leading article in the *Irish Times* on 21 February 1935 welcomed his statement on slum clearances. It commented that that portion of Dublin had been a plague spot for generations, and the report which the Housing Committee had received from its engineer showed that virtually every building in the district was in a ruinous or completely dilapidated condition. Whole families were huddled together in a single room, without proper sanitary facilities, without readily available water and in circumstances that would be a disgrace to a community of savages. Kelly described the constant stream of people coming to him looking for Corporation houses, bringing with them terrible evidence of the conditions under which they were living:

> Many of them come with glass bottles in their hands in which are filthy sewer slugs that crawl up the wall at night, and horrible looking beetles of a colour that I could not possibly describe. The children are brought in with their faces all marked with bug bites. At night the mothers have to tie a cloth over their faces in order to protect them. As for the evidence of sewer rats, over and over again have I got it ... Just imagine, when all other civilised people live under decent conditions and enjoy the summer, that is the time the slum dwellers hate most, because that is the period when the vermin are most active. When asked how long they had been living in that place, the reply very often is twenty or perhaps fifteen years.

Kelly estimated that the clearance of this area and the building of suitable houses would cost something in the region of £2,000,000 (€140million at 2005 prices). Then, not only would the city be rid of a festering sore, but constructive work would be provided for numbers of deserving citizens, who, through no fault of their own, found themselves without employment:

> I have material here that would probably keep me speaking for an hour, but what I want to make clear here to-night is that the Corporation has done its work, and if causes over which it has no control have operated to prevent further building being carried out, the Corporation is not to blame. I say, unhesitatingly, that I have never worked with a more

---

15 *DE*, 1934, pp. 1539-1545, 15 February 1934

competent body of men and women so wishful to do this work, so anxious to avoid all delays and so earnest in their job, as the present housing committee of the Corporation. Nothing has ever divided us. We all recognise that this question is a great human question.[16]

Kelly claimed that the new scheme would be carried out on the best town-planning lines, and that the solution of the housing problem was the most important task confronting the Irish Free State.

Less than a month later, at a site given by St. Ultan's Hospital, Kelly officiated at the opening of a new development of 33 flats with their own water, electric light and bathrooms, accommodating 114 persons and including 5 shops at Charlemont Street. This development was carried out by St. Ultan's Hospital Utility Society and Kelly referred to it as a splendid achievement. Michael Scott was the architect, and was present at the opening, as were Dr. Kathleen Lynn, Mrs. Wyse Power, and other dignitaries. The new buildings were to be let at the same rents which had been paid for the old tenements and cottages which they had replaced. Kelly stated that, at this time, over 60,000 people were living in new flats or houses erected by Dublin Corporation at a cost of only one shilling in the pound on the rates. The tenants would be helped and encouraged in every way to keep their flats in proper order, and no overcrowding or subletting would be allowed. Having declared the houses open, Kelly said that the Corporation had determined to destroy forever the one-room tenement system in Dublin, which had operated for generations, and which had brought about a situation that could not be tolerated any longer. The Corporation was currently faced with the problem of providing accommodation for fourteen or fifteen thousand families who were still living in one-roomed dwellings in the city, and a loan of £1,350,000 was at present being raised to provide housing for them. He invited those who could do so to invest in the loan.[17]

During the 1930s, Kelly was busy with numerous civic and public activities. Apart from his political and Corporation activities, he was elected chairman of the Committee of Management for the new municipal gallery at Charlemont House, which was opened on 19 June 1933. In 1934, he was chosen as first president of the newly formed Old Dublin Society. He held both of these positions until his death in 1942. In July 1935, he was crowned King of Dalkey Island, an ancient custom which had been revived after centuries, at a ceremony which saw his bowler hat exchanged for a crown of 'gold and precious stones' and he was given a twenty-one gun salute. In his speech he said that he hoped that one of the results of the day's proceedings would be the brightening up of the town of Dalkey. Miss Margaret Pearse TD was also present, and echoed his sentiments, and said she would like to see Dalkey developed as a tourist centre. An aeraíocht (outdoor fête) then followed, together with a number of competitions, all arrangements carried out under the auspices of the Dalkey Fianna Fáil cumann.[18]

---

16 *DE,* 21 April 1936, pp. 1232-1237
17 *Irish Press,* 6 March 1935
18 Ibid. 16 July 1934

The municipal elections of July 1936 saw Kelly returned as alderman, having topped the poll with 6,277 votes in his constituency of St. Stephen's Green. Dillon and Kelly continued sparring. Kelly complained that on every conceivable subject introduced in the Dáil, Dillon was on his feet making speeches on buttons, flannelette, pigs, malt, whether liquid or otherwise, beef and wheat. Kelly said he wondered what his age was, as he was like Peter Pan, the boy who never grew up, at the same time admitting that Dillon bore an honoured name in Irish history, and remembered well the time when his father John Dillon, William O'Brien and Michael Davitt were three men who had held the affection of the people of Dublin and the country to an extraordinary degree.[19]

Another controversy arose in May 1937 when the question of an appointment to the post of City Manager was being debated. John P. Keane, who had been acting in the post in succession to Gerald Sherlock, was overlooked by the Local Appointments Commission, and one of the ex-commissioners, P.J. Hernon, had been chosen in his stead. This caused much annoyance in the Council. Members of all parties paid great tribute to the abilities of Keane, and felt that the exercise was a blow to democracy, and an attempt to stifle the will of the people. Keane had been recommended for the position of City Manager, and not acting City Manager, as was now being claimed. He had been the choice of the Council, and was considered to have performed his duties in a most satisfactory manner in the eight intervening months. The decision had caused consternation amongst the staff of the Corporation. Alderman Cormac Breathnach said that he had no personal objection to the person nominated by the commissioners, but he held that a great injustice had been done to the man who had acted in the position for eight months. Not alone had the Corporation a high opinion of Mr. Keane, but the Minister himself, (Seán T. O'Kelly, Minister for Local Government and Public Health) had paid a tribute to him in the Dáil on 8 April.

Kelly spoke in praise of Keane, and said he would like to see him continued in the position, as he was a competent man and his character was above reproach. He thought, however, that the whole process amounted to the fact that the elected representatives of the people were held as being incompetent to do the work of the city, and reverted once again to the suppression of the Corporation when he said that he had been perfectly satisfied that no case had ever been made to justify that decision. The Lord Mayor, Alfie Byrne, was then asked if any member of the Appointments Commission had consulted him as to how Mr. Keane had carried out his duties. He replied in the negative. Criticism was also levelled at the type of questions put by the Appointments Commission Board to the candidates during their interviews, which were deemed ludicrous and betrayed little or no knowledge of civic administration.[20] This row dragged on for four months, after which the commissioners got their way, and Hernon was confirmed in the post. Keane returned to his former position as chief officer in charge of Finance. He was eventually appointed assistant City and County Manager and went on to serve the city and the state in several capacities over a long and distinguished career.

---

19 *DE,* 24 June 1936, pp. 254-255
20 *Irish Independent,* 29 May 1937

Kelly's participation in the meetings of the Fianna Fáil Party must also be mentioned. He had attended regularly at party meetings immediately after his election in 1933. On 2 March 1933, when it was noted that there were noisy crowds outside Leinster House on opening day, he urged that the Chief Whip be instructed to consult with the Dáil superintendent to ensure that when the Gallery had empty places the public could be admitted. On 20 July 1933, he was appointed to a special committee of the party to deal with the grievances of town tenants. On 30 November he raised the matter of the Dáil restaurant staff as it was proposed to dismiss a number of them for the Christmas recess period, and he was concerned that they would be left without their money for Christmas. He urged that they be treated sympathetically and their salary paid to them if at all possible. That such an arrangement was even thought about is another instance of how serious the Government's financial situation was at that period.

On 10 January 1934, Kelly inquired about the IRA prisoners in Arbour Hill who were being held under the Public Safety Act. He was rebuked by Éamon de Valera, who, inter alia, said that the propaganda of persuasion should not be encouraged. On 22 March, Kelly asked to be excused from attending party meetings because his presence was required at meetings of various public bodies of which he was chairman. He clearly felt that he could make a more significant contribution in those forums. This request was granted, and from then on his attendance at party meetings was on an occasional basis. On 5 July 1935, he was appointed to a party committee to deal with the matter of exorbitant rents being charged for tenement rooms.

Another sadness for the family occurred with the death of the Kellys' daughter Sallie, in America in 1937. She was a member of the community of the Sisters of St. Joseph of Peace, and her father and mother had visited her in America during her long illness. A vote of sympathy was expressed to the family by the Fianna Fáil Party on 25 February 1937. She was the second of the Kelly children to die an untimely death.

Kelly's next recorded attendance at a Fianna Fáil Party meeting was in February 1937, to hear proposals from President Éamon de Valera regarding the new Senate, and also to discuss the proposed draft of the new Constitution. On 3 June 1937, Deputy Mrs. Concannon asked a question on his behalf, and on behalf of Deputy Briscoe, regarding the numerous strikes in the city and their possible effect on the coming election. Fianna Fáil won this election with a small majority. At a meeting on 20 July, de Valera spoke of the necessity for all deputies to attend Dáil sessions in view of the disappointing results for the party, and stressed the need to keep secret the matters discussed at meetings. Kelly was present again on 21 October 1937, and raised a question on the problem of unemployment and the anxiety being expressed by the numerous deputations coming before him in the Corporation. Kelly's last recorded attendance at party meetings occurred on 10 November 1939, and there are no further references to him in the minutes until 22 April 1942, when a vote of sympathy, proposed by de Valera, was passed to his family at the time of his death.[21]

---

[21] Fianna Fáil Party archives consulted at Mount Street Dublin, courtesy Philip Hannon, then party archivist

In the autumn of 1941, Kelly gave a lecture entitled *Pallace Row* to the members of the Old Dublin Society, which dealt with the establishment of the municipal gallery and his friendship with Hugh Lane. He explained that the title he used gave him an opportunity to describe the location and history of Charlemont House, the site of the new municipal gallery. The land upon which Pallace Row was built was known as 'The Bunch of Keys', and originally belonged to St. Mary's Abbey. Pallace Row was subsumed into Rutland (later Parnell) Square, and became a row of family residences, in the centre of which was Charlemont House, described as 'most cheerfully situated on rising ground'. The remaining houses were occupied chiefly by members of the Irish parliament and some were superbly decorated and embellished with all the care that cultured taste and money could provide. Kelly went on then to talk about Hugh Lane and the setting up of the Harcourt Street gallery. He brought the story up to the time when the gallery was properly invested in the Corporation in 1913, when its financial status was assured. This lecture was subsequently published in the *Dublin Historical Record,* the journal of the Old Dublin Society. He finished the published version of this lecture, with a little personal anecdote concerning his long-time friend and colleague, Sarah Cecilia Harrison:

> I had not seen her for some time, and I knew she was not in good health. Her death was announced in the press of 23 July (1941), and her funeral appointed to be private. I respected the family's wishes and did not make any inquiry as to the place of interment, although I desired very much to be present. On the morning of Friday, July 25th, I was in Aungier Street just as the bell for the 11 o'clock Mass in the Carmelite Church was ringing, when a funeral slowly moved up consisting of a motor hearse, containing a flower-bedecked coffin, followed by seven or eight private motor cars. I said to myself: This is her funeral on its way to Mount Jerome. As I hoped she would not go away without saying farewell, and after a friendship of over thirty years, I believe my hope was fulfilled.[22]

A second lecture was planned to follow this. However, in the event the Pallace Row lecture was probably the last occasion on which Kelly spoke in public. It is fitting that in his last recorded speech, at a City Council meeting on 3 November 1941, his focus was, as always, on the welfare of the dispossessed people in Dublin. This speech followed the bombing of the North Strand by German aircraft which had taken place in May 1941, and proposed a vote of thanks to P.J. Hernon, the then City Manager, on his handling of the very difficult circumstances arising from the bombing of the North Strand. Kelly praised Hernon for 'his resourceful initiative and energy in devising the earliest possible relief and practical sympathy to the victims, and the provision of hundreds of houses and financial aid'. (It will be remembered that Hernon was one of the three reviled city commissioners).[23]

The Council minutes dated 6 February 1942 record a letter from Kelly's daughter, Eileen Carden, in which she wrote that her father had asked her to express his deep gratitude to the members of the Council for their concern for him during 'his recent serious illness'.[24] He hoped to return to his duties at an early date. Kelly died on 20 April that same year.

---

[22] Kelly, T. 'Pallace Row' in *Dublin Historical Record,* September/November 1941, Vol. IV, No. 1, p. 1
[23] *Minutes of Dublin City Council,* 3 November 1941, p. 131, DCA
[24] Ibid. 1942, p. 27, DCA

Chapter Sixteen: The Bookman and the Art Lover

Kelly was a man who had emerged from the great poverty of the Dublin slums and had developed, as we have seen, a wide appreciation of the social and political needs of the people. From his own experiences and background, he knew how important it was to create opportunities for others, and particularly for children. His work for the libraries and the Municipal Gallery shows he understood the value of providing the means of self-education, and demonstrated how literature, history and music could enhance the otherwise deprived lives of the underprivileged.

Because of his work with the Amnesty Association from 1891 onwards, until it was wound up in November 1899, he had come in contact with those who frequented the small literary and historical societies which existed throughout the city at the time which, with hindsight, can be seen as a seedbed of nationalism from the 1890s onwards.[1] One of the earliest of these was the Leinster Debating Club whose records show that both Arthur Griffith and Willie Rooney, both close associates of Kelly, were members.

The subjects discussed at the meetings of this club tended to be nationalist with literary leanings, such as a paper read by Griffith on Grattan and Flood. The first mention of Willie Rooney occurs in January 1891, and Rooney subsequently gave a paper on Art McMurrough Kavanagh, on 27 February 1891. The Leinster Debating Club changed its name to the Leinster Literary Society, and it and several of the smaller societies then amalgamated under the title of the Celtic Literary Society in 1893. It published its own magazine entitled *An Seanachaidhe* under the editorship of Rooney, and continued to publish material in the same vein, and gave great scope to local amateur historians.[2]

Griffith went to South Africa on 31 December 1896 and returned in 1898, at Rooney's suggestion, to contribute to the launch of a new national paper, which would be the *United Irishman* and was first published on 4 March 1899. Griffith was the editor, and at his side was Willie Rooney. The directors were Henry Dixon, Walter Cole, John O'Leary, Seamus MacManus, and Thomas Kelly. Apart from the political issues which were of central importance, the paper also concerned itself with much literary material, articles on historic events, critiques of books of Irish interest, pieces on various polit-

---

[1] The late Séan Ó Luing has written most interestingly on their significance in *Art Ó Gríofa*, pp. 28-36
[2] Minutes of the *Celtic Literary Society,* 1893-1896, NLI Mss 19, 934

ical heroes, poems and ballads and much else besides, some of it in the Irish language. Contributors in those early days included W.B. Yeats, Pádraic Colum, Bulmer Hobson, Oliver St. John Gogarty, and other distinguished writers of the time. Rooney died in May 1901 at the early age of twenty-seven, and was greatly mourned in the pages of the *United Irishman* and elsewhere. Many tributes were written on his life and work, as noted in Chapter Two.

In 1901, Kelly found himself chairman of the Public Libraries Committee in Dublin Corporation. Apart from his fellow councillors, the committee included members such as T.W. Lyster, librarian of the National Library of Ireland, T.W. Rolleston and Dr. George Sigerson, all well-known literary figures of the time. One of Kelly's first projects as chairman of the committee, and one close to his heart, was to work to increase the number of public libraries in the city. The acquisition of the site, and the building of the Great Brunswick Street (now Pearse Street) Library, was a significant enterprise undertaken by the Corporation in the early years of the century, and made possible by a generous grant of £28,000 from the Carnegie Trust. It was opened on 1 December 1911. Nearly a hundred years later, an extensive refurbishment of this imposing building has taken place, incorporating two adjoining buildings. It now houses the Dublin City Library and Archive and a conference room in addition to the public library. The citizens of today know it as a state of the art library facility made available to them by Dublin City Council in 2004.

In 1899, when the matter of acquiring the Sir John Gilbert Collection came under consideration, Kelly proposed a motion that, having regard to the importance of its acquisition by the Corporation, the catalogue should be prepared on the best modern lines.[3] It was decided that the person undertaking this task should bring to the work both scholarly execution and special knowledge. Douglas Hyde was the unanimous choice of the committee, and he was engaged for a fee of £350. The motion to appoint Hyde was proposed by Kelly and seconded by Councillor Lyons.[4] Kelly also supported a proposal to erect an extension to the Charleville Mall Library to accommodate the Gilbert Collection.

Kelly may well have written many articles for both the *United Irishman* and *Sinn Féin* (Griffith's second newspaper) over the years, but under a pseudonym, as was the custom at the time. In later years, he took to signing them with his own name. Griffith often signed himself in his own newspapers as 'Cuguan', a South African word meaning 'pigeon', and Henry Egan Kenny, who wrote copiously on many subjects, used the pseudonym 'Seán Ghall'. Willie Rooney, a frequent contributor to the same papers up to his untimely death in May 1901, signed himself 'Fear na Muintire' and also used several other names. In 1910, Kelly (under his own name) contributed to *Sinn Féin* a series of major articles entitled 'The Streets of Dublin', the first of which appeared on 29

---

3 The Gilbert Collection had been acquired by the Corporation in 1899, under the auspices of the Chairman of the Finance and Leases Committee, Joseph M. Meade. *Dublin Corporation Reports 1899,* Vol. 2, pp. 423-426. See also *Minutes of Dublin City Council,* 1900, pp. 393-401
4 *Minutes of Dublin City Council,* 6 January 1901, p. 35 1902, p. 35- 36

October 1910. These articles, thirty-five in all, concluded on 21 October 1911. The first article was entitled 'Francis Street and The Coombe' and the most significant streets of the old city were dealt with one by one. Article No. 4 (19 November 1910), for example, was entitled 'James's Street to the Back of the Pipes'. This article contains a comprehensive account of the many streets associated with the industries of the James's Street portion of the city. The decline of the once-thriving tanning trade was discussed, as were the difficulties besetting the weaving industry at the time. Aside from these two trades, seventy years previously (approx. 1840), the industries of the area had included bacon curing, starch-making, type founding, coach-making, brush-making, wool-stapling, corn factoring, parchment- and vellum-making, and a clothing factory. By 1910, the growth of Guinness's Brewery had greatly changed the neighbourhood. Kelly attributes the loss of the jobs associated with these industries as being responsible for its current poverty. Beside this great industry, it pained him to have to point out that within a stone's throw of Guinness's there existed the most painful evidence of utter want and misery. The author alluded to the women's night shelter in Basin Lane, where he saw hundreds of women lying on a hard floor covered only with rough blankets. He presumed that those in charge of this institution were doing their best, but felt there was no excuse for tolerating such conditions in twentieth-century Dublin. He also mentioned the generosity of Lord Iveagh 'about whom there can be nothing said but that which is good', as he had helped very materially towards the prosperity of the city.[5] Kelly went on to deal with the history of the area, going back two centuries, describing various historical events associated with it. He concluded with an account of the silk and poplin weaving, out of which at one time 22,000 persons were calculated to have made a respectable living, and claimed that 500 looms had been constantly kept going. The weavers' toast was to 'The Duchess of Leinster and the Fifteen Ladies', under whose patronage the trade flourished.

Enough information has been given to indicate the breadth of Kelly's knowledge of the history of his native city, and the many historical books on which he drew for his own writings. Many of these books were from his own collection. By the early part of the century then, Kelly was recognised as having an extensive knowledge of the history of Dublin and was much in demand for lecturing to groups and societies. On 2 July 1906, he spoke on the history of the Corporation at the Father Mathew Hall, at which gathering Fr. Aloysius, the well known capuchin, presided. He concluded by saying that while the citizens might not always have approved of everything the Corporation had done, he himself thought it had proved itself to be a bulwark of nationalism.[6] In December 1906, we find him involved in a debate on 'Free Libraries' under the auspices of the Calaroga Literary Society, which was reported on in the *Leader*. This discussion included Count Plunkett, T.W. Lyster and Rev. George O'Neill, SJ, as well as Mr. Fox, the reader of the paper. The auditor's paper was fully in favour of the Free Public Libraries movement. Then the discussion turned to the fact that some Irishmen regarded free libraries as a possible source of danger to faith and morals. This debate

---

5 *Sinn Féin,* 4 January 1913. Article no. 4 in series 'The Streets of Dublin'.
6 *Irish Independent,* 3 July 1906

generated many contributions from readers of the *Leader* during the ensuing week. A correspondent, signing himself 'Z', wrote that mixed committees made libraries undenominational and necessarily led to all kinds of undesirable literature. The composition of the Public Libraries' Committee of Dublin Corporation was analysed, and Alderman Kelly, the chairman, was described as a Catholic and nationalist. Mr. T.W. Lyster, who was not a Catholic, apparently found no difficulty in serving on this committee, which contained many Catholics and several eminent priests.[7]

Kelly's policy with regard to the provision of public libraries was well expressed in the *Irish Independent* on 3 December 1906. He said that he wished to see public libraries in all cities, towns and villages, as they were the only means of placing sound literature and the leading daily and weekly papers within the reach of all classes, especially the artisans and labourers, whose limited means denied them the privilege of buying books.

In *Sinn Féin*, in August 1910, Kelly wrote two articles on the valuable library of William Monck Mason, historian and bibliophile, whose collection had been sold by auction on 29 March 1858, in London. The catalogue of this auction had fallen into his hands, and interested him greatly. He described the collection vividly and comprehensively, and included the prices at which each item was sold. He lamented the fact that such a valuable collection had been allowed to leave Ireland, and had been dispersed for a relatively small sum. A goodly portion of this library was acquired by the British Museum, which included the manuscript of *Leabhar Fhearmuidhe (The Book of Fermoy)* which consisted of a collection of ancient compositions in prose and in verse from as early as 1256, and was originally the property of the Roche family. This collection sold for £71 (€9,710 at 2005 prices) at auction. Other manuscripts included *Leabhar Na Caemhnag* (sic), compiled by the O'Mulconrys for the Kavanagh family during the fifteenth century which was sold for £100, and the *Contention of the Bards*, transcribed in 1676, sold for £15. The second of Kelly's articles on the sale of the Monck Mason library contained much information on the works of Jonathan Swift and an account of Swift's importance and place in Irish history and literature, as well as his influence on English opinion from Boyle in Swift's own day, to Birrell in the twentieth century. Kelly was known to be a great admirer of Swift, and summed up his feelings on the sale of these works:

> The disposal in the chief town of the English of the life-long literary work and collection of a learned, cultured and patriotic gentleman for the benefit of the British Museum and others may be a very small matter. There are, unfortunately, much larger and greater fingerposts which indicate how far we are from nationhood.[8]

Another series of note, for which Kelly was responsible, was published in *Sinn Féin* in 1913, and was entitled 'The Best Hundred Irish Books'. The series was edited by Kelly, and ran for several months. It provoked a good deal of interest, and attracted contributions from historians and book lovers from all over Ireland.

---

[7] *The Leader,* 12 January 1907
[8] *Sinn Féin,* 3 September 1910

Then Kelly raised an important issue, namely that consideration should be given to the compilation of a national biography for Ireland. He described previous attempts which had been made to publish such a biography. One in particular was that by Alfred Webb, whom he called 'that Grand Old Man of the Home Rule Movement' who had done Ireland a great service when he published his biography in 1878. Kelly mentions Webb's contribution to 'The Best Hundred Irish Books' series to which Webb sent his personal recommendations for inclusion.[9] But Kelly pointed out, however, that 'with characteristic modesty he leaves out his own great work *The Compendium of Irish Biography*', which in Kelly's opinion was the best of its kind yet produced. 'No doubt his (Webb's) book is his best monument, but it is strange that no effort has as yet been made to show in any form an appreciation of the honest patriot that he was.' Kelly wrote that it seemed to him that patriotism and patience were all that was required, and felt that help should be available to compile a new national biography from the many talented young men and women who would give their time and industry to the work of research and recording:

> As to the editing, we should be able to get Arthur Griffith, Seán Ghall (pen name of Henry Egan Kenny, then Librarian at Dublin Castle, and a frequent contributor to the *United Irishman* and *Sinn Féin*) and possibly one or two others of our gifted writers to undertake the most important part of the work.

In a further comment on the possibility of undertaking such an enterprise, Griffith stated that he had discussed the idea with Seán Ghall and others and, after full consideration, it had been deemed feasible if the co-operation of the readers of *Sinn Féin* could be secured. Griffith said that if they could get such co-operation they would undertake on their part to compile a complete Irish national biography.[10] It is unlikely that any progress was made with this suggestion, as national events took over, and Griffith's papers were closed down.

Much later in his life, Kelly wrote an article for the *Dublin Metropolitan Magazine,* recommending suitable books concerning the history of Dublin to help students and others to acquire a good knowledge of the city. He refers back to Charles Haliday's work on the Scandinavian settlement, and to the *Holinshead Chronicles* of Richard Stanyhurst. He mentions the first general history of the city, written by Walter Harris, the son-in-law of Sir James Ware, in 1766. Various other works, such as those by Warburton, Whitelaw and Walsh, are recommended, but Kelly's opinion was that by far the best were the histories by Sir John Gilbert, published in 1854 in three volumes. He mentions a host of others which appeared later, such as W.F. Wakeman's articles on old Dublin, A. Peter's *Dublin Sketches*, T.D. Sullivan's *Dublin and County Dublin* and the Georgian Society's publication in five volumes of the *Records of the 18th Century.* He also mentions the histories of the county, and points out the considerable amount of

---

[9] *Sinn Féin,* 12 April 1913
[10] Ibid. 4 January 1913

Portrait by Seán Keating, 'Homage to Sir Hugh Lane'. 1920. The sitters are (standing, left to right): Thomas Bodkin, Dermot O'Brien, Thomas Kelly (sitting, left to right): W.B. Yeats, George Russell (AE), Colonel Hutchinson Poe, Richard Caulfeild Orpen; with in the background, John Singer Sargent's portrait of Sir Hugh Lane and Sir Edwin Lutyens' elevation of proposed Municipal Gallery spanning the river Liffey.
Dublin City Gallery: The Hugh Lane. © Keating family.

valuable work being published by the learned societies such as the Royal Society of Antiquaries, and the Society for the publication of Parish Records.[11]

Kelly's knowledge and appreciation of art were considerable, as already noted. At the same time as he became engaged on expanding the city libraries, he was working to persuade the Corporation to take advantage of Hugh Lane's generous offer to establish a new art gallery for the city. His role in the establishment of the Municipal Gallery, and his enthusiastic support for Hugh Lane in the fight to convince the Corporation and the public that such an enterprise was desirable and necessary, has been already been described. Lane and Kelly had always remained on friendly terms in spite of the disagreements with the Corporation, until Lane died in the sinking of the *Lusitania* in 1915. His aunt, Lady Gregory, afterwards wrote his story and included the following:

> To-day I am thinking of one who believed in him all through, and supported him against his own companions and fellow-workers for a long time, although at the last he gave his voice against him, through honest belief that in so doing he was upholding Ireland's right

---

[11] *Dublin Metropolitan Magazine,* Spring Number, 1935

Dublin Corporation Lane Bequest Claim Committee, photographed in 1933:
Back row (left to right): J.J. Reynolds, Curator, Municipal Gallery of Modern Art; Councillor James Gately;
Alderman J. Hubbard Clark; J.J. Rowe, Committee Secretary; Horace T. O'Rourke, City Architect; Councillor
David Coyle; Gerald J. Sherlock, City Manager and Town Clerk; R.S. Laurie, City Architect's Department;
Thomas J. O'Neill, Clerk to the Council.
Front Row (left to right): Councillor Senator Mrs. Kathleen Clarke; Miss S.C. Harrison; Councillor Thomas
Kelly, T.D., Chairman; Alderman Myles Keogh (acting Lord Mayor); Councillor Mrs. Mary S. Kettle

… I speak of Thomas Kelly, an alderman of Dublin. Hugh always held him in affection and respect. It was but a little while before he left Dublin for that last voyage that they, meeting in the street, talked over this matter of a building, and at Hugh's urgency, Kelly said: 'Why don't you give us a little more time, why are you in such a hurry? And the answer 'because I have not long to live', had lingered in Kelly's ears for some thirty days, when that fatal news from Queenstown turned it to an immutable memory.[12]

After Lane's untimely death, and Kelly's own preoccupations between 1916 and 1930, it was his great joy to participate in the opening of the new gallery in 1933. On 21 February, the old Harcourt Street Gallery closed its doors for the last time, when J.J. Reynolds, the curator, removed some 700 *objets d'art* to the splendid new premises at Charlemont House in Parnell Square. It had been Sarah Purser's suggestion that Charlemont House would be an appropriate location for the new gallery, and her proposal was accepted by President Cosgrave. The necessary work which was required to refurbish the building was entrusted to the City Architect, Horace O'Rourke. Kelly was chosen to be chairman of the committee known as the Dublin Corporation Lane Bequest Claim Committee and his old colleagues and friends from the Harcourt Street days, Sarah C. Harrison and Richard Caulfeild Orpen, were amongst those who came

---

12 Gregory, Lady Augusta, *Hugh Lane*, London 1921, pp. 109-110

together to ensure that the wishes of Hugh Lane were finally honoured. Their work is an achievement of lasting significance, although, alas, not always remembered.

Kelly always had in mind that a portion of the gallery should be made available as a museum of Dublin, and with this objective, in 1937, when he became first president of the Old Dublin Society, he suggested that the society should mount an exhibition of Dublin artefacts in the Municipal Gallery. It was he who made the exhibition feasible for the society by securing the use of rooms in the new gallery to house it. The cata-logue of the Old Dublin Society Loan Exhibition (September 1937) makes interesting reading. It was open to the general public daily from 4 p.m. to 10 p.m. and also to organised groups of schoolchildren. The average attendance was in excess of 160 visi-tors an hour. Kelly was one of those who lectured to the schoolchildren. Its object was intended to illustrate some phases of the chequered history of Dublin, and to display the work of Irish craftsmen, as well as to provide an opportunity to study the objects which were assembled from diverse sources. An examination of the catalogue reveals the range of the exhibits: maps of Dublin; collections of billheads, receipts and indentures; a working model of a poplin-weaver's loom, a candleholder and an oil lamp (provided by Messrs. Elliott & Sons, weavers); copies of early newspapers; architectural busts; paintings and sketches of illustrious Dubliners; engravings of buildings; theatre pro-grammes; part of a Bossi mantelpiece taken from Bossi's own house (lent by his daugh-ter); prints of Dublin, such as those by Malton, Brocas and others, lent by the National Gallery and by Messrs. Cambridge; 19 exhibits illustrating the early history of the Grand Canal, lent by the Grand Canal Company; collections of photographs by Thomas Mason Robert Gahan and others, showing parts of Dublin now demolished. Also noted were some old wooden water pipes; a portion of an oak pile from the foun-dations of the old Custom House; broadsides concerning Dublin issued during the Rebellion of 1798; a carving knife and fork made by John Read; swords, cutlery and watches made by Dublin craftsmen – the watches by identified makers – lent by C.W. Gannon; the Mace and City Sword from the muniment room at City Hall, together with charters and other items lent by Dublin Corporation. As a young man, future his-torian, and eminent conservationist, Kevin B. Nowlan was associated with the arrang-ing of this exhibition.

This is just a cursory glance at the contents of the loan exhibition catalogue, but it sure-ly suggests that Kelly's vision of a special building to mount a permanent exhibition of the artefacts of the city of Dublin would be of huge interest, and is long overdue. The lack of a municipal museum, with permanent and loan exhibitions, remains to the pres-ent time a serious cultural deficit, but it is still an aspiration. The need for such an insti-tution could easily be overlooked in an age of rapid economic change.

One sour note was struck by an article in the *Irish Times* attacking the exhibition on the basis that some of the exhibits were associated with Protestants and the ascendancy class.[13] Kelly strongly refuted this accusation and said that he was sorry that he had to

---

13 *Irish Times*, 9 October 1937

Portrait of Alderman Tom Kelly by Sarah Cecelia Harrison
Dublin City Gallery: The Hugh Lane

deal with such a distasteful matter. The writer (not identified) had taken exception to the fact that portraits of the La Touche family were included in the exhibition, and that the head of this particular family had bitterness against Catholics. Kelly referred to the quality of the paintings in question and was at a loss to understand why their inclusion should have given offence. He singled out for particular mention the poplin loom exhibit and spoke of the common misapprehension that the trade was only associated with the Huguenots, stating that it was very much a Catholic craft in the fourteenth century. The loom exhibited had belonged to a Catholic and this man's apprenticeship certificate was exhibited beside the loom. The writer of the article also took exception to the Georgian houses, features of which were included in the exhibition. Kelly said that these houses were admired by everybody of taste. They displayed the magnificent craftsmanship of the Dublin workmen of those days. The Custom House was also unacceptable to this critic, and Kelly pointed out that it had been built by Gandon, and declared it to be one of the most magnificent buildings in Europe. The amount of space which had been given to the exhibition in the *Irish Times* was also criticised, and the writer then went on to attack the amount of money being spent on the Municipal Gallery, Kelly replied that no national money had been spent on it, as it had been built with the money of the Dublin ratepayers. He also pointed out that there would have been no municipal gallery had it not been for the generosity of Hugh Lane, who was a Protestant, as was Miss Harrison, who had ably and consistently worked with Hugh Lane and whose life had been almost wholly devoted to the interests of the poor in Dublin. If the writer had gone through the Municipal Gallery, he would have found that many of the paintings donated to the Gallery were gifts of 'members of the ascendancy'. Kelly said he did not know what religion the members of the Old Dublin Society practised, as everyone who took an interest in the city was welcomed into the society.

A final aspect of Kelly's work in relation to civic art is not generally known. This is his involvement in the mural paintings in the Rotunda of the City Hall, which were unveiled in 1919. The history of these paintings goes back to a request made by James Ward, head of the Dublin Metropolitan School of Art in the early twentieth century. Ward had trained in the School of Art at Kensington, London, and had been appointed headmaster at the Dublin school in 1907. He wanted his students to gain some practical experience of mural painting, and in 1913 he approached the Estates and Finance Committee of the Corporation, of which Kelly was a member, with a request that his students be allowed to decorate the twelve recessed panels in the Rotunda of the City Hall. It was not intended by the architect (Thomas Cooley) that they should be decorated. Ward was known to Kelly, and both of them went on to serve on the committee of the Arts and Crafts Society in 1917. Permission for this project was given by the Corporation, on the condition, proposed by Kelly, that the subjects depicted should be related to the history of the city. Seemingly, his wish was that the subjects would focus on the themes of Dublin's continually expressed demands for independence and consideration for its Catholic beliefs. The proximity of Dublin Castle to the City Hall is not without significance, as it is possible to see the parallel between the themes of Irish history as depicted in the City Hall murals and those of the Castle where the triumphalism of the ceiling paintings depict the primacy of English influences. This aspect of the work may have escaped the attention of the councillors, as the proposal was voted through by the Corporation without any dissension. It is unlikely that Kelly was unaware of its significance. Sarah Cecilia Harrison, in her capacity as an artist, disagreed with the project, as she felt that the panels should have been left undecorated as the architect had obviously intended, and many would agree with her. Two specimen designs were completed by December 1914 for approval by the Lord Mayor and councillors, who agreed to their acceptance, but with reservations. Permission was granted to proceed but the work fell into abeyance due to the Rising in 1916, and was only subsequently completed in 1919.[14]

The impact of Thomas Kelly's influence on the cultural life of his city was considerable in both literary and historic terms. Above all, he triumphed in his efforts to establish a worthy municipal gallery of modern art which, in 2006, was extended, refurbished and renamed in honour of Hugh Lane. It is also appropriate that the portrait of Kelly, who was elected Lord Mayor and could not assume office, now graces the walls of the recently restored City Hall where he spent so much of his life and which has national as well as civic significance. This portrait, painted by his friend Sarah Cecilia Harrison, is a fitting monument to a man who served his country and his city for so long with integrity and devotion.

---

14 I am indebted to Philip McEvansoneya for his article History, Politics and Decorative Painting James Ward's Murals in Dublin City Hall, *Irish Arts Review Yearbook*, vol. 15, 1999, pp.142-147

Epilogue

Thomas Kelly died on April 20 1942, at the age of seventy-four, and was deeply mourned. His passing was a sad loss to his family. However, it was a miracle that he had survived so long, given the difficult life that he had led and the gravity of his illness as a result of his imprisonment in 1920. He died, as he would have wished, in his own bed, instead of in prison or shot on the Dublin streets like so many of his colleagues and friends.

The poor and dispossessed of Dublin saw his death as a personal tragedy, as he had always been there to listen to their sad stories, and to help them in their difficulties. From Liam Cosgrave, son of W.T., and former Taoiseach, the author learned that when Kelly lay dying, his father came to visit his old friend, and they shook hands, both of them big enough to do so despite past difficulties and demonstrating that, in public life, strong personal relationships can overcome political differences.

There were extensive tributes paid to Kelly in the newspapers, mourning his passing as a politician and corporator. The *Irish Times* called him one of the best-known public men in Dublin who had occupied many public offices in the affairs of the city and the nation, known as 'Honest Tom', an active helper of William Rooney and a staunch follower of Parnell. The article referred to his position in Sinn Féin and to his series of articles on the streets of Dublin in Griffith's newspaper of the same name. It dealt with his work in the Corporation and the establishment of the Housing Committee and of the Municipal Gallery, his interest in the development of public libraries, music, and scholarships for the children of the workers. It called him a master of Johnsonian directness of speech, and of a satire as strong but not as bitter as Swift's. It claimed that with him passed one of the capital's best-known citizens. The same edition of the *Irish Times* also carried an article in Irish, signed simply C., which betrayed a deep personal knowledge of Kelly, and spoke about his close relationship with Griffith, and the respect and affection with which he was regarded in the city of Dublin.[1]

The *Irish Press,* in its leading article, wrote of his involvement with early Sinn Féin, and remarked on how, one by one, those associated with its foundation were passing away. It described his unflinching efforts for the national movement, and his imprisonment. 'The Alderman was a Dubliner bred and born, and Dublin took note of his imprisonment in the most fitting and appropriate way. It elected him Lord Mayor'.[2]

---

[1] *Irish Times,* 21 April 1942
[2] *Irish Press,* 21 April 1942

Tom and Annie Kelly, with their youngest daughter Annie and two of their grandchildren, Eoin Carden and Tommy Cullen. Private Collection

Hanna Sheehy-Skeffington, in the *Irish Press,* wrote a personal tribute based on her own relationship with him. She called him 'the Alderman', as there was only one to Dublin's poor, and said that with his passing went a piece of Dublin itself, so associated was he with the life and ways of the old city, whose every stone he loved, and whose every by-way and out-of-the-way storied spot he knew. He was Dublin personified, the very embodiment of its spirit. She recollected the 1918 election when many illiterates voted simply for the 'Alderman'. There were about 15 candidates and that was the best they could do. Henry Campbell, who was the Town Clerk at the time, accepted the description. Referring to the fact that he never held the office of Lord Mayor, she wrote that it was one of the pities of life that such a man should never have held the city's highest office:

He never troubled about honours or glory, was shy and self-effacing, but with a lion's courage when action was needed. His comrades were shot under his cell window in Kilmainham day after day in 1916. In civic things he was a pioneer, a friend of temperance, a supporter of women suffrage, when championship meant ridicule and hostility. He was a pacifist in a war-mad world, a friend of the poor who never forgot his early struggles and who always remained a man of the people. Brusque sometimes in his ways, but kindly and sensitive underneath; a storehouse of anecdote and reminiscence, an ever-bubbling fountain of racy humour, a shrewd judge of human values and a hearty hater of cant and humbug. His little shop in Trinity Street was the haven of many a wanderer, many a suppliant, for he was to the last the most accessible of men. Never was a being who had less of the salesman about him: if he thought you could not afford a special book (he had many a rare one), he would refuse to sell but would 'loan' it to you. Selfless, sincere, interested in things of the mind and the spirit rather than of the world, a man of peace, a storehouse of rare knowledge, that tall, lean stooping figure with bushy brows and twinkling blues eyes will be sadly missed from its familiar haunts in old Dublin.[3]

One of Kelly's last projects was an exhibition of Sarah C. Harrison's paintings to be held in the Municipal Gallery. His last literary work was the Pallace Row article in the *Dublin Historical Record,* as already discussed.

---

3 *Irish Press,* 22 April 1942

The columnist known as Roddy the Rover (Aodh de Blacam) in the *Irish Press* also wrote of his memories three days later. He recalled the first time he met Kelly, which was at the opening of the Sinn Féin Headquarters in Harcourt Street more than thirty years previously, in the company of Arthur Griffith and the O'Rahilly and others, all gone now.[4]

The other national newspapers paid similar tributes, and over the following months various journals did also. At a meeting of the Old Dublin Society, Patrick Meehan spoke of Kelly's compassion for the poor, and said that he regarded his Dáil salary as public trust money to give away, as the poor people had always received first consideration. Meehan had known him to give away his last coppers and walk home at night. He also mentioned that he had left his sickbed recently to approach one of the ministers on behalf of the street traders of Henry Street.[5]

In the Dáil, the Taoiseach Éamon de Valera described Kelly's political life and recalled that the late deputy had been a member of the first, second and third Dáileanna. He remarked that his interventions were marked by a sound practical commonsense and by that inimitable humour which characterised everything he said, and that he never failed to win attention for the points he desired to make. 'Everything that touched the dignity of our native city in whose history he was a specialist, or the interests of its citizens, was a matter of concern to him. In the late Alderman and Deputy the workers of the city and the poor had a constant and devoted champion whom it will be hard to replace. By his death an outstanding figure has been removed from our municipal and national life'.[6]

Kelly has been criticised by some for supporting de Valera in the latter part of his life. He did so because he felt that he could best assist the poor of Dublin to whom he was most committed. He had never sought to get involved in national politics by choice; as we have seen, he was automatically caught up in the national movement because Dublin Corporation was the forum for national politics in the early decades of the century as there was no other. In a tribute in the *Father Mathew Record* at the time of his death, the writer (unidentified) made the point that Kelly had entered public life as an independent nominee of a workmen's club, and it might be said that his independence was never surrendered.[7] He had subscribed ardently to the doctrine of the Declaration of Independence regarding the rights of all citizens, a theme which Seán Ó Faoláin articulated so well when he turned to Wolfe Tone and his concern for the rights of man and respect for 'the men of that large and respectable class, the men of no property'. He was no socialist but a social thinker, who knew and loved the ordinary people of his city.[8]

---

4 *Irish Press,* 25 April 1942
5 Ibid. 21 April 1942
6 *Irish Press,* 22 April 1942
7 *Father Mathew Record,* June 1942
8 Quoted in *Survivors,* p. viii, Uinseann Mac Eoin, Argenta Publications, 1980

Kelly's funeral from St. Kevin's Church, Harrington Street, attracted large crowds, including de Valera, several ministers and other political colleagues, civic dignitaries, friends, neighbours and a large number of the citizens of Dublin. Among the wreaths were those from the Workmen's Club at York Street, the Old Dublin Society and the street traders of Camden and George's Streets. He is buried in Glasnevin Cemetery.

Bibliography

Primary Sources
National Archives, Dublin
   Thomas Kelly papers
The National Archives, Kew, London
   Thomas Kelly papers
   Midleton papers
National Library of Ireland
   Sinn Féin Standing Committee Minutes; Seán Ó Luing papers;
   Hanna Sheehy-Skeffington papers; Laurence O'Neill papers; Seán T. Ó Ceallaigh
   papers; Hugh Lane papers
Sisters of St. Joseph of Peace
   Records of the Order
Trinity College Dublin, Manuscripts Room
   Dublin Castle records
University College Dublin Archives
   Éamon De Valera papers; Ristéard Mulcahy papers
Dublin Diocesan Archives
   Archbishop William Walsh papers; Monsignor Michael Curran papers
Dublin Workmen's Club, 5 Harrington Street, Dublin 8.
   Records of Dublin Workmens' Association
Parnell House, 14 Parnell Square, Dublin
   Records of Registry of Friendly Societies
Fianna Fáil Party
   Archives: all available records until 1942
Allen Library
   Thomas Kelly papers
Private Collection
   Kelly Papers (family)

Official Publications
Dáil Éireann
   Proceedings 1921-1922, 1933-1942
Dublin City Library and Archive
   Minutes of Dublin City Council; Dublin Corporation Reports

Newspapers and Periodicals

Irish Independent
Irish Times
Irish Press
Dublin Historical Record
Capuchin Annual
Catholic Bulletin
Dublin Metropolitan Magazine
Evening Telegraph
Father Mathew Record
Freeman's Journal
The Leader
New Ireland
Sinn Féin
Sunday Press
United Irishman
Westland Row Centenary Record 1964

Published Writings

Aalen, F.H.A. 'The Working-Class Housing Movement in Dublin', in Michael J. Bannon (ed.), *The Emergence of Irish Planning 1880-1920* (Dublin, 1985)

Andrews, C.S. *Dublin Made Me* (Dublin, 1979)

Asquith, Margot. *Autobiography* (ed. Mark Bonham Carter), (London, 1985)

Barry, Tom. *Guerilla Days in Ireland* (Dublin, 1989)

Béaslaí, Piaras. *Michael Collins and the making of a new Ireland* (Dublin, 1926)

Birrell, Augustine. *Things Past Redress* (London, 1937)

Bodkin, Thomas. *Hugh Lane and his Pictures* (Dublin, 1934)

Breatnach, Labhrás. An Pluincéadach (Dublin, 1971)

Brennan, Robert. *Allegiance* (Dublin, 1950)

Carroll, Denis. *They Have Fooled You Again: Father Michael O'Flanagan* (1876-1942) (Dublin, 1993)

Colum, Pádraic. *Arthur Griffith* (Dublin, 1959)

Collins, Michael. *The Path to Freedom* (Dublin, 1922)

Comerford, Máire. *The First Dáil, January 21st 1919* (Dublin, 1969)

Connolly, Joseph. *Memoirs of Senator Joseph Connolly (1885-1962). A founder of modern Ireland* (ed. Gaughan, J. Anthony), (Dublin, 1996)

Coogan, Tim Pat. *Michael Collins, a biography* (London, 1990)
 – *De Valera: long fellow, long shadow* (London, 1993)

Daly, Mary E. *Dublin: The Deposed Capital* (Cork, 1984)
 – 'Housing Conditions and the Genesis of Housing Reform in Dublin', in Michael J. Bannon (ed). *The Emergence of Irish Planning 1880-1920* (Dublin, 1985)

Dillon, Geraldine Plunkett. *All in the Blood* (Dublin, 2006)

Davis, Richard. *Arthur Griffith and non-violent Sinn Féin* (Dublin, 1974)

Dwyer, T. Ryle. *The Squad and the intelligence operations of Michael Collins* (Cork, 2005)

Edwards, Ruth Dudley. *Patrick Pearse: The Triumph of Failure* (London, 1977)
Farrell, Brian. *The Founding of Dáil Éireann: parliament and nation-building* (Dublin, 1971)
 – *The Irish Parliamentary Tradition* (Dublin, 1973)
Fingall, Elizabeth Countess of. *Seventy Years Young* (Dublin, 1991)
FitzGerald, Desmond. *Memoirs of Desmond FitzGerald, 1913-1916* (London, 1968)
Fitzgerald, William (ed.) *The Voice of Ireland* (Dublin and London, 1924)
Foster, R.F. *Modern Ireland, 1600-1972* (London, 1988)
Fitzpatrick, David. *Harry Boland's Irish Revolution* (Cork, 2003)
Flynn, W.J. *Irish Parliamentary Handbook 1939* (Dublin, 1939)
Gaughan, J. Anthony. *Thomas Johnson, 1872-1963: first leader of the Labour Party in Dáil Éireann* (Dublin, 1980)
Gregory, Lady Augusta. *Hugh Lane* (London, 1921)
Hogan, David (Gallagher, Frank). *The four glorious years* (Dublin, 1953)
Irish Times. *The Sinn Féin rebellion handbook* (Dublin, 1917)
Keane, Maureen. *Ishbel: Lady Aberdeen in Ireland* (Dublin, 1999)
Kearns, Kevin C. *Dublin Tenement Life* (Dublin, 1994)
Kelly, Alderman Thomas, TD. 'I remember' in *Capuchin Annual*, (Dublin,1942)
 – 'Pallace Row' *Dublin Historical Record* (1941)
 – 'The History of the Dublin Streets' series in *Sinn Féin*, (9 October 1910 – October 1911)
Laffan, Michael. *The Resurrection of Ireland, the Sinn Féin Party 1916-1921* Cambridge University Press, 1999)
Lee, Joseph. *Ireland 1912-1985 Politics and Society* (Cambridge University Press, 1989)
Levenson, Leah. *With Wooden Sword, A Portrait of Francis Sheehy-Skeffington, Militant Pacifist* (Dublin, 1983)
Little, Patrick J. 'A 1916 Document – The Mystery of the Dublin Castle Cypher' in *Capuchin Annual* (Dublin, 1942)
Lyons, F.S.L. *John Dillon: a biography* (London, 1968)
Macardle, Dorothy. *The Irish Republic* (London, 1937)
Maher, Jim. *Harry Boland A Biography* (Cork, 1998)
Manning, Maurice. *James Dillon A Biography* (Dublin, 1999)
Maume, Patrick. *D.P. Moran* (Dublin, 1995); *The Long Gestation* (Dublin, 1999)
Martin, F.X. *Leaders and Men of the Easter Rising, Dublin 1916* (London, 1967)
Miller, Mervyn. 'Raymond Unwin and the Planning of Dublin' in Michael Bannon (ed.) *The Emergence of Irish Planning 1880-1920* (Dublin, 1985)
Mitchell, Arthur. *Revolutionary Government in Ireland: Dáil Éireann, 1919-22* (Dublin, 1995)
Morrissey, Thomas J., S.J. *William Walsh, Archbishop of Dublin, 1841-1921* (Dublin, 2000)
Mulcahy, Ristéard. *Richard Mulcahy 1886-1971 A Family Memoir* (Dublin, 1999)
Murphy, Brian P. *Patrick Pearse and the lost republican ideal* (Dublin, 1991)
MacAtasney, Gerard. *Seán Mac Diarmada: the mind of the revolution* (Manorhamilton, 2004)
McBride, Lawrence. *The Greening of Dublin Castle the transformation of bureaucratic and judicial personnel in Ireland 1892-1922* (USA, 1991)

McCoole, Sinéad. *No Ordinary Women: Irish Female Activists in the Revolutionary Years 1900-1923* (Dublin, 2003)

Mac Eoin, Uinseann. *Survivors* (Dublin, 1980); *The IRA in the Twilight Years 1923-1948* (Dublin, 1997)

McManus, Ruth. *Dublin, 1910 –1940: Shaping the city and the suburbs* (Dublin, 2002)

Nowlan, Kevin B. (ed.), *The Making of 1916* (Dublin, 1969)

O'Brien, William. *Forth the Banners Go: reminiscences of William O'Brien as told to Edward MacLysaght* (Dublin, 1969)

Ó Broin, Leon. *The Chief Secretary: Augustine Birrell in Ireland* (London, 1969)
  – *Dublin Castle and the 1916 Rising* (London 1970)
  – *No Man's Man: a biographical memoir of Joseph Brennan, civil servant, and first governor of the Central Bank* (Dublin, 1982)

Ó Broin, Seosamh. *Inchicore Kilmainham and District* (Dublin, 1999)

O'Casey, Seán. *The Irish Citizen Army* (Dublin 1919)
  – *Drums under the Windows* (London, 1945)

O'Donnell, Peadar. *The Gates Flew Open* (Reprint Cork, 1966)

Ó Duibhir, Ciarán. *Sinn Féin – the first election 1908* (Manorhamilton, 1993)

Ó Faoláin, Seán. *Constance Markievicz* (London, 1934)

O'Grady, John. *The Life and Work of Sarah Purser* (Dublin, 1996)

O'Hegarty, P.S. *The Victory of Sinn Féin* (Dublin, 1998)

Ó hÓgartaigh, Margaret. *Kathleen Lynn, Irishwoman, Patriot, Doctor* (Dublin, 2006)

Ó Luing, Seán. *Art Ó Gríofa* (Dublin, 1953)

O'Mahony, Seán. *Frongach: university of revolution* (Dublin, 1987)

Ó Maitiú, Séamus. *Dublin's Suburban Towns 1834-1930* (Dublin, 2003)

O'Malley, Ernie. *On Another Man's Wound* (London, 1936)

O'Neill, Marie. *From Parnell to de Valera: a biography of Jennie Wyse Power, 1858-1941* (Dublin, 1991)
  – 'Sarah Cecilia Harrison, Artist and City Councillor' in *Dublin Historical Record* (Dublin, 1989)
  – *Grace Gifford Plunkett and Irish Freedom: tragic bride of 1916* (Dublin, 2000)

O'Neill, Thomas P. 'The General Election of 1918' in *Capuchin Annual* 1968

Pakenham, Frank (Lord Longford). *Peace by Ordeal* (London, 1935)

Pearce, Edward. *Lines of Most Resistance, The Lords, the Tories and Ireland, 1886-1914* (London, 1999)

Ryan, Desmond. *The Rising: The Complete Story of Easter Week* (Dublin, 1949)

Stephens, James. *The Insurrection in Dublin* (Dublin, 1965)

Townshend, Charles. *Easter 1916, The Irish Rebellion* (London, 2005)

Van Voris, Jacqueline. *Constance de Markievicz In the Cause of Ireland* (USA, 1967)

Ward, Margaret. *Unmanageable revolutionaries: women and Irish nationalism* (London, 1983)

West, Trevor. Horace Plunkett, *Co-operation and Politics* (London, 1986)

Workers' Union of Ireland. *1913 – Jim Larkin and the Dublin Lock-Out* (Dublin, 1964)

Yeates, Pádraig. *Lockout Dublin 1913* (Dublin, 2000)

Index